America's Addiction to Terrorism

America's Addiction to Terrorism

HENRY A. GIROUX

MONTHLY REVIEW PRESS

New York

Library of Congress Cataloging-in-Publication Data
available from publisher—

ISBN 978-1-58367-570-0 paper
IBSN 978-1-58367-571-7 cloth

Monthly Review Press
146 West 29th Street, Suite 6W
New York, New York 10001
monthlyreview.org

Typeset in Dante Monotype

5 4 3 2 1

Contents

To Olivia Ward:
A brilliant and courageous writer and a dear friend.

Acknowledgments

Susan Searls Giroux cannot be thanked enough for the many conversations we have had over many of the ideas presented in this book. She is my intellectual muse and treasured companion and partner. I am indebted to Brad Evans and David Clark for intellectual nourishment and their generous and informative comments. My assistant, Maya Sabados, has been her usual self in reading every word of this book and offering indispensable editorial advice. Victoria Harper, Leslie Thatcher, and Maya Schenwar, my editors at *Truthout*, are my literary anchors, always willing to provide support and editorial advice. I am enormously grateful to Michael Yates who urged me to write this book and offered invaluable advice along the way. Highly modified versions of some of these articles have been published in, *Thesis 11, Third Text, Truthout, CounterPunch, Truthdig,* and *Arena Magazine*.

Foreword

HENRY GIROUX IS A PHENOMENON. He has written more than sixty books, authored hundreds of essays, won numerous awards, and been an outstanding teacher for nearly forty years. His influence on the field of critical pedagogy is without parallel, and he has made significant contributions to many other areas as well, including both cultural and media studies.

What distinguishes Giroux's writing is a combination of lucid analysis and incisive and justifiably harsh criticism of the deterioration of the human condition under the onslaught of a savage modern-day capitalism. However, his examination of this savagery does not stop with a description of the vicious attacks on working people by corporations and their allies in government. Nor is it content to enumerate the economic, political, and social consequences of these assaults, such as the rise in poverty, stagnating wages, unconscionably high unemployment, deteriorating health, the astonishing increase in the prison population, and a general increase in material insecurity, to name a few. Instead, he goes beyond these to interrogate the more subtle but no less devastating effects of neoliberal capitalism, and by implication capitalism itself, on our psyches and on our capacity to resist our growing immiseration.

In this book, he uses his consummate skills to examine what he terms "America's addiction to terrorism." As he makes clear in these essays, especially those on race (see chapters 5 and 6, "Racism, Violence, and Militarized Terror in the Age of Disposability" and "The Fire This Time: Black Youth and the Spectacle of Post-Racial Violence"), terrorism is as American as apple pie. This nation was founded upon terrorism, namely that of slavery, whose unspeakable degradations hardly ended with formal emancipation. Jim Crow, the Ku Klux Klan, thousands of lynchings, mass imprisonment, and an orgy of police torture and murder have tormented the lives of black men and women right up to the present day. Black men, women, and children became the nation's torture template, and what has happened to them set the stage for that directed at workers who dared defy their employers and to the peoples of the world as the United States rained misery down on its many enemies, reaching its apogee but by no means its end with the atomic bombing of Hiroshima and Nagasaki (see the chapter titled "Hiroshima, Intellectuals, and the Crisis of Terrorism"). Giroux excoriates all of this terror, as well its contemporary raw, naked, and ever-more diabolical forms: drone strikes, waterboarding, renditions, rape, presidential kill lists, and all of the horrors documented in the recent U.S. Senate "Committee Study of the Central Intelligence Agency's Detention and Interrogation Program."

To the casual observer, the fact that the Senate report has generated very little public outcry, no prosecutions, and indeed brought forth an outpouring of rancid and angry justifications by the fascist Bush administration officials who sanctioned the torture the Senate report detailed seems unbelievable. However, as Giroux explains in his Introduction, "The Neoliberalism Reign of Terror," the turn away from even a moderate social welfare state represented by the neoliberalism begun in the mid-1970s after the end of the post–Second World War era of rapid economic growth has first gradually and then rapidly and radically changed the political and ideological landscapes.

In the wake of falling profits and the perception by businesses that labor was too strong, corporations launched an all-out attack on workers, marked most ominously by Ronald Reagan's firing of air traffic controllers. Along with the assault on the working class, employers demanded and soon won an end to regulations on businesses, especially banks and other financial institutions, as well as the freeing of capital to move around the globe without political impediments. Soon manufacturing began a long decline, hollowing out hundreds of communities once dependent upon it, creating vast wastelands of empty streets, boarded-up houses, and destroyed local economies. The impact on racial minorities was especially devastating. The changes wrought by neoliberal capitalism weakened the strength of labor and raised significantly the degree of economic insecurity faced by those not already financially secure. This, in turn, greatly strengthened the power of those who controlled the economy's commanding heights, which today are dominated by financial capital. The inevitable result has been an unprecedented flow of money to those at the very top of the distributions of income and wealth. We are witnessing a new Gilded Age, with unimaginably wealthy people able to buy whatever they want and do whatever they please, the rest of us be damned.

Given that wealth is power and given that the newly minted billionaires desire nothing more than to increase both their wealth and power, and given these two facts, the super-rich will try by whatever means possible to destroy any impediments to their desires. We see all around us the fruits of their efforts. Nearly all of life, every aspect of it from birth to death, has been commodified, and every public service either eliminated or made subservient to the profit motive.

When we say that the powerful will exercise their financial supremacy to secure still more wealth, we should be clear exactly what we mean. Austerity, by which, to put it bluntly, the rich take from the poor, requires the threat of, and under certain circumstances, the use of force. Giroux makes a telling point when he states in "Death-Dealing Politics in the Age of Extreme Violence" that neoliberalism is itself a form of terrorism. Here he focuses on what he calls our war on young people, who are among the primary casualties of neoliberalism:

The pernicious effects of neoliberal policies . . . amount to an act of domestic terrorism in light of the suffering such policies and practices impose on children in the United States. Rampant poverty, senseless levels of inequality, lack of adequate health services, racially and economically segregated schools, the rise of the prison state, a crippling minimum wage, police violence directed against poor minority youth, the return of debtors' prisons, a generation of young people burdened by excessive debt, and the attack on public and higher education only scratch the surface of the effects of what might be called a culture of war aimed at children.

However, more needs to be said. The fact that the policies are terroristic requires also that their implementation has a veiled threat of violence to those who might oppose them. As Giroux makes transparent in this chapter and throughout the book, it has become crystal clear that neoliberalism necessitates a cruel state, one that must punish or threaten to do so to anyone who interferes with the smooth flow of commerce. And cruelty was given new life by the events of September 11, 2001, which the Bush administration used to speed up the transition from a weak democracy to a full-fledged police state.

Still, punishment is normally not enough to quell dissent, at least over the long haul. What was needed was a second arrow in neoliberalism's quiver, namely an ideological blitzkrieg. As income and wealth began to flow relentlessly to the top, those with the most money exercised their phenomenal economic and political might to gain commanding control over the media, the schools, and governments at all levels, and using this to inundate us with a plethora of "commonsense" propositions. Giroux expounds on these propositions in nearly every chapter in the book: We were, and are, bombarded daily with neoliberal "wisdom" on Fox News and CNN, in the *Wall Street Journal* and most large-circulation newspapers, from both Republican and Democratic politicians, from various think tanks, in films and reality television shows, and now even in our schools. The message is that only private enterprise can solve our problem; public enterprises, such as Social Security and Medicare, are inherently inefficient and corrupt; success is marked solely by our income and wealth; happiness

is a function of consuming; we reap what we sow and have only ourselves
to blame for our failures; those who fail and are thus poor are therefore
inferior people, and since blacks and Hispanics are overrepresented among
the poor, they must be especially inferior; poverty has much less to do with
crime than individual character, which explains why minorities occupy
most of our prison cells.

On top of this mass ideological brainwashing has been added a layer
of noxious nationalism, this especially promoted since September 11.
America is the envy of the world, the greatest nation on earth, ever. Many
people in the world are jealous of our freedoms, enough so to terrorize us.
The world has become so dangerous that the government must engage
in any methods, no matter how repugnant to the country's core values
(this is said with a straight face), to ensure our safety and the defeat of our
enemies. Of course, rabid nationalism is nothing new to the United States,
having been used to justify gross violations of human rights abroad and
at home. It is, itself, a form of ideological brainwashing. And it has always
played well, breaking down only with the Vietnam War and then after
many years of wanton slaughter. However, the war on terror declared by
Bush and his band of madmen has given the most virulent kind of jingo-
ism a renewed vigor. Our enemies are everywhere, waiting to kill us. They
are even among us, our fellow citizens. Anyone might be a terrorist, and
any activity might be aiding the terrorists' cause. Taking advantage of the
legitimate horror felt by Americans at the callous acts of murder perpetrated by the plane hijackers on September 11, the federal government
enacted a series of draconian laws, invaded Afghanistan and Iraq, made up
Orwellian interpretations of laws, and killed many times more people than
died in the Twin Towers. President Obama has continued these policies,
and has added the new touch of an official kill list, even claiming the right
to kill U.S. citizens.

The United States is now engaged in an endless war. If we can say anything about military conflict, it is that war breeds authoritarianism. Wars
are inimical in all respects to democracy, and a country perpetually involved
in them must perpetually subvert human rights both in foreign lands and

at home. To keep the public on board, propaganda has to be incessantly intensified, with new enemy horrors, home-grown terrorist sympathizers, red alerts, rumors presented as truth, punishment of "subversives," secret courts, psyops and covert operations. Efforts must be made at all times to get media support, whether by "embedding" journalists with the troops in the field, giving "scoops" to favored press lackeys, trumpeting pro-war movies, or by prosecuting journalists who get too close to the truth (see chapter 10, "Hollywood Heroism in the Age of Empire"). As veterans return from combat suffering from PTSD, mayhem on the homefront rises as they begin killing their spouses, other soldiers, and themselves. Police departments recruit mentally unstable former soldiers, who then treat those they confront on the streets as enemy combatants, with predictable results.

Giroux pays special attention to the transformation of education, which has been a prime target of neoliberals. For him, education has a special role to play in stimulating critical thought, challenging the powerful, and bringing forth citizens worthy of democracy. In fact, Giroux sees education as a form of transformative and regenerative politics, without which society is doomed to ignorance and autocracy. No democracy can function without the people having a strong sense of public values, seeing themselves in others, and willing to suppress self-interest for the common good. It is critical education that embodies and disseminates this sense.

To Giroux's horror, most of education's potential to fulfill its democratic promise has been debased or destroyed (see chapter 9, "Barbarians at the Gates: Authoritarianism and the Assault on Public Education" and chapter 8, "Academic Terrorism and the Politics of Exile"). Here it is best to let him speak:

> These are ominous times. . . . In a society controlled by financial monsters, the political order is no longer sustained by faith in critical thought and care for the other. As any vestige of critical education, analysis, and dissent are disparaged, the assault on reason gives way to a crisis in both agency and politics. The right-wing Republican Party,

their Democratic Party counterparts, and their corporate supporters despise public schools as much as they disdain taxation. . . . Not only are both parties attempting to privatize much of public education in order to make schools vehicles for increasing the profits of investors, they are also destroying the critical foundations that sustain schools as democratic public spheres in which learning actually takes place.

Some teachers are revolting against this, but not nearly enough. With notable exceptions, the teachers' unions have gone along with it, even offering strong support. In colleges and universities, tenured faculty have vacated their duty to "profess" critically, and instead have retreated into meaningless scholarship and offered their services to the highest bidders. There are almost no awful actions to which some scholars won't give their imprimatur, including torture and mass murder, as in Iraq and Afghanistan. Professors have stood idly by while their workplaces have been turned into academic factories, relying on cheap adjunct labor and using managerial control techniques that would make Frederick Taylor proud. Few professors now are public intellectuals, with a felt duty to speak and write about important social issues and not afraid to walk an independent path. They have helped to create a climate of fear among academics, who are either afraid to lose any opportunity for a secure job, or terrified that what happened to Steven Salaita and many other brave academics who dared to speak truth to power will happen to them.

The combination of a pitiless capitalism and the unremitting ideological bombardment telling us that what is happening is both inevitable and good for us has produced millions of warped personalities: afraid, full of worry, devoid of altruism, inward-looking, and uncritical, tending toward narcissism and callousness. In an inspired essay, Giroux uses the ubiquitous use of "selfies" as testament to the willingness of people to lay bare their images and explicit personal information on social media and thereby open themselves to further exploitation, in a way, torturing themselves (see chapter 2, "Terrorizing the Self: Selfie Culture in the Age of Corporate and State Surveillance"). Neoliberalism has spawned creatures in its own image and likeness, incapable of piercing the veil that masks reality and easily won to an extreme and violently vindictive politics. If this continues, soon we will be living the Orwellian nightmare and not even know it.

If Giroux ended his book with chapter 2, he would have authored a caustically brilliant jeremiad. Thankfully, he did not. All of the chapters contain a consistent refrain. We must resurrect and further develop critical education, making it an active component of all politics and every political agitation and movement. He sees great hope in youth, especially minority youth, who have begun to build a strong movement aimed not only at ending police oppression of black communities and young people but at constructing a radically new, democratic, and egalitarian society. What all of those who seek to participate in this new politics must do is infuse it with a democratic and radical spirit, one that, in Giroux's astute phrase, "flips the script." Using his own intellectual development as paradigmatic, he tells us that what turned his life around was seeing that the working-class character traits that the powerful viewed as weakness were actually his strengths. Working-class kids internalize behaviors that end up condemning them to lives of subservience to the very people they think they are rebelling against—aggressiveness, violence, racism and sexism, macho posturing, allowing hatred of school to become disdain for learning. What they need to do instead is to uncover, through both self- and more formal education, the values, often intentionally hidden by schools, churches, even parents, another set of working-class values—solidarity, compassion, collective self-help, fearlessness, hatred of official authority. As they do this, they will discover the myriad struggles that have embodied these values, both those that succeeded and those that failed. Those who are educators have a special duty to aid in any way we can this process of discovery and to make it an integral part of every contemporary social upheaval, of every organization that seeks to transform anger into radical political change. Only if we do this will it be possible for people to, first, envision a new society, and second, to create one. In these essays, Henry Giroux helps show us the way.

—MICHAEL D. YATES

August 1, 2015

—— *Introduction* ——

The Neoliberal Reign of Terror

The thought of security bears within it an essential risk. A state which has
security as its sole task and source of legitimacy is a fragile organism; it can
always be provoked by terrorism to become more terroristic.
—GIORGIO AGAMBEN

GEORGE ORWELL'S NIGHTMARISH VISION of a totalitarian society
has become a looming reality, casting a dark shadow over the United States.
The consequences can be seen in the ongoing and ruthless assault on the
social state, workers, unions, higher education, students, poor minorities, and any vestige of the social contract. Free-market policies, values,
and practices, with their emphasis on the privatization of public wealth,
the elimination of social protections, and the deregulation of economic
activity, now shape practically every commanding political and economic
institution. Public spheres that once offered at least a glimmer of progressive ideas, enlightened social policies, non-commodified values, and critical
dialogue and exchange have been increasingly militarized—or replaced by
private spaces and corporate settings whose ultimate fidelity is to increasing profit margins. Citizenship is now subsumed by the national security
state and a cult of secrecy, which together organize and reinforce the constant mobilization of fear and a collective sense of insecurity designed to

produce a pervasive form of ethical tranquilization and social infantilism. Under such circumstances, we are witnessing not only the breakdown of civil society and the elimination of those public spheres that provide the ethical grammar to keep the forces of militarization, violence, and a state terrorism in check, but also the proliferation of policies and institutions that generate what John Hinkson has called "an entrenched . . . culture of war,"[1] or what I would label a culture of terrorism, one marked by monstrous policies such as the support of torture, a permanent warfare state, and the rise of a racially skewed punishing state.[2]

Democracy in Crisis

To understand how the United States arrived at the current juncture, the present needs to be situated within a broader crisis of democracy that has impacted the United States and Europe since the 1970s, and even more since the rise of state terrorism that intensified after the September 11, 2001, attacks on the Twin Towers and the Pentagon. What we have seen in most countries has been the emergence of a savage form of free-market fundamentalism, often called neoliberalism, in which there is not only a deep distrust of public values, public goods, and public institutions, but also an unhesitating embrace of a market ideology that accelerates the power of the financial elite and big business. Together, the various regimes of neoliberalism have gutted the formative cultures and institutions necessary for democracy's survival while placing the commanding institutions of society in the hands of powerful corporate interests and right-wing bigots whose strangulating control over politics renders what remains of a democratic ethos corrupt and dysfunctional.[3] In other words, the source of the material and existential crises many Americans are now experiencing lies in the roots of neoliberalism, particularly since its inception in the 1970s, when social democracy proved unable to curb predatory capitalism and economics became the driving force of politics. After the 1980s, neoliberalism was no longer a template for only market relations; it became a template for governing the whole of social life and increasingly imposed market rationality on the entire social order. In doing so, it has waged a war on the welfare state, social provisions, unions, public goods, and any other institution at odds with the logic of privatization, deregulation, and commodification.

Contemporary neoliberalism is an updated and more ruthless stage in the history of modern capitalism, exceeding in its rapaciousness the free-market fundamentalism made famous by Friedrich Hayek and Milton Friedman.[4] Neoliberalism's quest to consolidate class power now has a global reach, even as it exhibits a brutal disregard for the social contract. As Robert McChesney has argued, it can be likened to "classical liberalism with the gloves off."[5] In other words, neoliberalism is liberalism untempered by a sense of social responsibility or any willingness to provide political concessions—a more predatory form of market fundamentalism that is as callous as it is orthodox in its disregard for democracy. The old liberalism believed in social provisions and partly pressed for greater social and economic justice for fear of a revolt among workers and other oppressed groups. Neoliberalism, in contrast, considers any claims made for equality, justice, and democracy quaint, if not dangerous. It seeks to trivialize all things public, to eviscerate public life, and to destroy any notion of the common good. More than simply an intensification of classical liberalism, contemporary neoliberalism represents a confluence, a historical conjuncture, in which the most vicious elements of capitalism have come together to create something new and more punishing, amplified by the financialization of capital and the development of a mode of corporate sovereignty that takes no prisoners.

Neoliberalism, as the latest stage of an always predatory capitalism, is part of a broader project that aims to restore the total control of capital and class power. It is a political, economic, and educative project that differs from its predecessors through its acknowledgment that securing power involves changing the way people think, and it uses a particular brand of ideology, mode of governance, policymaking, and form of public pedagogy to do just this. As an ideology, it endorses profit-making as the essence of democracy and consumerism as the only operable form of citizenship—grounding both in an irrational belief in the market's ability to solve all problems and to serve as a model for structuring all social relations. Under neoliberalism every individual is responsible for their own fate, and this skewed notion of freedom is reinforced by an emphasis on possessive individualism and the notion that personal advantage is far more important than the public good. As a mode of governance, it idealizes identities, subjects, and ways of life exempt from government regulation, driven by a survival-of-the-fittest ethic, grounded in the celebration of shark-like competition, and committed to the rights of ruling groups and institutions to accrue wealth removed from matters of ethics and social costs. As a policymaking and political project, neoliberalism is wedded to the privatization of public services, the selling off of state functions, deregulation of finance and labor markets, elimination of the welfare state and unions, liberalization of trade in goods and capital investment, and the marketization and commodification of society. As a form of public pedagogy and cultural politics, neoliberalism casts all dimensions of life in terms of market rationality. One consequence is that neoliberalism legitimates a culture of cruelty and harsh competitiveness, and wages a war against public values and those public spheres that contest the rule and ideology of capital. It saps the democratic foundation of solidarity, degrades collaboration, and tears up all forms of social obligation.

Under the regime of neoliberalism, democracy in the United States has been undermined and transformed into a form of authoritarianism unique to the twenty-first century. What is distinctive about the new mode of authoritarianism is that it is driven by a criminal class of powerful financial and political elites who refuse to make political concessions.[6] These elites have no allegiances to nation-states and do not care about the damage they do to workers, the environment, or the rest of humanity. They are unhinged sociopaths, far removed from what the Occupy movement called the "99 percent."[7] They are the new gated class who float above national boundaries, laws, regulation, and oversight. They are a global elite whose task is to transform all nation-states into instruments to enrich their wealth and power. The new authoritarianism is not just tantamount to a crisis of democracy: it is also about the limits now being placed on the meaning of politics and the erasure of those institutions capable of producing critical, engaged, and socially responsible agents. Under the tyranny of neoliberalism, public trust is invested in the market rather than either in a democratic conception of the state or need to address crucial social problems. In part, this is because the state has been taken over by financial interests whose power lies in the hands of the global financial elite.[8] The state has become synonymous with the rule of corporate capitalism, which marks an updated form of domestic terrorism that wreaks havoc on a working class deprived of its pensions, poor people ending up in jail because they cannot pay their bills, young people suffering under the weight of insufferable debt, and black and brown citizens brutalized by SWAT teams and militarized police forces. Terrorism and lawlessness have become the new norm under a form of casino capitalism that mimics the unbridled violence and greed of the first Gilded Age.

Increasingly, the slide into this market-based form of authoritarianism has appeared in the realm of politics. Money now drives and corrupts politics in the United States and most other countries.[9] Congress and both major political parties have sold themselves to corporate power. Campaigns are largely financed by the financial elite such as the right-wing Koch brothers, Sheldon Adelson, major defense corporations such as Lockheed Martin, and key financial institutions such as Goldman Sachs. As a 2013 Princeton University report pointed out, policy in Washington, DC, has nothing to do with the wishes of the people but is almost completely determined by the massively wealthy and big corporations, made even easier thanks to *Citizens United* and a number of laws supported by a conservative Supreme Court majority.[10] Hence, it should come as no surprise that Princeton University researchers Martin Gilens and Benjamin Page reached the conclusion that the United States is basically an oligarchy where power is wielded by a small number of elites.[11] As Chris Hedges has argued, "There is no national institution left that can accurately be described as democratic."[12]

Neoliberal societies, in general, exist in a perpetual state of war—a war waged by the financial and political elites against low-income groups, the elderly, minorities of color, the unemployed, the homeless, immigrants, and any others whom the ruling class considers disposable. But disposable populations consigned to lives of terminal exclusion now include students, unemployed youth, and the working poor, as well as members of the middle class who have no resources, jobs, or hope. They are the voiceless and powerless whose suffering is enveloped by the ghostly presence of the moral vacuity and criminogenic nature of neoliberalism. They are neoliberalism's greatest fear, and a potential threat in a society that has capitulated to market-driven forces.

What is especially disturbing about neoliberalism in the United States today is that the social contract and social wage have so few defenders, with the exception of a rising number of black social movements such as the Black Lives Matter movement, they are being destroyed by politicians and anti-public intellectuals who dominate the political spectrum. Liberty and freedom are reduced to fodder for inane commercials or to empty slogans used to equate capitalism with democracy. In other words, the public spheres and institutions that support social provisions and keep public values alive in the United States have come under a sustained attack. Such an assault has not only produced a range of policies that have expanded the misery, suffering, and hardships of millions of people, but also reinforced a growing culture of cruelty in which those who suffer the misfortunes of poverty, unemployment, low-skill jobs, homelessness, and other social problems become the object of humiliation and scorn.[13]

Clear indications of America's descent into barbarism can be seen in the increasing prominence of the punishing state along with the school-to-prison pipeline, both of which disproportionately affect children of color; a massive incarceration system; the militarization of local police forces; and the ongoing use of state violence against youthful dissenters.[14] The prison has now become the model for a type of "punishment creep" that has impacted public schools in which young children can be arrested for violating something as trivial as a dress code.[15] The punitive model of prison culture is also evident in certain social services where poor people are put under constant surveillance and punished for minor infractions.[16] Indeed, throughout the culture, we see the militarization of everyday life in the endless celebration of the military, the police, and religious fundamentalisms, all of which are held in high esteem by the American public, in spite of their overt authoritarian nature. What this list amounts to is the undeniable fact that, in the last forty years, the United States has launched a systematic attack not only on the practice of justice, but on the very idea of democracy itself.

At the same time, liberty and civil rights face a direct assault as racism spreads throughout U.S. culture like wildfire, exemplified in such trends as escalating police harassment of black and brown youth.[17] A persistent racism can also be seen in the attack on voting rights laws; the mass incarceration of African American males; and the racist invective that has become prominent among right-wing Republicans and Tea Party types, most of which is aimed at President Obama.[18] In addition, racism emerges as acts of domestic terrorism as witnessed in the all too frequent racist violence by white supremacists such as Dylann Roof, who argued that he wanted to start a race war, and then killed nine innocent African Americans during "a prayer service at a historic African American church in Charleston, South Carolina."[19] As reported in the *New York Times*, "Lethal attacks by people espousing racial hatred, hostility to government and theories such as those of the 'sovereign citizen' movement, which denies the legitimacy of most statutory law" are far more frequent and represent a much greater threat of domestic terrorism than by self-proclaimed jihadist and radical Muslims.[20] Domestic terrorism is as homegrown as Disney World.

State terrorism more recently has blazed across the American landscape as African Americans are subject to what appears to be a relentless number of murderous acts of police violence.[21] "Black Americans are more than twice as likely to be unarmed when killed during encounters with police as white people, according to a *Guardian* investigation, which found 102 of 464 people killed so far this year [in 2015] in incidents with law enforcement officers were not carrying weapons. [In addition], an analysis of public records, local news reports and *Guardian* reporting found that 32% of black people killed by police in 2015 were unarmed, as were 25% of Hispanic and Latino people, compared with 15% of white people killed."[22] Less shocking acts of domestic terrorism can be found in the right-wing war on women's reproductive rights, which are being aggressively undermined, along with attempts by extremist politicians to demonize and disenfranchise poor minorities by rolling back voting rights. There is also the war and ongoing attacks on immigrants and a growing presence of vigilante violence in America.[23] Patterns of domestic violence and terrorism are also fed by the pathology of a gun culture whose presence can be gauged by the fact that "the United States has the highest rate of gun ownership in the world—an average of 89 per 100 people."[24] The ubiquity of violence in the United States is matched by the presence of a population armed and in possession of over 300 million firearms. In addition, a war is also being waged against critical reasoning and the institutions that support it, such as public and higher education. As a result, education at all levels is increasingly defunded and redefined as a site of training rather than as a site of critical thought, dialogue, and critical pedagogy.[25]

Domestic Terrorism and the Politics of Disposability

What is more, since 9/11, American democracy has been all but crushed by the emergence of a national security and permanent warfare state. In the aftermath of 9/11's monstrous acts of terrorism, there was a growing sense among politicians, the mainstream media, and conservative and liberal pundits that history as we knew it had been irrefutably ruptured. If politics seemed irrelevant before the attacks on the World Trade Center and the Pentagon, it now seemed both urgent and despairing—lending credence to the view already percolating among a shaken populace that those traditional public spheres and elements of civil society through which people could exchange and debate ideas, and shape the conditions

that structured their everyday lives, have little significance or political consequence. The government quickly dispensed with democratic appeals,
using the terrorist attacks as justification for an expanded use of force,
spending billions of federal dollars on enhancing its war machine and pro-
ceeding to assign massive powers to itself. A series of laws was passed—the
USA PATRIOT Act, the Military Commission Act, the National Defense
Authorization Act, and many others—that essentially shred human rights
and due process by giving the executive branch the right to conduct war-
rantless wiretaps, hold prisoners indefinitely without charge or a trial, and
establish a presidential kill list. Both Bush and Obama claimed the right
to kill anyone considered to be a terrorist or to abet terrorism. Targeted
assassinations are now typically authorized and carried out by drones that
too often kill innocent children, adults, and bystanders.[26] There is also the
shameful exercise under Bush, and to a lesser degree under Obama, of
state-sanctioned torture coupled with a refusal on the part of the government to prosecute those CIA agents and others who willfully engaged in
systemic abuses that should be properly designated war crimes. But the
terroristic nature of post-9/11 America is evident not only in endless wars
waged abroad. As Edward Snowden and the relentless persecution of whistleblowers has made clear, the United States is now a security-surveillance
state illegally gathering massive amounts of information from diverse
sources on citizens who are not guilty of any crimes.[27] Already imperiled
before the terrorist attacks, democracy became even more fragile in the
aftermath of 9/11.

Then, in the wake of the economic crisis of 2008, we witnessed the
development of a collective existential crisis, signaled by the despair and
depoliticization that overtook much of the American populace. The economic crisis was not matched by a crisis of ideas, thus leading to the further surrender of many people to a neoliberal ideology that limits their
sense of agency—defining them primarily as consumers, subjecting them
to a pervasive culture of fear, blaming them for problems that are not of
their doing, and leading them to believe that violence is the only mediating
force available to them. As neoliberalism continues to colonize popular

culture and its pleasure quotient, people are led to assume that the spectacle of violence is the only way through which they can feel anything anymore. In a world in which the reality of extreme violence and the spectacle of violence merge, not only has violence become a form of entertainment and a sport, it becomes the principal means of mediation to which people turn to solve problems, advertise themselves, and commit monstrous acts in order to gain some measure of celebrity status. This is a pathology that is endemic to the growing culture of violence in the United States. How else to interpret polls that show that a majority of Americans support the death penalty, torture, government surveillance, drone warfare, the prison-industrial complex, and zero-tolerance school policies that punish children?[28] Trust, honor, intimacy, compassion, and caring for others are now viewed as liabilities, just as self-interest has become more important than the general interest and the common good.

In such a society, selfishness and an unchecked celebration of individualism become, as Joseph E. Stiglitz has argued, "the ultimate form of selflessness"[29]—that is, selfhood becomes equated with vacuous expressions supplied by the dominant culture and divorced from any genuine capacity for personal agency or social connection. In other words, a dire consequence of neoliberalism is that it makes a virtue out of producing a series of widespread crises that, in turn, create a collective existential crisis of personal meaning and identity and saps democracy of its vitality. Within the discourse of neoliberalism, larger social, political, and economic systems disappear, replaced by the mantra of individual responsibility. Deepening the collective sense of helplessness, individuals are now blamed exclusively for the problems they encounter, rendering them even more powerless in the face of larger structural modes of oppression. This contemporary politics of blame and culture of cruelty is intimately related to the internal workings of the neoliberal market fundamentalism that now pervades all aspects of life. Moreover, the economic crisis intensified its worst dimensions.

Neoliberalism's war against the social state continues to produce ever more forms of collateral damage. As security nets are destroyed and social bonds undermined, neoliberalism relies on a version of social Darwinism both to punish its citizens and to legitimate its politics of exclusion and violence, at the same time convincing people that the new normal is a constant state of fear, insecurity, and precarity. By individualizing the social, all social problems and their effects are coded as individual character flaws rooted in a lack of individual responsibility or, worse, a form of psychopathology.[30] As political concessions become relics of a long abandoned welfare state, any collective sense of ethical imagination and social responsibility toward those who are vulnerable or in need of care is hollowed out to serve the interests of global markets. Life is now experienced as a war zone, with growing numbers of people considered disposable, particularly those who are viewed as a liability to capitalism and its endless predatory quest for power and profits.

The death-haunted politics of disposability, evident in the wave of austerity measures at work in North America and Europe, is a systemic outcome of neoliberal capitalism as it actively engages in forms of social control and asset stripping by deriving profits from companies bought cheaply and sold for a profit, cutting back on pensions, reducing the wages of workers, imposing sales taxes that disproportionately affect the poor, and privatizing public goods in order to put money in the hands of shareholders.[31] Austerity is now code for an intensified form of class warfare. In recent years, the notion of disposability has become one of global neoliberalism's most powerful organizing principles, rendering millions superfluous according to the laws of a market that wages violence against the 99 percent on behalf of the new financial elites. Under the regime of neoliberalism, Americans live in a society where ever-expanding segments of the population are being spied on, considered potential terrorists, and subject to a mode of state and corporate lawlessness in which the arrogance of power knows no limits. As American society is increasingly militarized, the policies and practices of disposability have become a societal scourge that constitutes entire populations as excess, to be relegated to zones of social death and abandonment, surveillance, and incarceration.

Higher Education and the War on Youth

What has emerged in this particular historical conjuncture is the way in which young people, particularly low-income and poor minority youth, are increasingly denied any place in an already weakened social order.[32] The degree to which youth are no longer seen as central to how many neoliberal societies define their future is startling. One index of what might be called the war on youth can be seen in the increasing exclusion of low-income and poor minority youth from higher education.[33] What needs to be stressed is that the increasing corporatization of higher education will most certainly undermine its role as a democratic public sphere and a vital site where students can learn to address important social issues, be self-reflective, and learn the knowledge, values, and ideas central to deepening and expanding their capacities to be engaged and critical agents.

The mission and meaning of higher education should always involve teaching young people what it means not merely to be educated, but also to be socially and ethically responsible to each other and the world at large. This role of higher education is perceived by neoliberal acolytes as dangerous because it has the potential to educate young people to think critically and learn how to hold power accountable.[34] Unfortunately, with a corporate mentality now defining many aspects of college governance, curriculum, finances, and academic matters, higher education has become largely about training an elite class of managers and eviscerating those forms of knowledge that threaten the status quo. Any subject or mode of knowledge that does not serve the instrumental needs of capital—especially anything that might conjure up forms of moral witnessing and collective political action—is rendered disposable, suggesting that the only value of any worth is exchange value. The corporate university is the ultimate expression of a disimagination machine in its efforts to reduce pedagogical practice to nothing more than a commercial transaction; employ a top-down authoritarian style of governance; mimic a business culture; infantilize students by treating them as consumers; and depoliticize faculty by removing them from all forms of power. As William Boardman argues, the destruction of higher education

> by the forces of commerce and authoritarian politics is a sad illustration of how the democratic ethos (educate everyone to their capacity, for free) has given way to exploitation (turning students into a profit center that has the serendipitous benefit of feeding inequality).[35]

As a co-conspirator in the neoliberal takeover of the social order, higher education today has little to say about teaching students how to think for themselves in a democracy, how to engage with others, or how to address through the prism of democratic values the relationship between themselves and the larger world. Hence, students are treated like commodities and research data—or, worse, as institutional performance indicators—to be ingested and spit out as potential job seekers for whom education has become merely a form of career training. Students are now being taught to ignore human suffering and to focus mainly on their own self-interest; that is, they are being educated to exist in a political and moral vacuum. Education under neoliberalism is a form of radical depoliticization, one that kills the social imagination and any hope for a world that is more just, equal, and democratic.

It cannot be emphasized enough that the slow death of the university as a center of creativity and critique, a fundamental source of civic education, and a crucial public good sets the stage for the emergence of a national culture that produces and legitimates an authoritarian society. The corporatization of higher education may, in fact, qualify as one of the most serious assaults against democracy. Certainly, it gives rise to the kind of thoughtlessness that Hannah Arendt believed was at the core of totalitarianism.[36] A glimpse of such thoughtlessness has been on display at Rutgers University, which in 2014 presented an honorary degree to Condoleezza Rice while offering to pay her $35,000 to give a commencement speech. This gesture was clearly motivated by political interests, for how else to explain giving such a prestigious degree to someone whom a number of people consider to be a war criminal?[37] This example is only one of many that exhibit how higher education has now become firmly entrenched in what President Eisenhower once called the military-industrial-academic complex.[38]

One of the most troubling elements of the corporate university's attempt to wage a war on higher education is the ongoing attrition of full-time faculty, as numbers are mostly reduced or replaced by part-time instructors with minimal power, benefits, and security. Not only are part-time and non-tenured faculty in the United States demoralized as they increasingly lose their rights and power, but many now find themselves relying on food stamps and living slightly above the poverty level. Too many educators find themselves positioned as subaltern labor and staring into an abyss. As a result, with some exceptions, they have little time on their hands to make room to resist the oppressive structures of the university or they feel threatened to offer any resistance for fear of being fired. On the other hand, there are some faculty who have withdrawn into the language of specialization and professionalization, which has cut them off from connecting their work to larger civic issues and social problems. Hindered from developing a meaningful relationship to a larger democratic polity, the academy's retreat from public life leaves an ethical and intellectual void in higher education as it increasingly transforms critical educators into fully integrated supporters of the corporate university.

The seriousness of the declining numbers of public intellectuals who are willing to address important social issues, aid social movements, and use their knowledge to create a critical formative culture cannot be overstated. Moreover, the retreat of intellectuals engaged in the struggle against neoliberalism and other forms of domination is now, alarmingly, matched by the rise of anti-public intellectuals who have sold themselves to corporate power. While the list is too long to mention everyone, one would have to include the likes of cultural theorists such as Thomas Sowell, Shelby Steele, and John McWhorter, and arch supporters of neoliberalism such as Martin Feldstein, Glenn Hubbard, Frederic Mishkin, Laura Tyson, Richard Portes, John Campbell, and Larry Summers. These so-called intellectuals are the enemies of democracy and strive to legitimate modes of identification and values that buy into the notion that capitalism, rather than humanity, is the agent of history. They do not critique democracy for the sake of improving it; rather, they do everything they can to undermine democratic principles. These intellectuals are bought and sold by the financial elite and are nothing more than ideological puppets using their skills to destroy the social contract, critical thought, and all those social institutions capable of constructing non-commodified values and democratic public spheres. Their goal is to normalize the ideologies, modes of governance, and policies that reproduce massive inequities and suffering for the many, while generating exorbitant privileges for the corporate and financial elite. The growing presence of such intellectuals is symptomatic of the fact that neoliberalism represents a new historical conjuncture in which cultural institutions and political power have taken on a whole new life in shaping politics. And it is precisely on the ideological front that neoliberalism has surpassed any preceding versions of capitalism in gaining ground, through legitimating self-interest as a virtue, consumerism as the noblest act of citizenship, and militarism as a cherished ideal.

Indeed, the growing army of anti-public intellectuals who function largely as adjuncts of the military-industrial-academic complex and serve the interests of the financial elite is evidence of just how vast the neoliberal apparatus of pedagogical relations has become—an apparatus that privileges deregulation, privatization, commodification, and the militarization of everyday life. One could even argue that the corporate elite now so thoroughly controls the commanding cultural apparatuses—using them to produce and disseminate ideas, values, and ideologies that render market ideologies, policies, and practices as "common sense"—that the aforementioned crisis of ideas is barely perceptible. What must be constantly brought to our attention at this time in our history is that schools and colleges are not the only sites invested in education. The educational force of the wider culture has now become a major sphere in which identities, desires, and forms of agency are being shaped. This is particularly true for popular culture, which has been largely colonized by corporations and is increasingly used to reproduce a culture of consumerism and social illiteracy. Mainstream popular culture is a distraction through which people's emotions are channeled toward spectacles, often violent ones, while suffocating all vestiges of the imagination. Hijacked by neoliberal values, American popular culture now largely promotes the idea that any act of critical thinking is an act of stupidity, while offering up the illusion of agency and participatory democracy through gimmicks like voting on *American Idol*.

What is crucial to consider about popular culture today is that it is not simply about entertainment: it also functions to produce particular subjectivities that favor its own profitability and proliferation. It has become one of the most important and powerful vehicles for public education, or what I have called an oppressive form of public pedagogy.[39] Film, television, talk radio, video games, newspapers, social networks, and online media do not merely entertain us; they are also teaching machines that offer interpretations of the world and largely function to produce a public with limited political horizons. They both titillate and create a mass sensibility that is conducive to maintaining a certain level of consent, while legitimating the values, ideologies, power relations, and policies that maintain the dominance of a neoliberal regime. They also engage in forms of intellectual and symbolic violence by emptying words, images, and sound of any meaning, while bombarding the public with an endless spectacle of stupidity, idiocy, brutality, and carnage.

There are a number of registers through which a market-driven popular culture produces subjects willing to be complicit in their own oppression, further enhancing a culture that is wedded to violence and prone to domestic terrorism. Celebrity culture, for one, collapses the public into the private and reinforces a certain level of unthinking consumption. The advertising that imbues all elements of popular culture likewise functions to turn people into consumers and reinforces the view that the only obligation of citizenship is to shop, consume, and discard goods. Surveillance culture undermines autonomy and is largely interested in locking people into strangulating orbits of privatization and atomization. A militarized popular culture offers up violence and a hyper-masculine model of agency as both a site of entertainment and a mechanism with which to solve all personal and social problems. Indeed, violence as the exercise of power is portrayed as the most important force for mediating social relationships. All together, these elements work to depoliticize the population, distract people from recognizing their capacities as critically engaged agents, and empty out any notion of politics that would demand thoughtfulness, social responsibility, and civic courage.

The National Insecurity State

I think it is fair to say, following Hannah Arendt, that each country ravaged by neoliberalism and its attack on the social state will develop its own form of authoritarianism rooted in the historical, pedagogical, and cultural traditions that enable it to reproduce itself.[40] In the United States, a "soft war" is being waged on the cultural front aided by the new electronic technologies of consumerism and surveillance. There is a full-fledged effort to conscript the pedagogical influence of various cultural apparatuses, extending from schools and older forms of media, on the one hand, to new media and digital modes of communication, on the other. These educational tools are being used to produce elements of the authoritarian personality, while crushing as much as possible any form of collective dissent and struggle. With the continuation of such conditions, state sovereignty will be permanently replaced by corporate sovereignty, giving substance to the specter of totalitarianism that Michael Halberstam once stated "haunts the modern ideal of political emancipation."[41] What is more, there is ample evidence that any failure of this soft war to enthrall the citizenry is liable to provoke a "hard war" that deploys unremitting state violence against the American people. There has been an increase in military-style repression in order to deal with the inevitable economic, ecological, and political crises that will only intensify under the new authoritarianism. In this instance, justifications will continue to be issued regarding the need for state security and control, reinforced by a virulent culture of fear and an intensified appeal to overtly racist forms of nationalism. This has become particularly evident in the overt racism displayed by Donald Trump and his fellow

Republican Party candidates in the 2016 presidential primaries. The racist anti-immigrant discourse spewed forth in this campaign is as ruthless and cruel as it is politically reactionary. Mexican immigrants are now labeled as rapists, criminals, and moochers while their children born in the United States are derisively called "anchor babies."[42]

Chris Hedges crystalizes this premise in arguing that Americans now live in a society in which "violence is the habitual response by the state to every dilemma." [43] War is increasingly legitimized as a permanent feature of society and violence embraced as the organizing principle of politics. Under such circumstances, malevolent modes of rationality now impose the values of a militarized neoliberal regime on everyone, shattering what remains of any democratic modes of agency, solidarity, and hope. Amid the bleakness and despair, the discourses of militarism, danger, and aggression now fuel a war on terrorism that "represents the negation of politics— since all interaction is reduced to a test of military strength, war brings death and destruction, not only to the adversary but also to one's side, and without distinguishing between guilty and innocent."[44] Human barbarity is no longer invisible, or hidden under the bureaucratic language of Orwellian doublespeak. Its conspicuousness, if not celebration, emerged with the new editions of American exceptionalism ushered in by the post-9/11 war on terror.

Fourteen years after September 11, 2001, the historical rupture produced by the events of that day has transformed a terrorist attack into a war on terror that mimics the very crimes it pledged to eliminate. The script is now familiar: security trumped civil liberties as shared fears replaced any sense of shared responsibilities. Under Bush and Cheney, the government lied to the American public about the war in Iraq and manipulated the justice system in order to impose anti-terrorist laws that violate civil liberties. The Bush administration used a state of emergency to turn the United States into a torture state, rolling out a range of terrorist practices around the globe, including extraordinary rendition and state torture.[45] But it is Obama who has become the master of permanent war, seeking to increase the bloated military budget—close to a trillion dollars—while "turning to

lawless violence…translated into unrestrained violent interventions from
Libya to Syria and back to Iraq," including an attempt "to expand the war
on ISIS in Syria and possibly send more heavy weapons to its client government in Ukraine."[46] Obama has not only expanded the reach of the
militarized state, but has colluded with Democratic and Republican Party
extremists in preaching a notion of security rooted in personal fears rather
than rallying collective strengths against the deprivations and suffering
produced by war, poverty, racism, and injustice.[47] United in their efforts
to wage war abroad, both political parties have made it easier at home to
undermine those basic civil liberties that protect individuals against inva-
sive and potentially repressive government actions.

Under the burgeoning of what James Risen has called the "home-
land security–industrial complex," state secrecy and organized corporate
corruption have filled the coffers of the defense industry along with the
corporate-owned security industries—especially those providing drones—
who benefit the most from the war on terror.[48] This is not to suggest that
security is not an important consideration for the United States. Clearly,
the legitimate need to defend itself should not serve, as it has, as a pretext for American exceptionalism and the imperialist, expansionist goals of
political elites. No more should security serve as an excuse for abandoning
civil liberties, democratic values, and any semblance of justice, morality,
and political responsibility.

The war on terrorism has extended the discourse, space, location, and
time of war in ways that have made it unbounded and ubiquitous, turning everyone into a potential terrorist and bringing the battle home to be
fought in domestic sites as well as foreign ones. The philosopher Giorgio
Agamben has rightly warned that under the war on terrorism, the political landscape has utterly changed in the United States: "We are no longer
citizens but detainees, distinguishable from the inmates of Guantanamo
not by an indifference in legal status, but only by the fact that we have
not yet had the misfortune to be incarcerated—or unexpectedly executed
by a missile from an unmanned aircraft."[49] The war on terror has come
home. Fear has taken on a totalizing presence, as enemies of the state now

include not only those enemy combatants abroad who endure bombing, abduction, and torture, but also citizens of the United States who have seen a growing imposition of punitive measures at home through the use of the police and federal troops for interventions ranging from drug interdictions to the enforcement of zero tolerance standards in public schools to the arrest and criminalization of homeless people.

That the war on terror now manifests as state terrorism is made clear as poor neighborhoods are transformed into war zones with the police resembling an occupying army. Of course, terrorism is part of U.S. history, and its homegrown dimensions include the lynchings of thousands of black men and women in the first half of the twentieth century, the 1963 church bombing in Birmingham, and the more recent torture of black men by the Chicago police force in the 1960s—a practice that still continues.[50] Not only has this legacy been forgotten, but its most poisonous effects have returned with a vengeance. Racism is now normalized, even as it is being loudly proclaimed across the country that we live in a post-racial society, a statement that suggests both a tragic state of self-delusion and mass psychosis. The most lethal expressions of racism have become commonplace. In 2014, Eric Garner was brutalized and choked to death by a white policeman who believed he was selling cigarettes illegally. In 2015, unarmed black men such as Walter Scott and Eric Harris were both shot in the back by poorly trained cops. Racist violence has also touched the lives of black youth such as twelve-year-old Tamir Rice who was shot for holding a toy gun and Freddie Gray who died after his spine was broken while in police custody.[51] The prevalence of African American youth and adults being victimized by police violence has rightly provoked moral outrage and social protest. Such occurrences are shocking because they expose civility and color-neutrality as merely thin veneers that overlay the racism and barbarism that infuses American culture both past and present. Oliver Laughland, Jon Swaine, and Jamiles Lartey report in *The Guardian* that

Police in the United States are killing people at a rate that would result in 1,100 fatalities by the end of [2015], according to a *Guard-*

ian investigation, which recorded an average of three people killed per day during the first half of 2015. . . . When adjusted to accurately reflect the US population, the totals indicate that black people are being killed by police at more than twice the rate of white and Hispanic or Latino people. Black people killed by police were also significantly more likely to have been unarmed. [52]

What is also shocking is the apparent willingness of most of the general population to accept lethal violence in everyday life as a common event—indicative of the widespread desensitization that has occurred within the context of rising state terrorism and lawlessness. As Jeffrey St. Clair has pointed out, one indicator of how state-sanctioned violence has become normalized is the fact that the majority of Americans support torture, even though they know "it is totally ineffective as a means of intelligence gathering." [53] This suggests more than simple indifference; it implies an endorsement of cruelty that is mirrored in the American public's growing appetite for violence, whether it parades as entertainment or manifests itself in the growing demonization and incarceration of poor minority youth, Muslims, immigrants, and others deemed as disposable.

When the history and range of the cultural and systemic forces that promote violence in the United States are considered, it should really come as no surprise that the only issue on which the top 2016 Republican Party presidential contenders agree on is that guns are the ultimate symbol of freedom in America, a "bellwether of individual liberty, a symbol of what big government wants and shouldn't have." [54] Gun policies provide political theater for the new extremists, and are symptomatic less of some cockeyed defense of the Second Amendment than a willingness to capitalize on the pleasure of violence and a hyper-masculine aesthetic infused with patriotic fervor in order to buttress the case for using deadly force both at home and abroad. Far from deterring the growth of "big government," which is simply their code for the social state, they wish to arm and militarize society in order to justify the existence of a maximum security state and the authoritarian rule that is inevitably its corollary. When the campaign message of major political figures in the United States becomes "maximizing the pleasure of violence,"[55] as Rustom Bharacuha and Susan Sontag have argued in different contexts, surely we are bearing witness to a moment in history that "dissolves politics into pathology."[56]

Notions of democracy appear to be giving way to the discourse of revenge, domestic security, stupidity, and war. The political reality that has emerged since the shattering crisis of 9/11 increasingly points to a set of narrow choices that is being dictated by jingoistic right-wing extremists, the Defense Department, and neoconservative private foundations, all fueled by the dominant media. War and violence now function as an aphrodisiac for a public inundated with commodities and awash in celebrity culture idiocy. Capitalizing on the pent-up emotions of an angry, disillusioned, and grieving public, almost any reportage of a terrorist attack throughout the globe further amplifies the American media's hyped-up language of war, patriotism, surveillance, and retaliation—often infused by unchecked racism. Conservative talking heads write numerous op-eds and appear on endless talk shows fanning the fires of "patriotism" by calling upon the United States to expand the war against any one of a number of Arab countries that are considered terrorist states. For example, John Bolton, writing an op-ed for the *New York Times*, insisted that any attempt by the Obama administration to negotiate an arms deal with Iran would clearly be a sign of weakness. For Bolton, the only way to deal with Iran is to launch an attack on their nuclear infrastructure. The title of his op-ed sums up the organizing idea of the article: "To Stop Iran's Bomb, Bomb Iran."[57] Indeed, the current extremists dominating Congress require no encouragement to go to war with Iran, bomb Syria into the twilight zone, and further extend the reach of the American empire through its bloated war machine to any country that questions the use of American power.

Against an endless onslaught of images of jets bombing countries extending from Syria and Iraq to Afghanistan and Gaza, amply supplied by the Defense Department, the dominant media use the war abroad to stoke fears at home by presenting numerous stories about the endless ways in which potential terrorists might use nuclear weapons, poison the food supply, or unleash biochemical agents on the American population. Innumerable examples of fear-based, warmongering rhetoric can be found in the militarized frothing and Islamophobia perpetrated by the Fox News Channel, which frequently reaches fever pitch as a result of the bellicosity that informs the majority of its commentaries and reactions to the war on terror.

It is worth recalling that not only the most fanatical outlets but all American mainstream media supported Bush's fabrications to justify the invasion of Iraq, and never apologized for such despicable actions. Missing from the endless calls for security, vengeance, and the use of state violence has been any account of the massive lawlessness produced by the United States government through targeted drone attacks on enemy combatants, the violation of civil liberties, and the almost unimaginable human suffering and hardship perpetrated through the American war machine in the Middle East, especially in Iraq. Also missing has been the history of lawlessness, imperialism, and torture that supported a host of authoritarian regimes propped up by the United States. Mainstream media have similarly remained silent about the pardoning of those who tortured as a matter of state policy, and even more so about supporting the heroic actions of whistleblowers such as Edward Snowden, Chelsea Manning, Thomas Drake, John Kiriakou, Jeffrey Sterling, and others.[58]

At the same time, American mainstream media do little to resist publicly the emergence of a surveillance state and a domestic war on terror that produces a dangerous "culture of shadows and subterfuge" in which there is a holding back of dissent, openness, and resistance for fear that such actions could cost one a job, initiate government harassment, or worse.[59] To the contrary, glaring examples of support for increased securitization can be found in the constant and underanalyzed images and stories circulating in the media of the terrorists "in our midst" threatening to blow up malls, schools, and any other conceivable space where the public gathers. The fear and insecurity created by such stories simultaneously serve to support a militaristic foreign policy and legitimatize a host of anti-democratic practices at home—including "a concerted attack on civil liberties, freedom of expression, and freedom of the press,"[60] and a growing sentiment on the part of the American public that people who suggest that terrorism is, in part, caused by American foreign policy should not be allowed to teach in the public schools or work in the government.[61]

This legacy of suppression has a long history in the United States, and it has returned with a vengeance in academia, especially for those academics such as Norman Finkelstein and Steven G. Salaita who have condemned America's policies in the Middle East and the government's support of the Israeli government's policies toward Palestinians. The public's surrender to intimidation and fear is made all the more easy by the civic illiteracy now sweeping the United States. Climate change deniers, anti-intellectuals, religious fundamentalists, the "Love America" crowd, and others exhibit pride in displaying a kind of thoughtlessness bereft of historical consciousness. The consequence is that the people feel beset by a form of political and theoretical helplessness that opens the door to public acceptance of foreign and domestic violence.

The war on terror is the new normal. Its intensification of violence, militarization, and state terrorism now reaches into every aspect of American life. Americans complain over the economic deficit, but say little about the democratic and moral deficits that move the country ever closer to authoritarianism. The growing police presence in our major cities provides a visible sign of how the authoritarian state now flourishes. For example, with 34,000 uniformed police officers in its midst, New York City resembles an armed camp with a force that, as Thom Hartman points out, is "bigger than the active militaries of Austria, Bulgaria, Chad, the Czech Republic, Hungary, and Kenya."[62] At the same time, the Pentagon has given billions of dollars' worth of military equipment to local police forces all over America. Is it any wonder that minorities of color fear the police more than the gangs and criminals that haunt their neighborhoods? Militarism is one of the breeding grounds of violence in the United States and is visible in the ubiquitous gun culture, the modeling of schools after prisons, the exploding incarceration state, the paramilitarization of local police forces, the burgeoning military budget, and the ongoing attacks on protesters, dissidents, black and brown youth, and women.

Beyond these visible elements of an expanding culture of violence, identity and language itself have become militarized, fed by an onslaught of extreme violence that now floods Hollywood films and dominates American television. Hollywood blockbusters such as *American Sniper* glorify war crimes and reproduce demonizing views of Islam.[63] Television programs such as *Spartacus, The Following, Hannibal, True Detective, Justified,* and *Top of the Lake* intensify the pleasure quotient for viewing extreme and graphic violence to an almost unimaginable degree. Graphic violence appears to provide one of the few outlets for Americans to express what has come to resemble something like a form of spiritual release. Consuming extreme violence, including accounts of state torture, may be one of the few practices left that allows the American people to feel alive, to mark what it means to be close to the register of death in a way that reminds them of the ability to feel within a culture that deadens every possibility of life. Under such circumstances, the representation of violence is transformed into something more than entertainment; it becomes akin to a sacred experience that ritualizes and legitimates a carnival of cruelty. The privatization of violence through media spectacles does more than maximize the pleasure quotient and heighten macho ebullience; it also gives violence a fascist edge by depoliticizing a culture in which the reality of violence often takes the form of state terrorism.

The extreme visibility of both real and imagined violence in American culture represents a willful pedagogy of carnage and gore designed to normalize its presence and to legitimate its practice as a matter of common sense. Moreover, warmaking and the militarization of public discourse and public space also serve as an uncritical homage to a form of hyper-masculinity that operates from the assumption that violence is not only the most effective practice for mediating most problems, but also central to identity formation itself. Agency is now militarized and almost completely removed from any notion of civic values. We get a glimpse of this form of violent hyper-masculinity not only in the highly publicized brutality against women dished out by professional football players, but also in the endless stories of sexual abuse and violence now taking place in frat houses across America, many in some of the most prestigious colleges and universities. Violence has become the nervous system of warmaking in the United States, escalating under Bush and Obama into a kind of war fever that embraces a death drive. As Robert J. Lifton points out:

> Warmaking can quickly become associated with "war fever," the mobilization of public excitement to the point of a collective experience with transcendence. War then becomes heroic, even mythic, a task that must be carried out for the defense of one's nation, to sustain its special historical destiny and the immortality of its people. . . . War fever tends always to be sporadic and subject to disillusionment. Its underside is death anxiety, in this case related less to combat than to fears of new terrorist attacks at home or against Americans abroad—and later to growing casualties in occupied Iraq.[64]

Under the war on terrorism, moral panic and a culture of fear have not only redefined public space as the "sinister abode of danger, death and infection" and fueled the collective rush to "patriotism on the cheap," they have also buttressed a "fear economy" and refigured the meaning of politics itself.[65] Defined as "the complex of military and security firms rushing to exploit the national nervous breakdown,"[66] the fear economy promises big financial gains for both the Defense Department and the anti-terrorist security sector now primed to terror-proof everything from trash cans and water systems to shopping malls and public restrooms. The war on terrorism has been transformed into a new market in which to pitch consumer goods for the fearful, while the hysterical warmongers and their acolytes in the media turn politics into an extension of war. Fear is no longer an attitude as much as it is a culture that functions as "the enemy of reason [while distorting] emotions and perceptions, and often leads to poor decisions."[67] But the culture of fear does more than undermine critical judgment and suppress dissent. As Don Hazen observes, it also "breeds more violence, mental illness and trauma, social disintegration, job failure, loss of workers' rights, and much more. Pervasive fear ultimately paves the way for an accelerating authoritarian society with increased police power, legally codified oppression, invasion of privacy, social controls, social anxiety and PTSD."[68] Fear and repression reproduce, rather than address, the most fundamental antidemocratic elements of terrorism. Instead of promulgating a culture of fear, people need to recognize that the threat of terrorism cannot be understood apart from the crisis of democracy itself.

In the current historical moment, the language of indiscriminate revenge and lawlessness seems to be winning the day. This is a discourse unconscious of its own dangerous refusal to acknowledge the important role that democratic values and social justice must play to achieve a truly unified response and to prevent the further killing of innocent people, regardless of their religion, culture, and place of occupancy in the world. Authoritarianism in this context encounters little resistance in its efforts to turn politics "into a criminal system and keeps working toward the expansion of the realm of pure violence, where its advancement can proceed unhindered."[69] The greatest struggle faced by the American public is not terrorism, but a struggle on behalf of justice, freedom, and democracy for all of the citizens of the globe. This is not going to take place, as President Obama's policies will tragically affirm, by shutting down democracy, eliminating its most cherished rights and freedoms, and deriding communities of dissent.

American society is broken, corrupted by the financial elite, and addicted to violence and a culture of permanent war. The commanding institutions of American life have lost their sense of public mission, just as leadership at all levels of government is being stripped of any viable democratic vision. The United States is now governed by an economic and social orthodoxy informed by the dictates of religious and political extremists. Reform efforts that include the established political parties have resulted in nothing but regression, or forms of accommodation that serve to normalize the new authoritarianism and its war on terrorism. Politics has to be thought anew and must be informed by a powerful vision matched by durable organizations that include young people, unions, workers, diverse social movements, artists, intellectuals, and others. In part, this means reawakening the radical imagination so as to address the intensifying crisis of history and agency, and engage the emotional and ethical registers of fear and human suffering. To fight the neoliberal counterrevolution, social movements need to create new public spaces along with a new language for enabling people to relate the self to public life, social responsibility, and the demands of global citizenship.

Instead of viewing the current crisis as a total break with the past that has nothing to learn from history, it is crucial for the American public to begin to understand how the past might be useful in addressing what it means to live in a democracy at a time when democracy is viewed as nothing more than a hindrance to the wishes and interests of the new extremists who now control the American government. The anti-democratic forces that define American history cannot be forgotten in the fog of political and cultural amnesia. State violence and terrorism have a long history in the United States, both in its foreign and domestic policies, and ignoring this dark period of history means that nothing will be learned from the legacy of a politics that has indulged authoritarian ideologies and embraced violence as a central measure of power, national identity, and patriotism.[70]

At stake here is the need to establish an alternative vision of a genuinely democratic society and a global order that prioritizes the safeguarding of basic civil liberties and human rights. Any struggle against terrorism must begin with the pledge on the part of the United States that it will work in conjunction with international organizations, especially the United Nations; that it will refuse to engage in any military operations that might target civilians; and that it will rethink those aspects of its foreign policy that have allied it with repressive nations in which democratic liberties and civilian lives are under siege. Once again, the United States has a long history of supporting terrorist groups, upholding authoritarian regimes, and imposing atrocities and barbarous acts of violence on others—the more recent and well-known being Abu Ghraib, the torture dungeons of CIA-controlled black sites, the Predator and Reaper drone strikes "on at least eight wedding parties," and the brutalizing murders committed by the twelve-member "'kill team' that hunted Afghans 'for sport.'"[71] Crimes overlooked will be repeated and intensified, just as public memory is rendered a liability in the discourse of revenge, demonization, and extreme violence.

The political left in the United States is too fractured and needs to develop a more comprehensive understanding of politics, oppression, and struggles as well as a discourse that rises to the level of ethical assessment and accountability. Against the new authoritarianism and its ever-evolving forms of terror, progressives of all stripes need an inspiring and energizing politics that embraces coalition building, rejects the notion that capitalism equals democracy, and challenges the stolid vocabulary of embodied incapacity stripped of any sense of risk, hope, and possibility. If the struggle against the war on terrorism, militarization, and neoliberalization is to have any chance of success, it is crucial for a loyal and dedicated left to embrace a commitment to economic and social justice, understanding the educative nature of politics, and the need to build a sustainable political formation outside of the established parties.[72]

The United States is in a new historical conjuncture, and as difficult as it is to admit, it is a conjuncture that shares more with the legacies of totalitarianism than with America's often misguided understanding of democracy. Under the merging of the surveillance state, warfare state, and the harsh regime of neoliberalism, we are witnessing the death of the old system of social welfare supports and the emergence of a new society marked by the heavy hand of the national security state. For the American public, this has meant not only the depoliticization of public discourse and a pervasive culture of fear, but extreme inequities in wealth, power, and income, and a new mode of governance now firmly controlled by the major corporations, banks, and financial elite. This is a politics in which there is no room for democracy, and no room for reformism. The time has come to name the current historical moment as representative of the "dark times" that Hannah Arendt warned us against. We must begin to transform politics at a systemic level through social movements in which the promise of a radical democracy can be reimagined in the midst of determined, collective struggles. The war on terrorism has morphed into a new form of authoritarianism that imposes its own brand of terror and whose real enemy is not terrorism at all, but democracy itself.

1

America's Addiction to Torture

THE UNITED STATES IS ADDICTED TO TORTURE. Not only does this savage addiction run through its history like an overheated electric current, but it has become intensified as part of a broader national psychosis of fear, war, and violence. A post-9/11 obsession with security and revenge has buttressed a militarized culture in which violence becomes the first principle, an essential need, whether in the guise of a national sport, mode of entertainment, or celebrated ideal.

Foreign and domestic violence now mediate everyday relations and America's connection to the larger world. As such, terror, fear, war, and torture become normalized, and the work of dehumanization takes its toll on the American public as more and more people not only become numb to the horror of torture but begin to live in a state of moral stupor, a coma that relegates morality to the dustbin of history. How else to explain recent polls indicating that 58 percent of the American public believe that torture under certain circumstances can be justified and that 59 percent think that the CIA's brutal torture methods produced crucial information that helped prevent future attacks?[1] There is more at stake here than manufactured ignorance and an unconscionable flight from the truth. There is also a dangerous escape from justice, morality, and the most basic principles central to a democratic society. The celebration of brutality, spectacles of violence, and the affirmation of torture suggest that in a market-driven society with its unchecked individualism, sheer social Darwinism, and refusal to think about social costs or, for that matter, any notion of the public good, nurturing an addiction to cruelty, violence, and torture becomes only too easy. In the age of disposability and despicable gaps in wealth, income, and power, modern terror becomes normalized and points to the onslaught of a mode of totalitarianism that is more than an ephemeral moment in history. Violence is no longer marginal to American life; it is the foundation that now drives it. As Lawrence Wittner recently observed:

When it comes to violence and preparations for violence, the United States is, indeed, No. 1. In 2013, according to a report by the Stockholm International Peace Research Institute, the U.S. government accounted for 37 percent of world military expenditures, putting it far ahead of all other nations. (The two closest competitors, China and Russia, accounted for 11 percent and 5 percent respectively.) From 2004 to 2013, the United States was also the No. 1 weapons exporter in the world. Moreover, given the U.S. government's almost continuous series of wars and acts of military intervention since 1941, it seems likely that it surpasses all rivals when it comes to international violence.[2]

With the release of the Senate Select Committee on Intelligence's Report on Torture in December 2014, it became clear that the United States, in the aftermath of the loathsome terrorist attack of 9/11, has entered into a new and barbarous stage in its history, one in which acts of violence and moral depravity were not only embraced but celebrated.[3] Certainly, this is not to suggest that the United States had not engaged in criminal and lawless acts historically or committed acts of brutality that would rightly be labeled acts of torture. That much about our history is clear: indiscriminate violence and torture practiced through and with the right-wing Latin American dictatorships in Argentina, Chile, Uruguay, Paraguay, Bolivia, and Brazil in the 1970s; the willful murder and torture of civilians in Vietnam, Iraq, and Afghanistan; and, of more recent memory, the torture and prisoner abuse at Guantánamo and Abu Ghraib. The United States is no stranger to torture, nor is it free of complicity in aiding other countries notorious for their abuses of human rights. As Noam Chomsky and Edward Herman have reminded us: among "35 countries using torture on an administrative basis in the late 1970s, 26 were clients of the United States."[4]

In fact, the United States has a long record of inflicting torture on others, both at home and abroad, although it has never admitted to such acts. Instead, the official response has been to deny this history or do everything to hide such monstrous acts from public view through government censorship, appealing to the state secrecy privilege, or deploying a language that buries narratives of extraordinary cruelty in harmless sounding euphemisms. For example, the benign-sounding CIA "Phoenix Program" in South Vietnam resulted in the deaths of over 21,000 Vietnamese.[5] As Carl Boggs argues, the acts of U.S. barbarism in Vietnam appeared both unrestrained and never-ending, with routinized brutality such as throwing people out of planes jokingly labeled as "flying lessons" or "half a helicopter ride,"[6] while tying a field telephone wire around a man's testicles and ringing it up was a practice horrifyingly called "the Bell Telephone Hour."[7] Officially sanctioned torture has never been discussed as a legitimate concern; but, as indicated by a few well-documented accounts, it seems to be as American as apple pie.[8]

Torture for the United States is also part of a long history of domestic terrorism, as was evident in the attempts on the part of the FBI, working under a secret program called COINTELPRO, to assassinate those considered domestic and foreign enemies.[9] COINTELPRO was about more than spying; it was a legally sanctioned machinery of violence and assassination.[10] In one of the most notorious cases, the FBI worked with the Chicago police to set up the conditions for the assassination of Fred Hampton and Mark Clark, two members of the Black Panther Party. Noam Chomsky has compared COINTELPRO, which went on from the 1950s to the 1970s, to Wilson's Red Scare, while further asserting that COINTELPRO was "the worst systematic and extended violation of basic civil rights by the federal government."[11] What characterized these programs of domestic terrorism was that they were all shrouded in secrecy, yet allegedly were conducted in the name of national security and democratic rights.

Torture has also had a long-standing domestic presence as part of the brutalized practices that have shaped American chattel slavery through to its most recent "peculiar institution," the rapidly expanding prison-industrial complex.[12] The racial disparities in American prisons and criminal justice system register the profound injustice of racial discrimination as well as a sordid expression of racist violence. As the novelist Ishmael Reed contends, this is a prison system "that is rotten to the core . . . where torture and rape are regular occurrences and where in some states the conditions are worse than at Gitmo. California prison hospitals are so bad that they have been declared unconstitutional and a form of torture."[13]

One of the more recently publicized cases of prison torture involved the arrest of a former Chicago police commander, Jon Burge, who was charged with regularly torturing African American men "in order to force them to falsely confess to crimes they did not commit."[14] According to attorney Taylor Flint, "from 1972 to 1991, Burge led a group of white Chicago detectives who tortured over 100 African American men at stationhouses on Chicago's South and West Sides [routinely using] electric shock, suffocation with plastic bags and typewriter covers to obtain confessions from their victims."[15] One report claims that many of these men were beaten with telephone books and that "cattle prods were used to administer electric shocks to victims' genitals. They were suffocated, beaten, and burned, and had guns forced into their mouths. They faced mock executions with shotguns. . . . One tactic used was known as 'the Vietnam treatment,' presumably started by Burge, a Vietnam veteran."[16] The filmmaker Deborah Davis has documented a number of incidents in the 1990s of unmistakable torture within the American prison system and has argued that many of the sadistic practices she witnessed being used against prisoners were essentially exported to Abu Ghraib.

After 9/11, the United States slipped into a moral coma as President Bush and Vice President Cheney worked tirelessly to ensure that the United

States would not be constrained by international prohibitions against cruel and inhumane treatment. Their crusade against terror turned torture, as Mark Danner argues, into "a marker of political commitment," while their actions resulted in the construction of a vast secret and illegal apparatus of violence in which, under the cover of national security, alleged "terrorists" could be arrested and held without charges, made to disappear into secret CIA "black sites," become ghost detainees removed from any vestige of legality, or be secretly abducted and sent to other countries to be tortured. As Jane Mayer puts it:

> Simply by designating the suspects "enemy combatants," the President could suspend the ancient writ of habeas corpus that guarantees a person the right to challenge his imprisonment in front of a fair and independent authority. Once in U.S. custody, the President's lawyers said, these suspects could be held incommunicado, hidden from their families and international monitors such as the Red Cross, and subjected to unending abuse, so long as it didn't meet the lawyer's own definition of torture. And they could be held for the duration of the war against terrorism, a struggle in which victory had never been clearly defined.[17]

The maiming and breaking of bodies and the forms of unimaginable pain inflicted by the Bush administration on so-called enemy combatants were no longer seen as violations of either international human rights or a constitutional commitment to democratic ideals. The war on terror had now reduced governance in the United States to a legalized apparatus of terror that mimicked the very violence it was meant to combat. In the aftermath of 9/11, under the leadership of Bush and his neoconservative band of merry criminal advisors, justice took a leave of absence and the "gloves came off." As Mark Danner states, "The United States transformed itself from a country that, officially at least, condemned torture to a country that practised it."[18] But it did more. Under the Bush-Cheney reign of power, torture was embraced in unprecedented ways through a no-holds-barred approach to war that suggested the administration's need to exhibit a kind of ethical and psychic hardening—a hyper-masculine emotional callousness that expressed itself in a warped militaristic mindset. State secrecy and war crimes became the only tributes now paid to democracy. The latter is particularly evident in Cheney's morally irresponsible, if not depraved, response to the *Report on Torture* in which he stated: "I think that what needed to be done was done. I think we were perfectly justified in doing it and I'd do it again in a minute."[19] Cheney went so far on NBC's *Meet the Press* as to deny that waterboarding and related interrogation tactics were torture. In Cheney's dark world, there are no mistakes so long as the ends justify the means: "Asked again whether he was satisfied with a program that erroneously locked up detainees, [Cheney] replied, 'I have no problem as long as we achieve our objective.'"[20] This barbarous sanctioning of human suffering is reminiscent of statements provided by other war criminals such as Adolf Eichmann and Pol Pot who also denied that their actions were a violation of human rights. Hopefully, Cheney's admission that he engineered the CIA to torture people will one day require justification in a court of law in which he is charged as a war criminal.[21]

As Frank Rich has argued and the *Report on Torture* confirms, "Torture was a premeditated policy approved at our government's highest levels . . . psychologists and physicians were enlisted as collaborators in inflicting pain; and . . . in the assessment of reliable sources like the FBI director Robert Mueller, it did not help disrupt any terrorist attacks."[22] When the Torture Memos of 2002 and 2005 implicating the Bush-Cheney regime were eventually made public by the Obama administration, they revealed that the United States had been turned into a globalized torture state.[23] Conservative columnist Andrew Sullivan went so far as to claim that "if you want to know how democracies die, read these memos."[24] The memos, written by government lawyers John Yoo, Steven Bradbury, and Jay Bybee, advised the CIA under the Bush administration to use barbaric interrogation techniques on al Qaeda detainees held at Guantánamo and other secret detention centers around the world. They offered detailed instructions on how to implement ten techniques prohibited in the *Army Field Manual*, including facial slaps, "use of a plastic neck collar to slam suspects into a specially built wall,"[25] sleep deprivation, cramped confinement in small boxes, use of insects in confined boxes, stress positions, and waterboarding. All of these examples of physical and mental torment have been documented in the Senate report. In fact, the report claims that the most recent disclosures about torture used by the CIA demonstrate such practices were even more brutal and less effective than previously reported.

Waterboarding, which has been condemned by democracies all over the world, consists of the individual being "bound securely to an inclined bench, which is approximately four feet by seven feet. The individual's feet are generally elevated. A cloth is placed over the forehead and eyes. Water is then applied to the cloth in a controlled manner [and] produces the perception of 'suffocation and incipient panic.'"[26] The highly detailed, amoral nature in which these abuses were first defined and endorsed by lawyers from the Office of Legal Council (OLC) was not only chilling but also reminiscent of the harsh and ethically depraved instrumentalism used by those technicians of death in criminal states such as Emperor Hirohito's imperialist Japan and Nazi Germany. Andy Worthington's analysis suggests that there is more than a hint of brutalization and dehumanization in the language used by the OLC's Principal Deputy Assistant Attorney General Steven G. Bradbury's memo, which recommended

"nudity, dietary manipulation and sleep deprivation"—now revealed explicitly as not just keeping a prisoner awake, but hanging him, naked except for a diaper, by a chain attached to shackles around his wrists—essentially, techniques that produce insignificant and transient discomfort. We are, for example, breezily told that caloric intake "will always be set at or above 1,000 kcal / day," and are encouraged to compare this enforced starvation with "several commercial weight-loss programs in the United States which involve similar or even greater reductions in calorific intake" . . . and when it comes to waterboarding, Bradbury clinically confirms that it can be used 12 times a day over five days in a period of a month—a total of 60 times for a technique that is so horrible that one application is supposed to have even the most hardened terrorist literally gagging to tell all.[27]

The *New York Times* claimed in an editorial that "to read the . . . four memos on prisoner interrogation written by George W. Bush's Justice Department is to take a journey into depravity."[28] The editorial was particularly incensed over a passage written by Jay Bybee, who was then an assistant attorney general in the Bush administration. As the *Times* then pointed out, Bybee "wrote admiringly about a contraption for waterboarding that would lurch a prisoner upright if he stopped breathing while water was poured over his face. He praised the Central Intelligence Agency for having doctors ready to perform an emergency tracheotomy if necessary."[29] Bybee's memo is particularly disturbing, even repugnant, in its disregard for human rights, human dignity, and democratic values, not only describing how the mechanics of waterboarding should be implemented but also providing detailed instructions for introducing insects into confined boxes that held suspected terrorist prisoners. In light of mounting criticism, Bybee both defended his support of such severe interrogation tactics and further argued that "the memorandums represented 'a good faith analysis of the law' that properly defined the thin line between harsh treatment and torture."[30] Indeed, it seems that Bybee should have looked carefully at the following judgment pronounced by the American court in Nuremberg to the lawyers and jurists who rewrote the law for the Nazi regime: "You destroyed law and justice in Germany utilizing the empty forms of the legal process."[31]

As brutal as the reasoning revealed in the memos proved to be, the *Senate Report on Torture* documents even further revelations regarding millions of dollars spent on black sites, the amateurish qualifications of those who conducted interrogations, the complicity of unqualified psychologists who milked the government for $81 million to develop torture techniques, and the endless lies produced by both the CIA and the Bush-Cheney administration regarding everything from the use of secret prisons established all over the world to the false claims that the use of torture was responsible for providing information that led to the finding and killing of Osama Bin Laden by members of the Navy SEALs.[32] The report also stated that far more people were waterboarded than was first disclosed and that the sessions amounted to extreme acts of cruelty. Some members of the CIA choked up over the cruel nature of the interrogations and sent memos to Langley calling their legality into question, but were told by higher officials to continue with the practice. In fact, the interrogations were considered so inhumane and cruel by some CIA officers that they threatened to transfer to other departments if the brutal interrogations continued.

The United States was condemned around the globe for its support of torture and it was hoped that such extensive condemnation would take place once again in light of the Senate report. Fortunately, when President Obama came to office, he outlawed the most egregious acts practiced by the professional torturers of the Bush-Cheney regime. Yet undercurrents of authoritarianism die hard in the circles of unaccountable power. The Senate report made clear that the CIA engaged in lies, distortions, and horrendous violations of human rights, including waterboarding and other sordid practices. The report also revealed that the CIA used monstrous methods such as forced rectal feeding, dragging hooded detainees "up and down a long corridor while being slapped and punched," and threatening to kill or rape family members of the prisoners. But, in spite of the appalling evidence presented by the report, members of the old Bush crowd— including former vice president Cheney, former CIA directors George J. Tenet and Michael V. Hayden, and a number of prominent Republican Party politicians—are still defending the use of torture or, as they euphemistically contend, "enhanced interrogation techniques."

The psychopathic undercurrent and the authoritarian impulse of such reactions finds its most instructive expression in former Bush communications chief Nicolle Wallace, who, while appearing on the *Morning Joe* show, protested in response to the revelations of the Senate report: "I don't care what we did." Yet, as Elias Isquith, a writer for *Salon.com*, contends, "Grotesque as that was, though, the really scary part was [Wallace's implication that] waterboarding, sleep deprivation, stress positions and sexual assault is part of what makes America 'great.'"[33] Wallace's comments are more than morally repugnant; they embody the stance of so many other war criminals who either have been indifferent to the massive suffering and deaths they caused or actually took pride in their actions. They are the bureaucrats whose thoughtlessness and moral depravity Hannah Arendt identified as the rear guard of totalitarianism.

Illegal legalities, moral depravity, and mad violence are presented to the public wrapped in a whitewashed logic of such subterfuge that it rivals Orwellian doublethink. The rhetorical gymnastics used by the torture squad are designed to make the American public believe that if you refer to torture by some seemingly innocuous name, then the pain and suffering it causes will suddenly disappear.[34] The latter represents not just the discourse of magical thinking, but a refusal to recognize that "if cruelty is the worst thing that humans do to each other, torture [is] the most extreme expression of human cruelty."[35] These apostles of torture are politicians who thrive in some sick zone of political and social abandonment, and who unapologetically further acts of barbarism, fear, willful lies, and moral depravity. They are the new totalitarians who hate democracy, embrace a punishing state, and believe that politics is primarily an extension of war. They are the thoughtless gangsters reminiscent of the monsters who made fascism possible at another time in history. For them, torture is an instrument of fear; one sordid strategy and element in a global war that attempts to expand U.S. power and put into play a vast legal and repressive apparatus that expands the field of violence and the technologies, knowledge, and institutions central to fighting what they wish to be an all-encompassing war on terror. Americans now live under a government in which the doctrine of permanent warfare is legitimated through a state of emergency deeply rooted in a mass psychology of violence and culture of cruelty that are essential to transforming a government of laws into a regime of lawlessness.

Once the authoritarian side of political governance takes hold, it is hard to eradicate. Power is addictive, especially when it is reckless, and offers personal rewards for those politicians who follow the corporate script and stand to benefit from human misery. Witness the number of Republicans who still defend the practice of torture and deny the legitimacy of the Senate report. Ignoring that torture is an exercise of power based on willed amorality, they duplicitously attack the Senate report not for its content, but because they believe its release will anger the alleged enemies of the United States—as if that hasn't already been done by demonizing their religion, encircling them with nuclear weapons, bombing them alongside civilians in indiscriminate drone attacks, torturing them, and otherwise threatening or killing them through a range of savage military practices and diplomatic acts. Or they argue, somewhat more ingenuously, that the Senate report will embarrass the Bush-Cheney administration. As is well-known, the Obama administration has done nothing to address or bring to justice those indicted by the report.

Civility has not been the strong point of a Republican Party that is overtly racist, hates immigrants, shuts down the government, and twists logic in order to claim itself to be a victim of hate, all the while catering to every whim of the financial elite. Through such talking heads as Nicolle Wallace, the United States doesn't just alienate its enemies, it actively creates them by spreading hatred and lies. Principles are not being defended in these arguments—only the kind of raw, naked power that has come to mark authoritarian regimes. It gets worse. The defenders of the globalized torture state are neither deranged nor even confused; on the contrary, they are decisive and deliberate in their allegiance to capital and the corporate machinery of social, cultural, and political violence that will provide them with lucrative jobs once they finish the bidding of defense contractors and other proponents of the finance and warfare state.

To his credit, Republican Senator John McCain, himself a victim of torture during the Vietnam War, broke with the moral dinosaurs in his party and defended the release of the Senate report, insisting that the CIA's use of torture during the Bush-Cheney years "stained our national honor, did much harm, and little practical good." Most of his colleagues disagree and are now arguing that in spite of the evidence, torture produced actionable intelligence and helped to save lives, a claim the Senate report strongly negates. Once again, pragmatism trumps the levers of justice, and the principles of human rights as moral considerations give way to a kind of ghastly death-embracing dance with a debased instrumental rationality.

Not only has the United States lost its moral compass, it has degenerated into a state of political darkness reminiscent of dictatorships that maimed human bodies and inflicted unspeakable acts of violence on the innocent while embracing a mad utilitarianism in order to remove themselves from any sense of justice, compassion, and reason. This is the formative culture not simply of a society that is dehumanizing and ethically lost, but one that produces a society in alignment with the savage ethos and beliefs of an updated totalitarianism. The Senate report has brought one of the darkest sides of humanity to light, and it has sparked a predictable outrage and weak public condemnation. But, thus far, little has been said about either the conditions that made this journey to the dark side possible, or what moral, political, and educational absences had to occur in the collective psyche of both the American public and the U.S. government that not only allowed torture to happen but actually sanctioned its use? What made it so easy for the barbarians not only to implement acts of torture but to openly defend such practices as a legitimate government policy?

With the release of the Senate report, the supine American press finally has to acknowledge that the United States had joined with other totalitarian countries of the past in committing atrocities completely alien to any functioning democracy. America is no longer even a weak democracy. The lie is now more visible than ever. Nonetheless, the usual crowd of politicians, pundits, and mainstream media not only has little to say about the history of torture committed by the United States at home and abroad, but also about its own silence when it comes face to face with this dark side of American history. The possibility of a politically and morally charged critique has turned into a cowardly and evasive debate around questions such as: Does torture prevent terrorist acts from taking place? Is waterboarding really an act of torture? Is torture justified in the face of extremist attacks on the United States? Is the CIA being scapegoated for actions promoted by the Bush-Cheney-Rumsfeld administration? And so it goes. These are the wrong questions and reveal the toxic complicity the mainstream press has had all along with these anti-democratic practices. War crimes should not be debated; they should be condemned without qualification.

In an incredible act of bad faith, those responsible for state-sanctioned acts of torture are now interviewed by the mainstream media and presented, if not outright described, as reasonable men with honorable intentions. Rather than being condemned as agents of a totalitarian state and as war criminals who should be prosecuted, those who gave the orders to torture as well as those who carried out such inhuman practices are treated as one side of a debate team, anxious to get the real story out in order to provide the other side of the narrative. The appeal to balance offered by the mainstream media and others is more than a self-glorifying ritual that takes flight from naming the violence and barbarism imposed by states that practice torture; it also hides the voices, thus further dehumanizing those who are the victims of torture. If torture kidnaps, hides, and maims the bodies of those it savagely violates, the apologists for torture willfully erase the voices and humanity of those victims who have been dehumanized. As Glenn Greenwald makes clear:

Ever since the torture report was released last week, U.S. television outlets have endlessly featured American torturers and torture proponents. But there was one group that was almost never heard from: the victims of their torture, not even the ones recognized by the U.S. Government itself as innocent, not even the family members of the ones they tortured to death. They don't show all sides. They systematically and quite deliberately exclude the victims of the very policies of the U.S. Government they pretend to cover. And they do that because including those victims would be too informative. . . . At the very least, it would make it impossible for many people to deny to themselves the utter savagery and sadism carried out in their names. Keeping those victims silenced and invisible is the biggest favor the U.S. television media could do for the government over which they claim to act as watchdogs. So that's what they do: dutifully, eagerly and with very rare exception.[36]

There is more than a hint of moral depravity here; there is also what I have called elsewhere the violence of organized forgetting.[37] Discussions of torture should never involve a cowardly appeal to balance. The only reasonable approach any democracy can take toward torture is both to condemn it and to prosecute those responsible for it as well as those who practice it. In this case, that would include the highest elected officials such as George W. Bush, Dick Cheney, Donald Rumsfeld, members of the CIA, the subcontractors who tortured, and all those who engaged in despicable acts designed to create physical torment and mental anguish for other human beings—whether this involved hanging people upside down, raping them rectally, subjecting them to freezing temperatures while chained to a floor, or any number of horrific treatments—all the while looking askance, even when torture ended in murder.

For a society to regard torture as a reasonable practice worthy of informed debate reveals a death-dealing virus deeply embedded in the American social and political psyche, partly produced by those commanding cultural apparatuses that believe the only value that matters is rooted in acts of commerce and the accumulation of capital at any cost—and that willingly glean massive profits from the carcinogenic culture of the mainstream media that sell pervasive spectacles of violence and the unchecked militarism of American society as entertainment. Ideas matter, education matters, morality matters, and justice matters in a democracy. People who hold power in America should be held accountable for what actions they take and what actions they permit, especially when they violate any and every standard of human rights and decency.

Maybe it is time to treat the *Senate Report on Torture* as just one register of a series of crimes being committed under the regime of a savage neoliberalism. After all, an economic policy that views ethics as a liability, disdains the public good, and enshrines self-interest as the highest of virtues provides a petri dish not just for testing a range of state-sanctioned torture methods abroad, but also for the growth of lawless and cruel policies at home. Maybe it's time to connect the dots between the government's use of waterboarding and a history that includes the killing of Black Panther

Fred Hampton by the Chicago police, the illegal existence of COINTEL-PRO, the savage brutality of the Phoenix Program in Vietnam,[38] the rise of the post-Orwellian surveillance state, the militarization of the local police, the transformation of underserved American cities into war zones, the creation of Obama's kill list, the use of drones that indiscriminately execute people, and the latest killings of Michael Brown, Eric Garner, Tamir Rice, Freddie Gray, and others at the hands of a militarized police force that now acts with impunity.[39] And most of all, the savage system of organized torture that made the nation's economic dominance possible in the first place—slavery.

Is it not reasonable to argue that the lawlessness that creates the torture state and provides immunity for killer cops also provides protection for those in the government and the CIA who extended the tentacles of the globalized torture state? Is it too far-fetched to argue that Eric Garner's utterance "I can't breathe, I can't breathe" is a reminder of the many foreign nationals under the control of the torture state who might have uttered the same words as they were being tortured? Connect these dots and there is more at play here than retreat into a facile high moralism that condemns torture as a "stain on our values." Instead, what becomes evident is that the United States engaging in torture has become symptomatic of something much larger than an errant plunge into immorality and lawlessness. What begins to be revealed is a more systemic entrenchment in what Robert Jay Lifton has described as "a death-saturated age"[40] in which matters of violence, survival, and trauma inescapably bear down on daily experience while pushing the United States into the dark recesses of a new authoritarianism. The mad and naked horror of torture has now become standardized, a kind of mad common sense, rather than thought to be unimaginable, just as radical evil fails to provoke moral outrage and degenerates into the fog of everyday banality. The Senate report reveals only one moment in an endless upsurge of lawlessness that has come to characterize the United States' long, slow plunge into totalitarianism. How else to explain a paper written and published by a West Point professor, William Bradford, who argues that lawful targets in the war on terror should include "law school facilities, scholars' home offices and media outlets where they give interviews. . . . Shocking and extreme as this option might seem, [dissenting] scholars, and the law schools that employ them, are—at least in theory—targetable so long as attacks are proportional, distinguish noncombatants from combatants, employ non-prohibited weapons, and contribute to the defeat of Islamism."[41] The killing of dissidents is what the war on terror morphs into when its most vile impulses are presented as reasonable policy measures. Americans now inhabit a society in which the delete button holds sway and the ethical imagination withers. And what is being erased is not only any vestige of a sense of commitment, but also public and historical memory and the foundations of any viable notion of justice, equality, and accountability. That is a story that also needs to be told.

This book is about another kind of torture, one that is more capacious and seemingly more abstract but just as deadly in its destruction of human life, justice, and democracy. This is a mode of torture that resembles the "mind virus" mentioned in the Senate report, one that induces fear, paralysis, and produces the toxic formative culture that characterizes the reign of neoliberalism. Isolation, privatization, and the cold logic of instrumental rationality have created a new kind of social formation and social order in which it becomes difficult to form communal bonds, deep connections, a sense of intimacy, and long-term commitments. Neoliberalism has created a society of monsters for whom pain and suffering are viewed as entertainment or deserving of scorn; warfare is a permanent state of existence; torture becomes a matter of expediency; and militarism is celebrated as the most powerful mediator of human relationships.

Under the reign of neoliberalism, politics has taken an exit from ethics, and thus interventions in the world are now divorced from any consideration of their social costs. This is the ideological metrics of political zombies. The key word here is *atomization*, and it is the curse of both neoliberal societies and democracy itself. A radical democracy demands a notion of educated hope capable of energizing a generation of young people and others who connect the torture state to the violence and criminality of an economic system that celebrates its own depravities. It demands a social movement unwilling to accept temporary technological fixes or cheap reforms. It demands a new politics for which the word *revolution* means going to the root of the problem and addressing it nonviolently, with dignity, civic courage, and the refusal to accept a future that will only mimic the present. The return of torture should provoke discussion and thought beyond matters of state policy and spectacles of violence: it should bring to mind the moral paralysis and deadening legacy of a dark period in American history; it should serve as a point of identification for all victims of neoliberal tyranny and the extreme terror it perpetrates across the globe; and it should be utterly condemned as a war crime and challenged in all of its dreadful registers.

— 2 —

Terrorizing the Self: Selfie Culture in the Age of Corporate and State Surveillance

AMERICAN SOCIETY IS IN THE GRIP of an ethical tranquillization marked not only by a crisis of history, memory, and agency but also the proliferation of a kind of paralyzing infantilism. Everywhere we look the refusal to think, engage in troubling knowledge, and welcome robust dialogue and engaged forms of pedagogy are now met by the fog of rigidity, anti-intellectualism, and a collapse of the public into the private. A politics of intense privatization and its embrace of the self as the only viable unit of agency appears to have a strong grip on American society as can be seen in the endless attacks on reason, truth, critical thinking, and informed exchange, or any other relationship that embraces the social and the democratic values that support it. This might be expected in a society that has become increasingly anti-intellectual, given its commitment to commodities, violence, privatization, the death of the social, and the bare bones relations of commerce. But it is more surprising when it is elevated to a national ideal and fashion craze wrapped in a kind of self-righteous moralism marked by an inability or reluctance to imagine what others are thinking. Or as Kant once said: "to think from the standpoint of everyone else."[1] That this type of ideological self-righteousness fueled by a celebrity culture and elevation of self-interest is seen as the only value that matters is especially dispiriting when it accommodates rather than challenges the rise of the surveillance state and the demise of the public good along with those modes of solidarity that embrace a collective sense of agency.

Surveillance has become a growing feature of daily life wielded by both the state and the larger corporate sphere. This merger registers both the transformation of the political state into the corporate state as well as the transformation of a market economy into a criminal economy. One growing attribute of the merging of state and corporate surveillance apparatuses is the increasing view of privacy on the part of the American public as something to escape from rather than to preserve as a precious political right. The surveillance and security-corporate state is one that not only listens, watches, and gathers massive amounts of information through data mining necessary for monitoring the American public—now considered as both potential terrorists and a vast consumer market—but also acculturates the public into accepting the intrusion of surveillance technologies and privatized commodified values into all aspects of their lives. Personal information is *willingly* given over to social media and other corporate-based websites such as Instagram, Facebook, Twitter, and other media platforms and harvested daily as people move from one targeted website to the next across multiple screens and digital apparatuses.

As Ariel Dorfman points out, many "social media users gladly give up their liberty and privacy, invariably for the most benevolent of platitudes and reasons," all the while endlessly shopping online and texting.[2] While selfies may not lend themselves directly to giving up important private information online, they do speak to the necessity to make the self into an object of public concern, if not a manifestation of how an infatuation with selfie culture now replaces any notion of the social as the only form of agency available to many people. Under such circumstances, it becomes much easier to put privacy rights at risk as they are viewed less as something to protect than to escape from in order to put the self on public display.

When the issue of surveillance takes place outside of the illegal practices performed by government intelligence agencies, critics most often point to the growing culture of inspection and monitoring that occurs in a variety of public spheres through ever-present digital technologies used to amass information, most evident in the use of video cameras that inhabit every public space from the streets, commercial establishments, and workplaces to the schools our children attend as well as in the myriad scanners placed at the entry points of airports, stores, sporting events, and the like. Rarely do critics point to the emergence of the selfie as another index of the public's need to escape from the domain of what was once considered to be the cherished and protected realm of the private and personal. Privacy rights that were once viewed as a crucial safeguard in preventing personal and important information from being inserted into the larger public domain are now regarded as a liability by many young people. Formerly defended as a key democratic principle that ensures citizens' autonomy from the state, the right to privacy has now been reduced to the right to participate, anonymously or otherwise, in the seductions of a narcissistic consumer culture. Privacy was also seen as a sphere of protection from the threat of totalitarianism made infamous in George Orwell's *1984*. In the present oversaturated information age, the right to privacy has become a historical relic and for too many people privacy is no longer a freedom to be cherished and protected.

Privacy has become a curse, an impediment that subverts the endless public display of the self. Zygmunt Bauman echoes this sentiment, arguing:

> These days, it is not so much the possibility of a betrayal or violation of privacy that frightens us, but the opposite: shutting down the exits. The area of privacy turns into a site of incarceration, the owner of private space being condemned and doomed to stew in his or her own juice; forced into a condition marked by an absence of avid listeners eager to wring out and tear away the secrets from behind the ramparts of privacy, to put them on public display and make them everybody's shared property and a property everybody wishes to share.[3]

Privacy has mostly become synonymous with a form of self-generated, nonstop performance—a type of public relations in which privacy is valued only for the way it makes possible the unearthing of secrets, a cult of commodified confessionals, and an infusion of narcissistic, self-referencing narratives. Of course, there is a notable exception here regarding people of color, especially poor dissenting blacks, for whom privacy has never been an assumed right. The right to privacy was violated in the historical reality of slavery, the state terrorism enacted under deep surveillance programs such as COINTELPRO, and in the current wave of mass incarcerations. What has changed, particularly since 9/11, is that the loss of privacy now extends to more and more groups, who are all too willing to view it as a form of self-generated, nonstop performance, a type of public relations in which privacy is rarely valued. Unfortunately, in too many cases the loss of privacy is done voluntarily rather than imposed by the repressive or secret mechanisms of the state.

This is particularly true for many young people who cannot escape from the realm of the private fast enough, though this is not surprising given neoliberalism's emphasis on branding, a "contextless and eternal now of consumption,"[4] and the undermining of any viable social sphere or notion of sociability. The rise of the selfie offers one index of this retreat from privacy rights and thus another form of legitimation for devaluing these once guarded rights altogether. A case in point is the ubiquity of self-portraits endlessly posted on social media. In 2013, *BBC News Magazine* reported:

A search on photo-sharing app Instagram retrieves over 23 million photos uploaded with the hashtag #selfie, and a whopping 51 million with the hashtag #me. Rihanna, Justin Bieber, Lady Gaga and Madonna are all serial uploaders of selfies. Model Kelly Brook took so many she ended up "banning" herself. The Obama children were spotted posing into their mobile phones at their father's second inauguration. Even astronaut Steve Robinson took a photo of himself during his repair of the Space Shuttle *Discovery*. Selfie-ism is everywhere. The word "selfie" has been bandied about so much in the past few years that it is now included in the Oxford Dictionary Online.[5]

What this new politics of digital self-representation suggests is that the most important transgression against privacy may not only be happening through the unwarranted watching, listening, and collecting of information by the state. What is also taking place through the interface of state and corporate modes of the mass collecting of personal information is the practice of normalizing surveillance by upping the pleasure quotient and enticements for young people and older consumers. These groups are now constantly urged to use the new digital technologies and social networks as a mode of entertainment and communication. Yet they function largely to simulate false notions of community and to socialize young people into a regime of security and commodification in which their identities, values, and desires are inextricably tied to a culture of private addictions, self-help, and consuming.

The usual criticism of selfies is that they are an out-of-control form of vanity and narcissism in a society in which an unchecked capitalism promotes forms of rampant self-interest that both legitimizes selfishness and corrodes individual and moral character.[6] In this view, a market-driven moral economy of increased individualism and selfishness has supplanted any larger notion of caring, social responsibility, and the public good. For example, one indication that Foucault's notion of self-care has now moved into the realm of self-obsession can be seen in the "growing number of people who are waiting in line to see plastic surgeons to enhance images they post of themselves on smartphones and other social media sites."[7] Patricia Reaney points out: "Plastic surgeons in the United States have seen a surge in demand for procedures ranging from eye-lid lifts to rhinoplasty, popularly known as nose job, from patients seeking to improve their image in selfies and on social media."[8] It appears that selfies are not only an indication of the public's descent into the narrow orbits of self-obsession and individual posturing but also good for the economy, especially plastic surgeons who are generally among the rich elites. The unchecked rise of selfishness is now partly driven by the search for new forms of capital, which recognize no boundaries and appear to have no ethical limitations.

The plague of narcissism has a long theoretical and political history extending from Sigmund Freud to Christopher Lasch.[9] Freud analyzed narcissism in psychoanalytic terms as a form of self-obsession that ran the gamut from being an element of normal behavior to a perversion that pointed to a psychiatric disorder. According to Lasch, narcissism was a form of self-love that functioned less as a medical disorder than as a disturbing cultural trait and political ideology deeply embedded in a capitalist society, one that disdained empathy, care for "the Other," and promoted a cutthroat notion of competition. Lasch argued that the culture of narcissism promoted an obsession with the self under the guise of making selfishness and self-interest a cherished organizing principle of a market-based society. For Lasch, these traits became visible in the cinematic critique of the megalomaniac and utterly narcissistic Gordon Gekko, the main fictional character in Oliver Stone's 1987 film *Wall Street*, who has become immortalized with his infamous "Greed is good" credo. Both theorists saw these psychological and cultural traits as a threat to one's mental and political health. What neither acknowledged was that in the latter part of the twentieth century they would become normalized, commonsense principles that shaped the everyday behavior of a market-driven society in which they were viewed less as an aberration than as a virtue.

In the current historical moment, Gordon Gekko looks tame. The new heroes of contemporary American capitalism are now modeled after a marriage of John Galt, the character from the infamous Ayn Rand novel *Atlas Shrugged,* who transforms the pursuit of self-interest into a secular religion for the ethically bankrupt, and Patrick Bateman, the more disturbing character in Bret Easton Ellis's novel and the 2000 film *American Psycho* who literally kills those considered disposable in a society in which only the strong survive. Today, fiction has become reality, as the characters Gordon Gekko, John Galt, and Patrick Bateman are personified in the real-life figures of the Koch brothers, Lloyd Blankfein, and Jamie Dimon, among others. The old narcissism looks mild compared to the current retreat into the narrow orbits of privatization, commodification, and self-interest. Lynn Stuart Parramore gets it right in her insightful comment:

> If Lasch had lived to see the new millennium, marked by increased economic inequality and insecurity, along with trends like self-involved social networking and celebrity culture, he would not have been surprised to hear that the new normal is now pretty much taken for granted as the way things are in America. Many even defend narcissism as the correct response to living with increased competition and pressure to win. According to one study, Americans score higher on narcissism than citizens of any other country. Researchers who study personality find that young Americans today score higher on narcissism and lower on empathy than they did 30 years ago.[10]

Under the regime of neoliberalism, narcissism becomes the defining characteristic of not only spoiled celebrities, brutish and cruel CEOs, and fatuous celebrities, it also speaks to a more comprehensive notion of deformed agency, an almost hysterical sense of self-obsession, a criminogenic need for accumulating possessions, and a pathological disdain for democratic social relations. Mainstream selfie culture may not be entirely driven by a pathological notion of narcissism, but it does speak to the disintegration of those public spheres, modes of solidarity, and sense of inclusive community that sustain a democratic society. In its most pernicious forms it speaks to a flight from convictions, social responsibility, and the rational and ethical connections between the self and the larger society. Selfie culture pushes against the constructive cultivation of fantasy, imagination, and memory, allowing such capacities to deteriorate in a constant pursuit of commodified pleasure and the need to heighten the visibility and performance of the self. The culture of atomization and loneliness in neoliberal societies is intensified by offering the self as the only source of enjoyment, exchange, and wonder. How else to explain the bizarre behavior of individuals who have their faces altered in order to look good in their selfies. As Jennifer Reynolds points out after having plastic surgery, "I definitely feel more comfortable right now with my looks if I need to take a selfie; without a doubt, I would have no problem."[11]

In a society in which the personal is the only politics there is, there is more at stake in selfie culture than rampant narcissism or the swindle of fulfillment offered to teenagers and others whose self-obsession and insecurity takes an extreme, if not sometimes dangerous, turn. What is being sacrificed is not just the right to privacy, the willingness to give up the self to commercial interests, but the very notion of individual and political freedom. The atomization that, in part, promotes the popularity of selfie culture is nourished not only by neoliberal fervor for unbridled individualism, but also by the weakening of public values and the emptying out of collective and engaged politics.

Not only is the political and corporate surveillance state concerned about promoting the flight from privacy rights, but it also attempts to use that power to canvass every aspect of people's lives in order to suppress dissent, instill fear in the populace, and repress the possibilities of mass resistance against unchecked power.[12] Selfie culture is also fed by a spiritually empty consumer culture driven by, in Jonathan Crary's words, never-ending "conditions of visibility . . . in which a state of permanent illumination (and performance) is inseparable from the nonstop operation of global exchange and circulation."[13] Crary's insistence that entrepreneurial excess now drives a 24/7 culture points rightly to a society driven by a constant state of "producing, consuming, and discarding" photos as disposable—a central feature of selfie culture.[14] Selfie culture is increasingly shaped within a mode of temporality in which quick turnovers and short attention spans become the measure of how one occupies the ideological and affective spaces of the market with its emphasis on speed, instant gratification, fluidity, and disposability. Under such circumstances, the cheapening of subjectivity and everyday life are further intensified by social identities now fashioned out of brands, commodities, relationships, and images that are used up and discarded as quickly as possible. Under such circumstances, pleasure is held hostage to the addiction of consuming with its 24/7 discharging of impulses, fast consumption, and mass exodus at the expense of purposeful thought and reflection.

Once again, too many young people succumb to the influence of neoliberalism and its relentless refiguring of the public sphere as a site for displaying the personal by running from privacy, making every aspect of their lives public. Or they limit their presence in the public sphere to posting endless images of themselves. In this instance, community becomes reduced to the nonstop production of shared images in which the self becomes the only source of agency worth validating. At the same time, the popularity of selfies points beyond a pervasive narcissism or a desire to collapse the public spheres into endless and shameless representations of the self. Selfies and the culture they produce cannot be entirely collapsed into the logic of domination. Hence, I don't want to suggest that selfie culture is only a medium for various forms of narcissistic performance. Some commentators have suggested that selfies enable people to reach out to each other, present themselves in positive ways, and drive social change. There are many instances in which transgender people, people with disabilities, women of color, undocumented immigrants, and other marginalized groups use selfies in proactive ways that do not buy into mainstream corporate selfie culture. For instance, women of color are using selfies to connect with other women of color and engage in a politics of representation not controlled by mainstream media. As one black feminist writer argues:

So, why invest so much energy into discussing selfies? For marginalized communities, these signs of life are important. Self-publications are flickers of life, assuring you that there are others out there like you, surviving and thriving. I am here. Look at me. Those who experience difficulties or dangers in finding and associating with other members of their community in real life can now find and communicate with them on the Internet. We can find people like us who exist in one or multiple communities, and engage in discourse and provide support. Learning about past and present narratives is easier than before. Social media sites have led to the creation of safe spaces for people of color to manufacture their own visibility and share their narratives in the face of erasure and forced silence.[15]

Many young people claim that selfies offer the opportunity to invite comments by friends and to raise their self-esteem, and that they offer a chance for those who are powerless and voiceless to represent themselves in a more favorable and instructive light.[16] For instance, Rachel Simmons makes a valiant attempt to argue that selfies are especially good for girls.[17] Though this is partly true, I think Erin Gloria Ryan is right in responding to Simmons's claim about selfies as a "positive-self-esteem builder" when she states: "Stop this. Selfies aren't empowering; they're a high-tech reflection of the fucked-up way society teaches women that their most important quality is their physical attractiveness."[18] It is difficult to believe that mainstream, corporate-saturated selfie culture functions constructively to mostly build self-esteem among young girls who are reduced to salacious sexual commodities and fodder for dating sites in the context of a never-ending market that defines them as titbits of a sensationalized celebrity culture. What is often missing in the marginalized use of selfies is that for the most part the practice is driven by a powerful and pervasive set of poisonous market-driven values that frame this practice in ways that are often not talked about. Selfie culture is now a part of an economy that encourages selfies as an act of privatization and consumption, not as a practice that might support the public good, and fails to recognize that some groups are using selfie culture to expand public dialogue rather than turn it over to commercial interests. For instance, a number of people with disabilities are using selfies to connect with others who are marginalized and often disparaged because of their illnesses.[19] Citing a *Vice* website article on "Hospital Selfies Are Therapeutic, Not Narcissistic," Michelle K. Wolf points out:

There are more than 400,000 Millennials living with disabilities in America alone, with an untold number sharing their lives on Instagram. . . . To those on the other side of the lens, graphic images are a way of forcing others to confront a reality most would rather not: that while the body may break, life limps on, just as complex and human as it was before.[20]

At the same time, there is considerable research indicating that "the reality of being watched results in feelings of low self-esteem, depression and anxiety. Whether observed by a supervisor at work or Facebook friends, people are inclined to conform and demonstrate less individuality and creativity."[21] Moreover, the more people give away about themselves, whether through selfies or the emptying out of their lives on other social media such as Facebook, "the more dissatisfaction with what they got in return for giving away so much about themselves."[22] Is it any wonder that so many college students in the age of the selfie are depressed?

A romanticized and depoliticized view of the popularity of selfies misses the point that their mass acceptance, proliferation, and commercial appropriation, filling the public space that once focused on important social problems, show that a sense of social responsibility is in decline. This is especially true among young people whose identity and sense of agency is now shaped largely through the lens of a highly commodified celebrity culture. Ironically, there is an element of selfie culture that does not fall into this trap but is barely mentioned in mainstream media. For example, mainstream selfie culture ignores groups with disabilities that are using selfies to redefine how they are represented in the wider social order. In addition, many Palestinians and Israeli youth are using selfies to draw attention to the suffering inflicted on the inhabitants of Gaza.[23]

We now live in a market-driven age defined as heroic by the conservative Ayn Rand, who argued in her book *The Virtue of Selfishness* that self-interest was the highest virtue and that altruism deserved nothing more than contempt. This retreat from the public good, compassion, and care for the other, and the legitimation of a culture of cruelty and moral indifference are often registered in strange signposts and popularized in the larger culture. This new celebrity-fed stupidity is exemplified by the widely marketed fanfare over reality TV star Kim Kardashian's appropriately named book, *Selfish*, the unique selling feature of which is that it contains 2,000 selfies.

There is more at work here than the marketing of a form of civic illiteracy and retrograde consumer consciousness in which students are taught to mimic the economic success of alleged "brands." There is also the pedagogical production of a kind of insufferable idiocy that remakes the meaning of agency, promoted endlessly through the celebration of celebrity culture as the new normal of mass entertainment. As Mark Fisher points out, this suggests a growing testimony to a commodified society in which "in a world of individualism everyone is trapped within their own feelings, trapped within their own imaginations . . . and unable to escape the tortured conditions of solipsism."[24]

Under the surveillance state, the greatest threat one faces is not simply the violation of one's right to privacy, but the fact that the public is subject to the dictates of authoritarian modes of governance it no longer seems interested in contesting. And it is precisely this existence of unchecked power and the wider culture of political indifference that puts at risk the broader principles of liberty and freedom, which are fundamental to democracy itself. According to Quentin Skinner,

> The response of those who are worried about surveillance has so far been too much couched, it seems to me, in terms of the violation of the right to privacy. Of course it's true that my privacy has been violated if someone is reading my emails without my knowledge. But my point is that my liberty is also being violated, and not merely by the fact that someone is reading my emails but also by the fact that someone has the power to do so should they choose. We have to insist that this in itself takes away liberty because it leaves us at the mercy of arbitrary power. It's no use those who have possession of this power promising that they won't necessarily use it, or will use it

only for the common good. What is offensive to liberty is the very existence of such arbitrary power.[25]

The rise of the mainstream appropriation of selfies under the surveillance state is only one register of neoliberal inspired flight from privacy. As I have argued elsewhere, the dangers of the surveillance state far exceed the attack on privacy and warrant more than simply discussion about balancing security against civil liberties.[26] The critique of the flight from privacy fails to address how the growth of the surveillance state and its appropriation of all spheres of private life are connected to the rise of the punishing state, the militarization of American society, secret prisons, state-sanctioned torture, a growing culture of violence, the criminalization of social problems, the depoliticization of public memory, and one of the largest prison systems in the world—all of which "are only the most concrete, condensed manifestations of a diffuse security regime in which we are all interned and enlisted."[27] The authoritarian nature of the corporate-state surveillance apparatus and security system, with its "urge to surveill, eavesdrop on, spy on, monitor, record, and save every communication of any sort on the planet,"[28] can only be fully understood when its ubiquitous tentacles are connected to wider cultures of control and punishment, including security-patrolled corridors of public schools, the rise in supermax prisons, the hyper-militarization of local police forces, the rise of the military-industrial-academic complex, and the increasing labeling of dissent as an act of terrorism in the United States.[29] Moreover, it must be recognized that the surveillance state is at its most threatening when it convinces the public to self-monitor themselves so that self-tracking becomes a powerful tool of the apparatus of state spying and control.

Selfies may be more than an expression of narcissism gone wild—the promotion of privatization over preserving public and civic culture with their attendant practice of social responsibility. They may also represent the degree to which the ideological and affective spaces of neoliberalism have turned privacy into a mimicry of celebrity culture that both abets and is indifferent to the growing surveillance state and its totalitarian revolution, one that will definitely be televised in an endlessly repeating selfie that owes homage to George Orwell. Once again, it must be stressed that there are registers of representation in selfie culture that point in a different direction.

Some elements of selfie culture neither subscribe to the Kardashian model of self-indulgence nor limit the potential of an alternative selfie culture to comments by a handful of mainstream feminists talking about photos being self-esteem builders. Another trajectory of selfie culture is at work that refuses the retreat into a false sense of empowerment and embraces modes of self-representation as a political act intent on redefining the relationship between the personal and the social in ways that are firmly wedded to social change. These non-mainstream groups are concerned with far more than building self-esteem in the superficial sense. For example, women of color, transgender and disabled people are using selfies to promote communities of healing and empowerment while also challenging a culture of cruelty that marks those who are different by virtue of their age, disability, sexual orientation, and race as disposable.[30]

As Alicia Eler observes, "The selfie is an aesthetic with radical potential for bringing visibility to people and bodies that are othered."[31] And as writer D.K.A. notes:

> The selfie is a new framework for women of color to create their own visibility and subvert dominant truths. Regardless of the content of the image, it is made with the subject's own volition and published with their consent. It is a genuine image, created privately with minimal filtration. The selfie represents a marginalized human being as a human being, instead of countless dehumanizing stereotypes. To control our image and how it is presented is one of the many ways we reclaim our bodies and celebrate our identities. We are converting a tool used to erase us into means to fashion our visibility.[32]

What is crucial to recognize here is that selfie culture can itself be a site of struggle, one that refuses to become complicit either with the politics of narcissism or the growing culture of surveillance. In this case, various individuals and groups are using selfie culture to expand the parameters of public dialogue, public issues, and the opportunity for different political identities to be seen and heard. This is a growing movement whose public presence has largely been ignored in the mainstream press because it connects the personal to the task of rewriting notions of self-presentation that stress matters of difference, justice, and shared beliefs and practices aimed at creating more inclusive communities.

Hannah Arendt has written that "totalitarian domination as a form of government is new in that it is not content with . . . isolation and destroys private life as well. It bases itself on loneliness, on the experience of not belonging to the world at all, which is among the most radical and desperate experiences of man."[33] Selfie culture cannot be viewed as synonymous with a totalitarian politics however it reorganizes and rearranges private life, and in some instances is fighting such a politics. In a totalitarian state, selfie culture can be used to sell dangerous drugs, shame immigrants, promote bullying, and sexually oppress young girls.

The good news is that selfie culture can also be used to rewrite the relationship between the personal and the political and in doing so expand the vibrancy of public discourse and work to prevent the collapse of public life. In this case, selfie culture moves away from the isolation and privatization of neoliberal culture and further enables those individuals and groups working to create a formative critical culture that better enables the translation of private troubles into public issues and brings a further understanding of how public life affects private experiences. In contrast to the mainstream appropriation of selfie culture, this more empowering use of selfies becomes part of what might be called an emergent public dedicated to undermining what Alex Honneth has called "an abyss of failed sociality."[34] Selfie culture is not all of one piece and is emblematic of such a struggle and at its best becomes an act of empowerment and a vehicle for social change. What selfie culture will become presents a crucial site of struggle to address both the collapse of the public into the private and the rise of the punishing and surveillance state—a fight desperately worth waging. Yet, though I don't want to underplay the possibilities for resistance in selfie culture, it is crucial to recognize that little is being said in the culture in general about the enormous power of the surveillance state and the diverse ways in which it welcomes the flight from privacy in order to position people "at the mercy of arbitrary power."[35] Selfie culture will continue to provide a backdoor for state terrorism as long as it does not address the crucial notion that the surveillance state is incompatible with any viable notion of democracy. Privacy rights are crucial as one bulwark against the surveillance state.

Digital promiscuity is not a virtue or a legitimate attempt to establish connections with others. On the contrary, it is a free pass for state and corporate power to spy on its citizens by encouraging their flight from privacy. As long as selfie culture lacks a self-consciousness and political understanding about what the implications are for giving up one's privacy in a surveillance state, it speaks less to new modes of resistance than it does to becoming complicitous with a new mode of state terrorism.

3

Death-Dealing Politics in the Age of Extreme Violence

HOW A SOCIETY TREATS ITS CHILDREN is a powerful moral and political index of its commitment to the institutions, values, and principles that inform the promises of a real democracy. When measured against such a criterion, it is clear that the United States has not only failed, but continues to embrace death-dealing policies that will surely result in democracy's further demise. According to a report released by the Southern Education Foundation, for the first time in history half of U.S. public schoolchildren live in poverty.[1] The U.S. Department of Education reported in 2013 that there were 1.3 million homeless children enrolled in U.S. schools, up 85 percent since 2008; and the organization Feeding America has estimated that 16 million U.S. children, or 21.6 percent, live without food security.[2] As Jana Kasperkevic points out:

> Those numbers are representative of the growing problem of child poverty in the U.S. Overall, one in five U.S. children live in poverty. It has only recently been dropping, with 14.7 million U.S. children living in poverty in 2013, down from 16.1 million in 2012. In 2012, out of 35 economically developed countries, only Romania had a higher child poverty rate than the U.S.[3]

Add to these shameful figures the fact that the United States incarcerates more young people than any other country in the world, keeping over 70,000 youth locked up in juvenile detention facilities while trying, sentencing, and incarcerating an estimated 250,000 youth through the adult criminal justice system each year.[4] With the social contract all but dead, children no longer count for much in a society that makes virtues out of self-interest and greed, and measures success almost entirely in terms of the accumulation of capital. Under the regime of a ruthless neoliberalism, children and working- and middle-class families have become the new casualties of a system that brazenly disdains the rule of law, compassion, and a concern for others. Systemic inequality has become one of the weapons now used not only to exacerbate and reinforce class divisions, but also to wage a war on young people.

The pernicious effects of neoliberal policies—ranging from an attack on the welfare state and the imposition of cruel austerity measures to the selling of public services to private contractors and the redistribution of wealth upward to the 1 percent—amount to an act of domestic terrorism in light of the suffering such policies and practices impose on children in the United States. Rampant poverty, senseless levels of inequality, lack of adequate health services, racially and economically segregated schools, the rise of the prison state, a crippling minimum wage, police violence directed against poor minority youth, the return of debtors' prisons, a generation of young people burdened by excessive debt, and the attack on public and higher education only scratch the surface of the effects of what might be called a culture of war aimed at children.[5] Surely, it would be irresponsible not to view this horrendous disinvestment in young people and the violence it produces as an act of domestic terrorism, made all the worse by massive levels of inequality that bear down on so many young people.

Paul Buchheit in his article "The Reality Tale of Two Education Systems" maps out how systemic inequality needlessly ruins the lives of millions of children in the public school system.[6] He makes clear that public schools succeed when there are fewer children who suffer from the debilitating effects of poverty. He points to the success of schools that are adequately funded and the importance of adequate support for early childhood education and programs such as Head Start, all of which have been defunded by the new extremists and will be further defunded as long as the apostles of free market fundamentalism are in power. As if funding cutbacks are not disadvantaging students enough, underprivileged schools are increasingly required to implement educational policies and classroom practices such as "teaching for the test" that impose on students an authoritarian regimen of repressive discipline and conformity. In fact, a widespread culture of repression that attacks unions, discredits teachers, and punishes children has become the new norm in America, backed up by members of both the Democratic and Republican parties. When it comes to educational policy, the logic of privatization and capital accumulation are the real forces at work in destroying public schools, and done ironically under the name of reform.

Ken Saltman, Diane Ravitch, Joel Westheimer, and many others have written eloquently about how both the Bush and Obama administrations have turned schools into testing and sorting factories that have little to do with learning and a great deal to do with enforcing a pedagogy of repression among students, on the one hand, and redefining schools as a lucrative market for profits on the other. Children and the public spheres they inhabit, along with the federal programs that provide them with crucial social provisions, have become targets in a larger campaign against democracy and the public institutions that support it. Educational reform is just code for an intensive assault now being waged by the financial elite and billionaires to decimate all elements of the public good in order to generate new financial investments and huge profits for private investors; it is also a strategy for producing thoughtless workers who will do what they are told.

The sordid ideological logic informing the government's educational and economic policies was suggested by a recent example involving the ethically bankrupt leaders of the House and Senate, John Boehner and Mitch McConnell, who claimed in a CBS News interview with Scott Pelley on January 22, 2015, that they were against funding Obama's free Community College Program because it would increase the deficit. The appeal to austerity as a rationale to punish students overburdened by debt, eviscerate the social state, and redistribute wealth upward to rich elites has, by now, become an oft-repeated defense that serves to legitimate economic injustice and a certain transformation to "a world in which political economy has become a criminal economy."[7]

Amy Goodman, host of *Democracy Now*, asked Pablo Iglesias, the secretary general of Podemos, a left-wing political party in Spain, how he defined austerity and his answer highlights the elements of class warfare waged in its name and the threat it poses to any viable democracy. He states that:

> Austerity means that people [are expelled from] their homes. Austerity means that the social services don't work anymore. Austerity means that public schools have not the elements, the means to develop their activity. Austerity means that the countries have not sovereignty anymore, and we became a colony of the financial powers and a colony of Germany. Austerity probably means the end of democracy. I think if we don't have democratic control of economy, we don't have democracy. It's impossible to separate economy and democracy, in my opinion.[8]

Guy Standing goes further and argues that austerity constitutes a form of "social cleansing" and "social zoning" in its passing of measures such as the closing of public libraries and public schools, shutting down of affordable housing programs, defunding of public transportation, elimination of arts programs, and elimination of sports programs for working-class kids.[9] One disturbing example of how austerity works to punish children is obvious in the recent call by Republican Governor Sam Brownback of Kansas. In order to make up for his crippling tax cuts, he has enacted legislation designed to cut "classroom funding for Kansas schools by $127 million and push[ing teacher] pension fund payments off into the future."[10] Rather than acknowledge that his massive tax cuts are hurting his state's finances, he implements brutal policies that further undermine the public school system, punishing students and teachers alike. This is a form of financial terrorism in which policies that benefit the rich and big corporations are enacted irrespective of the misery they impose on young people and the most important public spheres in which they are served. What such policies make clear is that the neoliberal support for austerity barely conceals a ruthless logic and oppressive politics that are at the heart of the new authoritarianism. Austerity measures under neoliberalism is an extortion racket "designed to callously extract money from the most vulnerable and funnel it upward to the elites." [11]

Some liberals such as Paul Krugman argue that the current batch of right-wing and Republican extremists are indifferent to reason and evidence and should rightly be viewed as reactionaries "threatened by any expansion of government."[12] This is only partly true. First, the new extremists at various levels of political power—local, state, and federal—have no trouble expanding and using the power of government to benefit the powerful and financially privileged. Nor do they have second thoughts about using state violence to beat back protests, demonstrations, and collective modes of dissent to contain any outbreaks of collective resistance and class struggle. Second, they are not simply dumb or morally vacant, though many of them appear rather thoughtless. Instead, they are pawns of corporate power and have sold themselves out to the highest bidders. Their power is dependent on doing the bidding of the billionaires such as the Koch brothers and Sheldon Adelson along with their obsequious unfettered support for the interests of oil companies, banks, hedge funds, the defense industry, big corporations, and other financial behemoths. They are not stupid, but they are corrupt. Their politics suggest less a lack of intelligence than the workings of systemic forms of predatory capitalism, which fosters iniquitous class-based relations of power that do great harm to both the American public and democracy itself. The extremists who now control the American government are the new warriors of authoritarianism, proudly implementing the crushing ideologies, values, and policies of a failed state that they have all but handed over to the financial ruling classes.

Painful truths about political corruption, economic injustice, and the rise of the corporate state; the increasing gap between the rich and poor; and the shocking conditions in which children live in the United States are buried within efforts to enforce savage austerity measures. Hence, it is not surprising that there is no mention by politicians such as Boehner, McConnell, and their cronies about how economics and militarism now drive politics. Boehner and McConnell are silent about how the new extremists created the deficit through tax breaks for corporations, deregulation, letting lobbyists write banking bills, the expense of two wasteful wars, pouring money into building more prisons than schools, and maintaining a nuclear arsenal and wasteful military-industrial complex at a huge cost to the American people. Such policies and practices not only impose a precarious and harsh existence on young people, poor minorities, working-class families, and others in the United States, they also pose a direct threat to the planet itself.

American society lives under the lie that free markets and free societies translate into the notion that capitalism and democracy are synonymous, in spite of an abundance of evidence to the contrary given the history of free-market regimes such as Turkey, Chile, China, and South Korea. Domestic terrorism thrives on this lie, as it benefits from neoliberalism's ongoing efforts to make power invisible, remove ethical considerations from the workings of the market, create the conditions that enable finance capital to rule all commanding institutions, and develop modes of schooling and education that function largely to eliminate critical thinking and depoliticize the polity by defining citizenship as merely the act of consuming. The power of neoliberal capital and its commanding economic structures is matched by its ideological machinery and its power to normalize its values, interests, and view of the world. Susan Buck-Morss captures the violence at the heart of neoliberalism and the forces that make it incompatible with democracy and supportive of state violence and authoritarian regimes. She writes that under the regime of neoliberalism

money rules. Finance capitalism integrates a global oligarchy that includes economic actors of every ethnicity and every religion. This system has resulted in grotesque disparities of wealth, both between nations and within them. Capitalist social relations are based on the extraction of value from labor and from nature in order for the system to thrive. The privatization and enclosure of any productive force from which profit can be obtained is encouraged. The social costs of the production process, so-called externalities, are left unpaid. Human misery is discounted. Risks to citizen health are measured in terms of the trade-off between benefits and costs. The trivialization of life for profit is a common occurrence. Deregulation rewards capitalists even when they fail. Banks survive, and citizens— entire national populations—are forced by authorities to pay the price. One does not have to accept Marx's theory of class warfare to conclude that, given extreme disparities of wealth, democracy as an expression of the general will becomes untenable.[13]

Under such circumstances, it is not difficult to grasp what will become of the lives and futures of young people, who represent but one way to measure the growing threat of authoritarianism in American society. The violence inflicted by the authoritarian state driven by financial capital also has a range of less perceptible and perhaps farther-reaching effects. Under the existing regime of market fundamentalism, there has been a weakening of social values and a hardening of the culture that makes it easier to live in a world in which demonization replaces compassion, a self-righteous coldness eviscerates the democratic imagination, and the bonds of trust are replaced by bonds of fear. While it is largely recognized that the United States is wedded to mass incarceration and displays an utter disregard for the public good, what is often ignored is the degree to which it has become a class and racially based punishing state. The assault on public education, for example, has particularly devastating effects on low-income and poor minority youth.

Under such circumstances, racism has become not simply more visible, but more violent and repulsive in its attempts to kill young black men, turn back voting rights laws, and in many cities across the country empower the police to become an occupying army, fully aware of the fact that they can act with impunity. Militaristic violence is the new face of racism, the specter that haunts poor minority youth and adults, who are considered disposable in a society in which the flight from responsibility on the part of the financial elite is only matched by the rate in which their wealth increases yearly. As the bonds of sociality and social obligations dissolve, every human relation is measured against the yardstick of profit. Retribution and punishment now replace any vestige of restorative justice, just as low-income and poor minority urban youth are offered jail rather than a quality education and decent jobs.

Racial violence and discrimination explode in a furious display of impunity as local polices forces and right-wing racists from Ferguson, Missouri, and Cleveland to Baltimore to Charleston, South Carolina, shoot unarmed African Americans, some as young as twelve. The alleged age of post-racial society under the presidency of Barack Obama is betrayed by the reality of a legacy of institutional racism with its 350-year legacy of slavery and Jim Crow segregation that cannot be erased either through the election of an African American or by simply removing the outward symbols of racism such as the Confederate flag.[14] Harsh and often violent police tactics in black neighborhoods cannot be separated from the rise of the punishing state, high levels of poverty and unemployment, "the systemic abandonment of black neighborhoods," and the "failed war on drugs."[15] As Keith Ellison points out:

> Cities, starved of funding by austerity-obsessed leaders in Washington and state capitals, write tickets and charge fees for residents already struggling to avoid hunger and eviction. Crimes like loitering, spitting, jay-walking—many of which have been de facto legalized in affluent communities—are frequently used today to harass and imprison people of color.[16]

Nor can such violence be removed from the increasing criminalization of a range of behaviors that extend from punishing schoolchildren who violate dress codes to entire populations who are brought before the courts for an endless array of administrative violations that include "parking tickets, or tickets for unmowed lawns or improperly placed trash receptacles—[none of which are] criminal matters."[17] On the contrary, they are violations of administrative codes that result in costly fines and sometimes jail sentences on the poor, often to provide revenue for local police administrations. For example, in Ferguson, Missouri, the Department of Justice revealed a pattern of "policing through profit," in which "just about every branch of Ferguson government—police, municipal court, city hall—participated in 'unlawful' targeting of African-Americans residents" as part of the goal of raising revenue rather than satisfying "public safety needs."[18] In 2015, the DOJ reported that such "fines and fees would account for 23% of the budget or $3.09 million of $13.26 million in general fund expenses."[19] In this case, not only did the police and courts engage in a form of racist-based extortion, but they also arrested people for trivial, trumped-up charges, put them under extreme duress, and put multiple impediments in their lives. (I explore this issue in more detail in chapter 9.) This is the invisible underside of domestic terrorism, one fueled by the connection between state violence and economic impoverishment. The war on poverty under neoliberalism has been transformed into the criminalization of poverty. The notion of war rings true not as an assault on poverty but as a practice that transforms a serious social, economic, and political problem into a police matter. The increasing criminalization of young people, poor minorities of class and color, and other disposable populations also makes clear that there is no discourse of empathy, morality, and justice under the regime of neoliberal authoritarianism. Consequently, older discourses that provided a vision of a better future have been all but rendered useless. As Hannah Arendt once argued, the very nature of the political in the modern period has been dethroned.[20]

The consolidation of class power by the financial elite has passed into a new historical moment in American history. The unbridled power now on display is indifferent to the problems of long-term unemployment, homelessness, increasing levels of poverty, and the desperate state of American youth. Political concessions to labor and other groups on the part of the financial elite is viewed as a sign of weakness in this hyper-masculine form of social Darwinism. What most of the American public are experiencing under this mode of governance is a level of oppression, violence, poverty, and loss of social provisions that seems unparalleled—especially given the grip that big money has on all the commanding institutions of American life.

To claim that the United States has become an oligarchy, as a recent Princeton University study has done, reveals more subterfuge than insight. Oligarchy sounds tame next to the savage form of free-market capitalism that operates in a field of lawlessness, extreme violence, and wild injustice in which a failed sociality reigns, and social death and individual misery are the norm. Anything that impedes market relations is suspect and deserving of state violence. Moreover, the increasing manifestations of state violence mark a radical shift away from even the slightest vestige of democracy to the more prevalent use of state terrorism. The militarization of American society, the failed war on drugs, the rise of the incarceration state, and the paramilitarization of local police forces coupled with the ongoing killings of unarmed young black men by the police has put on full display only the most obvious registers of the violence of a racist authoritarian state.

The machinery of governance and the commanding institutions of the United States are now controlled by corporate political zombies who savor and reproduce death-dealing institutions that extend from paramilitarized police forces to schools modeled after prisons. These are the same politicians who claim they hate big government but love big corporations, who deride the poor and slash health provisions but claim they are the new face of compassionate politics, and who turn corruption into a virtue and honesty into a political liability. These are the new extremists who support state torture, glorify militarism, and are responsible for the death of millions. Instead of investing in young people and schools, they invest in prisons and support a corrupt corporate state and institutions controlled by the financial elite.[21] The new extremists substituted a war on the poor for a war on poverty while at the same time, beginning in the 1990s, did everything possible to underfund and starve programs aimed at reducing poverty and, as Ellison argues, instead "made choices to keep 'law and order' in ways that exacerbated the problems facing low-income communities."[22] In a different historical period, they would have fit in well with the likes of Pinochet, apartheid South Africa, the military dictatorships in Greece, and other ruthless authoritarian regimes.

These people are truly the walking dead who inhabit what can only be called a world in which ethical and social responsibilities have been replaced by a moral coma, a culture of fear, and a politics of misery that produces a regime of violence, huge inequities in wealth and power, and a disdain for helping others, including young people. What is new about the emerging authoritarianism is that it takes ideology seriously and is marked by both a rampant and depoliticizing culture of consumerism and celebrity culture and the rise of an expansive punishing and surveillance state. As the language of the market replaces social categories, it hides power relations while isolating people in orbits of privatization and consumption. And it is this increasing culture of atomization, privatization, and reification that further erases the connected forms of experience and belonging needed to produce a new politics and collective struggle in the name of social and economic justice.

The current regime of neoliberalism acts without accountability, despite its ruthlessness, moral blindness, and evident willingness to destroy the planet to preserve its hoarding of power and wealth. The ongoing appeal to fear, insecurity, and uncertainty by the financial elite and its corporate-controlled cultural apparatuses defines the contemporary cultural zeitgeist, and lulls people into accepting a rise in violence and the increasing use of punitive practices in a growing number of public spheres. The war on terror has morphed into a form of domestic terrorism aimed not only at whistleblowers but at all those people, from poor minorities to immigrants, who are now considered disposable. For instance, under the rubric of preventing terrorism, France, England, and Canada have invoked policies that eviscerate personal freedoms and rule-of-law protections. In England, such laws sanction: "Arbitrary house arrest. Electronic tagging,

Prohibitions against free association. Travel restrictions."[23] In addition, "postal correspondence can be checked [and] buildings and vehicles can be bugged."[24] In France, "all Internet user data can be monitored and civil liberties have been eliminated with little debate."[25] In the name of anti-terrorism, passports can be confiscated, people can be sentenced to jail for up to 10 years for "consulting terrorist websites or receiving terrorist training."[26] In Canada, the state has more power to conduct surveillance, and under bill C-24 "the government has the discretion to strip citizenship of any dual citizen convicted of terrorism, treason, or spying abroad" without due process or trial.[27] Dual nationals now "run the risk of being treated as somehow less Canadian." The violence of the terrorist state now renders entire populations disposable, that is, subject to what Richard Sennett terms the "specter of uselessness that denies gainful employment and self-respect." Sennett calls this a "new wrinkle in neoliberal capitalism."[28] It is also a new form of terrorism.

Domestic terrorism has become the default response to social problems that increasingly affect all the individuals, groups, and communities that constitute "the 99 percent." The extremists in power patently refuse to address social problems, regardless of how serious they are. Instead, the behaviors exhibited by people victimized and injured by such problems are criminalized. Debtor prisons have made a comeback in a society in which incarceration has become the default position for dealing with the poor. Students, mostly poor minorities, who violate zero tolerance policies such as using their hand to simulate a gun or bringing a two-inch toy gun to trivial rules such as not wearing school uniform are routinely arrested and escorted away in police cars;[29] the strong arm of the punishing state appears to target those who are the most vulnerable, such as the homeless. For instance, Alex Chastain points out that "cities across the United States have been cracking down on homeless people with ordinances and laws that go as far as to prevent the homeless from sleeping with a blanket, or even kicking them out of town. People in 31 cities across America can also be legally punished for feeding the homeless. Instead of preventing veterans or citizens from being forced to live on the streets, cities are punishing them. The homeless are punished for sleeping in parks, and so it goes."[30]

Everyone outside of the corporate, financial, and political elite is a potential enemy in America, and this includes not only those populations considered disposable but also those who question authority and refuse to bend to the will of a politically corrupt ruling power. Even as more and more individuals are subject to punitive forms of punishment, financial terrorism, and the suffocating tentacles of the market and surveillance state, they are led to believe that all problems originate from within themselves, and are simply a matter of character. All social problems, according to this logic, are reduced to a matter of lifestyle, and provoke a demand that the impoverished and marginalized get up and make something of themselves.

If one face of the new authoritarianism is the militarization of all aspects of society, the other side is the rabidly individualized and privatized "self-help" culture that extends from Oprah Winfrey to the various screen cultures of the mainstream media. As Mark Fisher has noted, under neoliberalism's "'empire of the self' everyone is trapped in their own feelings, trapped within their own imaginations, and unable to escape the tortured conditions of solipsism."[31] This is one of the most distinctive features of the new authoritarianism: how it reproduces its own power and control over the American public not only through the imposition of harsh economic policies and the use of state repression but also through powerful forms of affective management prevalent in the wider culture.

The ideological and affective spaces that support the new authoritarianism do not simply produce powerful myths or function as an ideological drug that legitimates the elimination of broader structural, economic, and political forces. Nor do such spaces function only as a kind of disimagination machine working to make invisible the material relations of race, power, and class. They also work primarily as a powerful educative force that has succeeded extremely well in depoliticizing large numbers of the American public. Neoliberalism relies not only on ideology to legitimate market-based values and produce consent, it also mobilizes needs, desires, and hopes and "in doing so erode(s) the symbolic, affective dimensions of social existence."[32] The authoritarian mindset is central to a consumer culture marked by an endlessly repeating call to celebrate selfishness, waste, and privatization. Such cultural and educative toxins are peddled by the entertainment and advertising industries, celebrity culture, mainstream media, and the anti-public intellectuals who trade on other people's misery. More than just a popular addiction, consumerism is the new religion in the United States and engages in a swindle of fulfillment through its glitzy promise of a graveyard of rapidly disposable goods as the measure of the good life. Markets now define not only how people live but who they are.

The prison house of consumption succeeds at the expense of any viable notion of critical citizenship, social responsibility, and the skills and resources necessary to be an engaged individual and social agent. This prison house of self-interest and consumption cuts across the ideological spectrum, as is evident by the fact that even union members buy into this logic. No doubt encouraged by their leadership, they have often traded higher wages and other benefits for a class-conscious membership seeking to make work meaningful and production socially useful. Of course, this reshaping of the public is a perfect supplement to state terrorism because it replaces a personalized therapeutic language for a political vocabulary. Left unchecked, a rampant consumer culture will lead to historical and political amnesia; already it gives rise to what appears to be a form of collective insanity as the new extremists, marching forward with their death-dealing policies, seem increasingly to garner support among the American public.

Americans are witnessing a new moment in history in which the symbiosis among cultural institutions, power, and everyday life is shaping the very nature of politics and the broader collective public consciousness with an influence unlike anything we have seen in the past. Economics drives politics, and its legitimating apparatuses have become the great engines of a manufactured ignorance. This suggests the need for the political left and its allies to take seriously how identities, desires, and modes of agency are produced, struggled over, and taken up. The left and other progressive movements need to revisit Pierre Bourdieu's insistence that they have "underestimated the symbolic and pedagogical dimensions of struggle and have not always forged appropriate weapons to fight on this front"—that is, political interventions capable of challenging modes of domination that "lie on the side of the symbolic and pedagogical dimensions of struggle."[33] Couple this responsibility to understand and address the educative nature of politics with the need for a more comprehensive vision of change and the organization of broad-based social movements, and it may become possible once again to develop a new political language, new forms of collective struggle, and a politics for radical change rather than cravenly center-right reforms.

As Hannah Arendt, John Dewey, and others told us many years ago, there is no democracy without an informed public. This is a lesson the right took very seriously after the democratic uprisings of the 1960s. Acknowledging the failure of public culture in the United States is not a matter of criticizing the public for its partial views, but of trying to understand the role of culture and power as a vital force in politics and how these have been marshalled to support values and policies that enshrine massive inequities in wealth and income. The financial state promotes a form of ideological terrorism, and the key issue is how to expose it and then counter its cultural apparatuses with the use of the social media and other diverse apparatuses of communication, new political formations, and ongoing, collective educational and political struggles. This means asking, first, how to make the ideologies, policies, and structures that play such a powerful role in the expanding forms of indebted citizenship, poverty, and mass incarceration more visible in order to challenge and change them. Such questions must be taken seriously; otherwise, groups such as students, low-income families, immigrants, and poor minorities will continue to be treated as disposable and be increasingly unable to offer any collective resistance given their struggle to suffer and survive under harsh conditions of state repression.

Lies, misinformation, and the spectacle of entertainment frame how issues are presented to the North American public by the vast cultural machinery of education that extends from mainstream news media to conservative think tanks. For instance, in the aftermath of the 2014 election, ABC, CBS, and NBC all claimed that the government will be more sharply divided as a result of the Republican takeover of both houses of Congress. What the mainstream media failed to point out is that both parties have more in common than what divides them. The parties both support the consolidation of power in the hands of the financial and corporate elite. Both parties have passed policies that cut back on social provisions for the needy while providing tax breaks for the wealthy. That is to say, both parties, as Aron Gupta points out, have enacted "policies that increase the wealth and power of those on the top of the economic pyramid."[34] Moreover, at an essential level, both parties need the financial support of the financial elite to get elected in an authoritarian society in which money rules politics and kills any vestige of democracy. Meanwhile, the established press played up Obama's claim that he is willing to cooperate with the Republican Party—as if this represents a new era of bipartisanship in the United States. What is missed in this rush to judgment is that these parties have been cooperating for years on maintaining the privileges of the ultra-rich, corporations, and bankers, while at the same time punishing the poor, unions, the working class, immigrants, and minorities of color.

The only major difference between the two U.S. political parties is that the Republicans wage naked class warfare without any apologies or political concessions, while the Democrats offer a few painkillers to soften the blow. Yet, in some cases, Democratic leaders such as Bill Clinton and Barack Obama outdid their Republican counterparts in consolidating class power and imposing enormous hardships and misery on the poor and middle class. Clinton expanded the punishing state, callously removed millions of poor women and children from the welfare system, expanded the war on drugs, and dissolved the Depression-era Glass-Steagall Act, which helped pave the way for the financial crisis of 2008.[35] In several ways, Obama makes George Bush look tame given his unprecedented war on whistleblowers, use of the sweeping state secrecy doctrine, escalating violations of civil liberties, waging of drone warfare that has often resulted in the indiscriminate death of civilians, and the reckless establishment of an illegal kill list with the power to name U.S. citizens for assassination. To make matters worse, Obama has refused to prosecute corrupt bankers or CIA agents who engaged in torture, and has deported and imprisoned record numbers of immigrants.

In spite of what the established media claim, the 2014 election results contained a hidden order of politics that do not suggest a popular shift to the right, but a failure of both parties, especially the Democratic Party, to address the needs and mood of an ailing electorate. How else to explain that a number of states voted to raise the minimum wage? Joseph Kishore writing on the *World Socialist Web Site* gets it right in arguing:

> The Democratic strategy of appealing to affluent layers of the middle class on the basis of identity politics while working with the Republicans to step up attacks on workers' jobs, wages and living standards produced an electoral disaster. In a contradictory way, reflecting a system monopolized by two-right parties of big business, the election showed that appeals on the basis of race, gender and sexuality move only a small fraction of the population, while the broad masses of people are driven by more fundamental class issues—issues on which the Democrats have nothing to offer.[36]

As Paul Buchheit points out, capitalism is spreading like a tumor in American society,[37] and the key is to halt its ability to convince people that there are no other alternatives, that the market should govern all of social life including politics itself, and that the government's only role is to protect the benefits of big business and the interests of the super-rich. Terrorism and the culture of fear have become the malignant tissue holding together a society that relies more on ethical tranquillization and the forces of the punishing state than on any semblance of social justice. Terror is no longer simply a reference to foreign and domestic threats, however real these might be, but has become an alibi for state terrorism, whether it takes the form of a massive state-sponsored spying apparatus, the gutting of social provisions, the criminalization of social problems, the war on women, or the endless police violence used against innocent black youth.

The argument that things will inevitably get worse and push people into action is politically naive because there are never any political guarantees of how people will act in the face of massive repression. They could for all intents and purposes go either left or right. There are no guaranteed opportunities for action in any society. Political outcomes have to be the result of coordinated struggles waged by mass movements using a diversity of tactics extending from boycotts and strikes to sit-ins and direct action. The biggest challenge facing those who believe in social justice is to provide alternative discourses, educational apparatuses, vision, and modes of identification that can convince the American public that a real democracy is worth fighting for—and that such struggles need to begin immediately before ethically bankrupt leaders and the financial interests they serve close down any hope of a future in which matters of justice and equality prevail.

Though it is clear that American society is in a free-fall decline, what is not so clear is why discussions of economic and political crises are rarely matched by discussions about the crisis of ideas and the crisis of subjectivity and agency. As all vestiges of social and economic equality disappear, public provisions evaporate, and the machinery of politics come under the control of the financial elite, what is desperately needed are calls for new modes of subjectivity, a new understanding of power, and the mechanisms for creating new modes of resistance capable of struggling for a radical democracy. The interplay between the propagation of authoritarian values and the production of new modes of identity must be understood within the networks that combine culture, power, and what might be called neo-liberal forms of public pedagogy. At stake here is acknowledgment of the educative nature of politics and the centrality of education to any form of resistance. We need to create a critical formative culture in which individuals can reimagine what a radical democracy might look like and how it might be achieved. Politics matters when it changes the way people think, but it must do more. It must not only inform but also energize people to take collective action within deeply committed bonds of solidarity. The crisis of democracy and the slide into authoritarianism point not only to an economic crisis but also to a crisis of agency, subjectivity, and desire. Making education central to politics means developing a culture through which people are inspired to take modes of collective resistance seriously and act as new historical agents of change.

Democracy is quickly withering in the United States. A society is being constructed that no longer believes in the social contract or justice, is addicted to greed and power, and unabashedly displays its savage willingness to use state violence to manage its problems. The strong winds of authoritarianism are wreaking havoc all over the United States; with the new extremists now in power, it is only a matter of time before darkness descends. When this happens, lawlessness not compassion, violence not thoughtfulness, corruption not justice, will define America's future in a way similar to how the reactionary revolutions of the 1930s defined that horrendous genocidal and militarized period in history. Before then, let's hope that a thousand movements of resistance will flower and join together in ridding the earth of this neoliberal poison. Jacques Derrida once referred to hope as "an unrelenting fidelity—an entrusted trace, a renewed promise and an endless responsibility before 'the ghosts of those who are not yet born or who are already dead.'"[38] It is precisely at the intersection of justice, responsibility, and the civic imagination that hope inspires and energizes—not only as a repository of memory and moral witnessing, but as a budding recognition of how one's self and others are weighed down by forces of oppression and what it would mean to overcome them. In dark times, hope speaks to the need for realistic assessment and actions that extend the horizons of justice both by struggling against the obscene stupidity and reckless use of power that inform neoliberal capitalism and by making education central to imagining a democratic future that is worth fighting for.

— 4 —

Class Warfare and the Advance of Austerity Policies under the New Authoritarianism

RIGHT-WING CALLS FOR AUSTERITY suggest more than a market-driven desire to punish the poor, working class, and middle class by distributing wealth upward to the 1 percent. They also point to a politics of disposability in which the social provisions, public spheres, and institutions that nourish democratic values and social relations are being rapidly dismantled, including public and higher education. Neoliberal austerity policies embody an ideology that produces zones of abandonment and forms of social and civil death while also infusing society with a culture of increasing hardship. Urged by powerful corporations, right-wing billionaires such as the Koch brothers, and conservative pundits to lower corporate taxes and cut social services, governments are slashing salaries, imposing onerous financial demands on the poor, and taking an ax to alleged entitlements such as job training, health care, workers' rights, and retirement benefits. The foundations of economic and social stability that are part of the social contract—personal, political, and social rights—have been weakened, creating a great social malaise across populations in the United States and Europe. Dissent is now at the mercy of the surveillance state; collective bargaining rights are being undermined, especially in states ruled by right-wing governors such as Scott Walker in Wisconsin;[1] quality health care is rationed out along class lines; massive inquality undermines almost every vestige of democracy; and meaningful work and wages are disappearing. All the while education is being defunded, spending on prisons is increasing, and the financial elite are being taxed less and less while their wealth and power increases exponentially.

The financial crisis has produced an especially onerous social malaise in countries such as Greece, Italy, and Ireland, "leading to an alarming spike in suicide rates."[2] For example, between 2007 and 2009, suicides motivated by the economic difficulties and austerity policies have increased among men in Greece "more than 24 percent," in Ireland "suicides rose more than 16 percent," and in Italy, suicides "increased 52 percent" by 2010.[3] A more recent 2014 study in *Social Science and Medicine* found a direct link between spending cuts and increased suicide rates among Greek men, and a 2013 paper found a similar connection in Spain following the financial crisis.[4] What these reports make clear is that the weapons of class warfare do not reside only in oppressive modes of state terrorism such as the militarization of the police, but also in policies that inflict misery, immiseration, and suffering on the vast majority of the population. By imposing such measures on Greece and other countries, the troika—the International Monetary Fund, European Union, and European Central Bank—unleashes a form of financial terrorism.[5] The Greek people were brought to their knees under the imperatives of "a brutal austerity experiment imposed on Greece since 2010 [one that has] proved outstandingly counterproductive."[6]

Capitalism has learned to create host organisms, and in the current historical conjuncture one of those organisms is young people, many of whom are jobless and forced to live under the burden of crushing debt.[7] In the midst of growing gaps in wealth, income, and power, it is also the case that single mothers, immigrants, and poor minorities are being plunged into either low-paying jobs or a future without decent employment.[8] The sick and elderly are increasingly faced with making a choice between food and medicine. Austerity now drives a social system in which the only value that matters is exchange value. For students, this means paying increased tuition that generates profits for banks and credit companies and allows the state to lower taxes on the rich and megacorporations.[9]

Under this regime of widening inequality that imposes enormous constraints on the choices people can make, austerity measures function as a set of hyper-punitive policies and practices that produce massive amounts of suffering, rob people of their dignity, and then humiliate them by suggesting that they bear sole responsibility for their plight.[10] This is more than the scandal of a perverted form of neoliberal rationality; it is the precondition for an emerging authoritarian state with its proliferating extremist ideologies and its growing militarization and criminalization of all aspects of everyday life and social behavior.[11] Richard D. Wolff has argued: "Austerity is yet another extreme burden imposed on the global economy by the capitalist crisis (in addition to the millions suffering unemployment, reduced global trade, etc.)."[12] He is certainly right, but it is more than a burden imposed on the 99 percent. It is the latest stage of market warfare, class consolidation, and a ruthless grab for power waged on the part of the global financial elite, which is both heartless and indifferent to the mad violence and unchecked misery its neoliberal policies impose on much of humanity.

According to Zygmunt Bauman, "Capitalism proceeds through creative destruction. What is created is capitalism in a 'new and improved' form—and what is destroyed is the self-sustaining capacity, livelihood and dignity of its innumerable and multiplied 'host organisms' into which all of us are drawn / seduced one way or another."[13] Creative destruction armed with the death-dealing power of ruthless austerity measures benefits the financial elite and at the same time destroys the social state and lays the foundation for the punishing state, which now makes prison the default institution for those pushed out of the sanctuary of so-called democracy.[14] Both neoliberal governments and authoritarian societies share one important factor: they care more about consolidating power in the hands of the political, corporate, and financial elite than they do about investing in the future of young people and expanding the benefits of the social contract and common good.

The stories that now dominate the European and North American land-scape are not about economic reform, despite how they may be framed. Instead, the stories peddle what stands for common sense among market and religious fundamentalists in a number of mainstream political parties: shock-and-awe austerity measures; tax cuts that serve the rich and power-ful and destroy government programs that help the disadvantaged, elderly, and sick; attacks on women's reproductive rights; attempts to suppress voter-ID laws and rig electoral college votes; full-fledged assaults on the environment; the militarization of everyday life; the destruction of pub-lic education, if not critical thought itself; and ongoing condemnations of unions, social provisions, Medicaid expansion, and meaningful health care reform. These stories are endlessly repeated by the neoliberal and neocon-servative walking dead who roam the planet sucking the blood and life out of everyone and everything they touch—from the millions killed in foreign wars to the millions at home forced into unemployment, underemploy-ment, foreclosure, poverty, or prison.[15]

Right-wing appeals to austerity provide the rationale for slash-and-burn policies intended to deprive government-financed social and educational programs of the funds needed to enable them to work, if not survive. This is particularly obvious in the United States, though it is even worse in coun-tries such as Portugal, Ireland, and Greece. Along with health care fund-ing cutbacks, public transportation, Medicare, food stamp programs for low-income children, a host of other social provisions are being defunded as part of a larger scheme to dismantle and privatize all public services, goods, and spheres. The passion for public values has given way to the ruthless quest for profits and the elevation of self-interest over the common good. The educational goal of expanding the capacity for critical thought and the outer limits of the imagination has given way to the instrumental desert of a mind-deadening audit culture. We cannot forget that the deficit argument and austerity policies advocated in its name are a form of class warfare designed largely for the state to be able to redirect revenue in sup-port of the commanding institutions of the corporate-military-industrial complex and away from higher education, health care, jobs programs, workers' pensions, and other crucial public services and social protections. Of course, the larger goal is to maintain the ongoing consolidation of class power in the hands of the 1 percent.

I argue that austerity measures also serve another purpose conducive to the interest of the financial elite. Such measures go hand-in-hand with ideologies, policies, and practices that depoliticize large portions of the population, particularly those who are homeless or have lost their homes, are unemployed or tied to low-paying jobs, are experiencing devastating poverty, suffering under the weight of strangulating debt, or struggling just to survive. For example, in Greece where austerity policies have been aggressively implemented, belt-tightening measures have left millions in misery while leaving the resources and lifestyles of the rich untouched. The unemployment rate in Greece hovers around 27 percent, and "suicides have shot up. Cars sit abandoned in the streets. People sift garbage looking for food [and] about 900,000 of the more than 1.3 million who are out of work have not had a paycheck in more than two years, experts say."[16] The famed economist Thomas Piketty states that the austerity measures imposed upon Greece have resulted in a colossal humanitarian crisis: "40 percent of children now live in poverty, infant mortality is skyrocketing and youth unemployment is close to 50 percent."[17] Throughout Greece, people now inhabit what might be called zones of abandonment, spaces defined by the need to simply survive. These are spaces inhabited by people who lack viable employment, adequate food, health care, and sustainable pensions.

As of June 2015, Greece's creditors—the troika referenced above—are insisting that Greece impose severe tax hikes and pension cuts in order to secure much needed loans. The level of cruelty behind such policies seems unimaginable in the twenty-first century. For example, according to political economist C. J. Polychroniou, "If this proposal for overhauling the nation's pension system were to be accepted by the Greek government, it would mean that a person who today receives a monthly pension for the amount of, say, 500 euros [$560]—close to 50 percent of Greek pensioners receive pensions below the official poverty line—would be deprived of nearly 200 euros [$223]."[18] Similar problems face Spain, Italy, Portugal, France, and to a lesser degree the United States.

Politically paralyzed under the ideological fog of a hyper-individualism that insists that all problems are the responsibility of the same individuals who are victimized by larger systemic and structural forces, it is difficult for people to embrace any understanding of the common good, let alone recognize that the private troubles that plague their lives are connected to larger social issues. Without this crucial awareness, there is little motivating individuals to launch a vigorous campaign in defense of the social contract. Nothing will change without many people together acknowledging the necessity of engaging in collective action to dismantle the neoliberal system of violence and cruelty, which to some degree the Greeks have done, though they were betrayed by the July 2015 compromise of the Syriza government with the troika, especially since the final agreement imposed conditions much worse than those suggested before the Greek referendum.[19] For all intents and purposes, Greece is now run by the bankers and financial elite of Europe.

Austerity measures not only individualize social issues, they also produce massive disparities in wealth, income, and power that impose constraints on people's well-being, freedom, and choices, while serving to undermine any faith in government, politics, and democracy itself. The distrust of public values and egalitarian approaches to governance—coupled with wariness, if not disdain, for group solidarities and compassion for the Other—promotes a dislike of community engagement, social trust, and democratic public spheres. Austerity policies produce neither a world with safety nets nor the social and political formations necessary to embrace democratic forms of solidarity. Clinging "fiercely to neoliberal ideals of untrammeled individualism and self-reliance," many young people not only embrace therapeutic models of selfhood but develop a deep distrust, if not resentment, of any notion of the social and shun obligations to others.[20]

Austerity measures purposely accentuate the shark-like relations emphasized by the economic Darwinism of neoliberalism, and in doing so emphasize a world of competitive hyperactive individualism in which asking for help or receiving it is viewed as a pathological condition. The notion that one should rely only on one's self—and celebrate self-reliance and resilience to the point of excluding anything or anyone else—functions largely to privatize social problems and depoliticize those who buy into such a logic. The danger here is that the sense of atomization and powerlessness that neoliberalism produces also makes people prone to extremist politics. That is, distrust of the social contract, government, democratic values, and class-based solidarities also nourishes the conditions that give birth to extremist groups who demonize immigrants, push a strident nationalism, and appeal to calls for racial purity as a way of addressing the misery many people are experiencing, all the while deflecting attention away from the poisonous violence produced by neoliberalism and ways in which it can be confronted and challenged through a host of democratic approaches that reject austerity as a tool of reform.[21]

By eroding the middle class and punishing working-class and poor minorities, neoliberal policies make it that much more difficult for radical movements to emerge, and consequently politics gets drained of any hope for a democratic future. In the midst of a culture of mere survival and the normalization of violence, thoughtlessness prevails as time is focused largely on the need to simply stay alive. Under such circumstances, time becomes a luxury, making it difficult for individuals to reflect at length, think critically, grapple with complex problems, and resist neoliberal notions of citizenship, which define citizens largely as consumers. As time is transformed into a deprivation for many people, critical thought withers, citizenship is reduced to an empty voting exercise, and democracy is reduced to the limiting and depoliticizing parameters of a hyper-consumerism, a raging effort to privatize everything, and an ongoing concentration of power by the upper 1 percent. Under such circumstances, democracy is emptied of any substance, and politics falls prey not only to a reactionary cynicism, but also to a slew of antidemocratic demands on the part of right-wing extremists. These include an attack on immigrants, unions, public servants, and those made vulnerable because they lack the material resources to be able to survive in a consumer based society. What becomes clear is that austerity signals a terrifying new horizon of politics, one in which the conditions that produce the curse of totalitarianism become more and more evident. As democratic values are erased, public spheres eliminated, and the common good gives way to casino capitalism, what emerges is the dark side of authoritarianism. This dark side of politics constitutes the waging of a counterrevolution on the part of the new extremists and is evident in the United States in the corporate control of all the commanding institutions of society, the militarization of everyday life, and the ongoing production of a culture of misery and hardship enforced by the corporate state and financial elite. Economics drives politics and the concentrated power of the financial elite wages a war on the ideals of democracy and those individuals, movements, and institutions that defend it.

The turn to authoritarian capitalism is on the rise globally and can be found in "Russia's Vladimir Putin, Recep Tayyip Erdogan of Turkey, and Chinese President Xi Jinping."[22] The principles of authoritarian capitalism are also on full display in the austerity policies pushed without apology by Republican Party extremists and their Democratic Party cohorts in the United States. Channeling Ayn Rand, right-wing politicians such as Paul Ryan, Ted Cruz, and Marco Rubio argue for the most extreme austerity policies, asserting a twisted logic that attributes moral weakness and greediness to the debased characters of citizens who struggle for financial support and social provisions in the age of austerity.[23] Republican presidential contender Jeb Bush amplified the austerity logic by asserting that the crisis of unemployment could be fixed, in part, by insisting that "people need to work longer hours."[24] Bush ignores economic data that makes clear that "Americans overall work longer hours on average than peers in many other rich industrialized nations."[25] He also appears clueless by not acknowledging that what the United States lacks are meaningful jobs, not unproductive workers. In this discourse, hardworking Americans and their money must be protected from all the dissipated others. It is not surprising that austerity measures find their ideological legitimation in the notion that self-interest is the foundational element of agency and that self-sufficiency, however illusory, is the highest civic virtue. Margaret Thatcher's selfish insistence that "there is no such thing as society" when coupled with an aggressive assault on all things public and social does more than disparage democracy: it becomes a blueprint for the rise of fascism. Even liberals such as Paul Krugman are sounding the alarm in the midst of rising inequality and the emergence of extremist ideologies, circumstances that are ripe for the return of the totalitarian values that gave birth to the horrors of Fascism and Nazism in Europe in the 1930s.[26]

Austerity measures within the existing configurations of power represent the undercurrent of a new form of authoritarianism—one that refuses political concessions and has no allegiances except to power and capital. There is no hope in trying to reform neoliberal capitalism, because it is broken and will simply adapt in response to any partial reform strategy. Nor is there any hope in believing that the Democratic Party can be used to fix the system, given that the rich liberal elite fund it. As Bill Blunden reminded me in a personal correspondence, "the Democratic Party is the graveyard of social movements—[Democrats] quack like progressives but answer to billionaires." John Stauber gets it right in arguing that the financialization of American society is, among other things, a money machine for the Democratic Party and that the latter's notion of reform is dead on arrival. Any notion that the rich elite, the 1 percent, are going to fund "radical, democratic, social and economic change" is as disingenuous as it delusional.[27] What is one to make of a political party that claims to be the umbrella for a progressive reform movement when, as Michael Hudson points out, "the supposedly liberal Democrats [in 2015] are in the lead for scaling back pension funding, Social Security and labor protection in general"?[28]

Neoliberal capitalism is parasitic and sociopathic, and it needs to be replaced by a form of radical democracy that refuses to equate capitalism with democracy. These may be dark times, but the drumbeat of resistance is growing among workers, the poor, minorities, young people, artists, educators, and others. The key is to form social movements and political parties that have a comprehensive view of politics and struggle and are imbued with the spirit of collective resistance and the promise of a radical democracy. The cycle of brutality, suffering, and cruelty in which we are now caught appears overwhelming in light of the normalization of the intolerable violence produced by the politics of austerity and neoliberalism. The realms of imagination that might lead to a new vocabulary of struggle, politics, and hope appear in short supply. Yet, even as time is running out, the struggle has to be waged. What has been produced by humans, however inhuman and powerful, can be undone. In spite of what the apostles of casino capitalism would have us believe, history is open and far from frozen in the alleged politics of economic Darwinism.

The stakes in this battle are high because the struggle is not simply against austerity measures, but the institutions and economic order that produce them. One place to begin such a struggle is with a new sense of politics driven by a notion of educated hope. Hope turns radical when it exposes the violence of neoliberalism—acts of state and corporate aggression against democracy, humanity, and ecological stability itself. Hope has to make the workings of power visible, and then it has to offer thoughtful critiques of this machinery of death. But hope must do more than critique, dismantle, and expose the ideologies, values, institutions, and social relations that are pushing so many countries today into authoritarianism, austerity, violence, and war. Hope must and can energize and mobilize groups, neighborhoods, communities, campuses, and networks of people to articulate and advance insurgent discourses in the movement toward developing a broader insurrectional democracy. Hope is an important political and subjective register that enables people not only to think beyond the neoliberal austerity machine—the chronic and intergenerational injustices deeply structured into all levels of society—but also to advance forms of egalitarian community that celebrate the voices, wellbeing, inherent dignity, and participation of each person as an integral thread in the ever-evolving fabric of a living, radical democracy. Hope only matters when it turns outward, confronts the obstacles in its path, and provides points of identification that people find meaningful so that they choose to become critical agents capable of engaging in transforma-tive collective action.

The financialization of neoliberal societies thrives on a cruel, hyper-individualistic, survival-of-the fittest ethic. This is the ethic of barbarians, the thoughtless and cruel financial elite. While fear and state violence may be two of their weapons, the politics of austerity is one of the strongest forms of control in their arsenal because it imposes a poverty of mind and body that leads to not just a crisis of agency but its death. It is time to take social change seriously by imagining a future beyond the austerity policies and power relations that produce the misery and violence of a neoliberal social order. It is also time for human beings to discover something about the potential of individual and social agency, a sense of which can inspire, energize, educate, and challenge with the full force of social movements those undemocratic forces that make a mockery of social, economic, and political justice. As Pierre Bourdieu once argued, the time is right for the collective production of realist utopias, and with that opportunity comes the need to act with passion, courage, and conviction.

— 5 —

Racism, Violence, and Militarized Terror in the Age of Disposability

We revolt simply because, for many reasons, we can no longer breathe.
—FRANTZ FANON

THE LARGER REASONS BEHIND THE KILLING of Eric Garner, Freddie Gray, Walter Brown, and Tamir Rice, among others, seem to be missed by most commentators. The issues in question should not be limited to police misconduct and racist acts of police brutality, however deadly. What is also critical and needs to be explored is the growing use of systemic terror on a scale that summons to mind Hannah Arendt's notion of totalitarianism. When fear and terror become the organizing principles of a society in which tyranny has been expanded by the despotism of an unaccountable market, violence becomes the only valid form of control. The system has not failed. As social critic Jeffrey St. Clair has pointed out, it is doing exactly what it is supposed to do, which is to punish those it considers dangerous or disposable—extending to more and more individuals and groups as power and wealth become concentrated in fewer hands. Arendt was right in arguing that "if lawfulness is the essence of non-tyrannical government and lawlessness is the essence of tyranny, then terror is the essence of totalitarian domination."[1]

In an age characterized by an utterly commodified and privatized culture, the delete button quickly erases all vestiges of memory and commitment. It has become easy for a society to remove itself from those sordid memories that reveal the systemic injustices and presence of state violence and terrorism. Not only do the dangerous memories of bodies being lynched, beaten, tortured, and murdered disappear in the fog of celebrity culture and the 24/7 entertainment/news cycle, but the historical flashpoints that once revealed the horrors of unaccountable power and acts of systemic barbarism are disconnected from any broader understanding of domination and vanish into a past that no longer has any connection to the present.[2] The murder of Emmett Till; the killing of the four young black girls, Addie Mae Collins, Cynthia Wesley, Carole Robertson and Denise McNair, in the 1963 church bombing in Birmingham, Alabama; the assassination of Dr. Martin Luther King, Jr.; the killing by four officers of Amadou Diallo; the recent killings of countless young black children and men and women, coupled with the ongoing and egregious incarceration of black men in the United States—none of these is an isolated act or unexpected failure of a system. They are the deliberate expression and essence of the system, a system of authoritarianism in the United States that has intensified without apology since 9/11.

Rather than being viewed and swiftly forgotten as demented expressions of extremism, these incidents should be seen as part of a growing, systemic pattern of violence and terror that has emerged at a time when the politics and logic of disposability, terror, and expulsion have been normalized in American society. Indeed, violence has become the default position for solving all social problems, especially as they pertain to poor minorities of color. If police brutality is one highly visible expression of the politics of disposability, mass incarceration is its invisible underside. How else to explain that 77 percent of all inmates out of a population of 2.3 million are people of color? Or that "the United States incarcerates a higher proportion of blacks than apartheid South Africa did [and in] America the black-white wealth gap today is greater than it was in South Africa in 1970 at the peak of apartheid"?[3]

When ethics and any remnant of social responsibility and the public good are trampled beneath the hooves of the militarized finance state, there will be nothing left to sustain democratic values or justice. We live in an age of disposability—a historical period of increasing barbarism ruled by financial monsters and, as some studies show, psychopaths.[4] They offer no political concessions and are compelled by a death-drive to terrorize those individuals and populations considered vulnerable and superfluous in a market economy, such as poor minority youth and immigrants, as well as those public spheres such as public and higher education that offer a space for the development of critical ideas, thoughtfulness, informed exchange, and modes of democratic solidarity. How else to explain the publication of a paper by an assistant professor at West Point calling for drone strikes against dissenting intellectuals, making clear what my colleague David L. Clark calls "the endgame of the war on thought."[5]

Democratic values, commitments, integrity, and struggles are under siege in the age of neoliberal misery and disposability. The purpose of the terrorist state and its overlords is to crush any sense of dissent, civic morality, and political courage by instilling fear and squashing the very capacity for democratic beliefs, principles, and convictions. Under such conditions, power is not only made unaccountable, but divorced from any sense of moral and political conviction. Hence, the punishing state emerges as a way to govern all of social life. In this context, life is deemed disposable for most, but especially for poor minorities of color.

I think bell hooks is right when she states that "the point of lynching historically was not to kill individuals but to let everybody know: 'This could happen to you.'" This is how a terrorist state controls people. It individualizes fear and insecurity and undercuts the formation of collective struggle. Fear of punishment—of being killed, tortured, or reduced to the mere level of survival—has become the government's weapon of choice. The terrorist state manufactures ignorance and relies on induced isolation and privatization to depoliticize the population. Beliefs are reduced to the realm of the private, allowing the public realm to sink into the dark night of barbarism, terror, and lawlessness. Without the ability to translate private troubles into public issues, Americans face a crisis of individual and collective agency as well as a historical crisis.

As an endless expression of brutality and the ongoing elimination of any trace of equality and democratic values, the killing of innocent black children and adults by the police makes clear that Americans now inhabit a state of unapologetic lawlessness and extreme violence, one that both fills Hollywood screens with prurient entertainment and testifies to the presence of a growing culture of cruelty—and, unfortunately, provides confirmation of the ravaging violence that marks everyday life as well. Of course, this is not simply a domestic issue or one limited to the United States. As post-colonial theorist Arif Dirlik points out:

> Life in general is being devalued for entire sections of populations across the globe. Let's not forget the callousness with which people are being murdered by drones, U.S. troops, Israel, Han Chinese (Tibetans, Uighurs). The assassination of blacks by the police across the U.S. gives the impression of a vulnerable population being used as guinea pigs, to warn the rest of what to expect if we get out of line.[6]

Totalitarianism is on the rise across the globe, just as growing numbers of people who are vulnerable are being treated as disposable due to modes of governance wedded to militarism, unchecked market forces, corporate sovereignty, and updated forms of authoritarianism. Calls for minor reforms such as retraining the police, hiring more minorities in police forces, equipping police with body cameras,[7] or making the grand jury system more transparent will not change a political and social system that has lost its connections to the ideals, values, and promises of a democracy.[8] And calls for punishing the Wall Street crooks who caused the 2008 financial crisis will not reform the system that produced the financial debacle. In fact, pleas for reform have been more often made by apologists for the punishing state in the aftermath of highly publicized examples of police brutality, botched executions, the shootings of unarmed black teenagers, and numerous reports of torture, solitary confinement, and the ongoing criminalization of social problems.[9] President Obama, for one, responded to the police violence and national uprisings by chastising blacks for looting and rioting. This is not merely another blame-the-victim narrative—it is an act of moral duplicity, though perhaps unsurprising from a president who makes George W. Bush look liberal when it comes to violating civil liberties and punishing whistleblowers while expanding the killing of civilians through the use of indiscriminate drone warfare. There is also former attorney general Eric Holder, who refused to prosecute Wall Street criminals, and yet assured the American public that the government would conduct independent investigations in the interests of the powerless. Credibility was more than stretched in this instance. Willful deception and lying is like a disease sweeping the country: authority figures say one thing, but clearly think and act in ways that belie their public statements.

More to the point, there is New York City Police Chief Bill Bratton, who vowed to retrain 22,000 police officers, but evaded questions about the police force using chokeholds on innocent victims. And then there is former New York City mayor Rudolph Giuliani, appearing on *Fox News Sunday*, who suggested that some police reforms might be necessary, but then invoked the racist argument that blacks inhabit a culture of criminality. His comments are worth examining: "But I think just as much, if not more, responsibility is on the black community to reduce the reason why the police officers are assigned in such large numbers to the black community. It's because blacks commit murder eight times more per capita than any other group in our society."[10] As if this argument justifies the beatings, shootings, and killing of innocent individuals at the hands of the police. These calls for reforms are not only disingenuous coming from people entrenched in supporting the punishing state and its interests, they are invoked to hide the real causes of misery and violence in the United States—which arise from a society immersed in racism, economic inequality, and poverty, and increasingly shaped by the redistribution of wealth away from the public sector, the ongoing destruction of the welfare state, and a political system now controlled by financial elites.

The face of state terrorism has been captured in images of the police spraying tear gas into the crowds of peaceful protesters in New York City. It can be seen in reports of the police choking students, firing hundreds of rounds of bullets into the cars of civilians, and shooting an unarmed man in an apartment stairwell. It can also be seen in the comments of right-wing fundamentalists who try to incite moral panic over the presence of immigrants, protest movements, and any other form of resistance to the authoritarian state. How else to explain the comments made on national television news by Pat Lynch, the head of the New York City police union, who stated that Officer Daniel Pantaleo deserved to be acquitted by the grand jury in the death of Eric Garner because Garner was able to utter the words "I can't breathe," which allegedly indicated there was no choke-hold applied to his neck, in spite of what the video displayed or what the medical examiner concluded? Even Orwell could not make this up. Lynch overlooked not only the evidence provided by the video of Garner's brutal killing and the verdict of the medical examiner but also the fact that Officer Pantaleo had a history of racial misconduct in the police force. Pantaleo was not indicted, proving once again that "The first step to controlling the police is to get rid of the fantasy, once and for all, that the law is on our side. The law is firmly on the side of police who open fire on unarmed civilians."[11]

But, more important, the New York City police force as a whole has a long history of racist practices and violence, extending from an aggressive policy of racial profiling to bullying people in the name of the "broken windows theory," which is a synonym for harassing young black men.[12] It is only getting worse as fatal police encounters with black men reach epidemic proportions.[13] Necropolitics—or the presence of sovereign power that exercises control even over one's mortality—now drives the everyday existence of poor minorities. As race theorist David Theo Goldberg points out, how else to explain

the account Darren Wilson has given publicly about his sense of Michael Brown as a large, violent, probably armed young black man? Or the shooting with absolutely no warning of 12-year-old Tamir Rice for carrying a pellet gun in an otherwise empty snow-filled park? . . . Or the luckily unsuccessful shooting at a black father by mistaking for a weapon the 6-year-old daughter he was rushing to save from a severe asthma attack?[14]

It doesn't end there, as nightmare videos appear like the one of a cop viciously beating a fifty-year-old, mentally ill black woman along a busy Los Angeles highway, and another report surfaces of a young black man being killed in a Walmart store for allegedly "brandishing" an air rifle, which he had been holding and leaning on as if it were a walking stick. What ties all of these events together is the fact that these acts of violence, corruption, and incompetence are not isolated practices, but add up to the new face of domestic terrorism in post-9/11 America.

Yet none of the alleged reformers situate the violence done to Tamir Rice, for instance, within a wider context of state violence. Rice's death is never analyzed in the face of the charge that the Cleveland police force is a corrupt and lawless institution. No connection is made between how the police are trained and regulated and the evidence that the killing of a twelve-year-old black child was committed by a cop deemed incompetent by his previous department. Only recently has the militarization of local police forces become national news, but this has remained largely unassociated with the rise of a permanent warfare state and the militarization of the entire society. Little is learned from the ongoing evidence that black Americans are mostly terrified of the police, who act like an occupying force in their neighborhoods that consequently are treated like war zones. Social commentator Chase Madar is right in arguing that lawlessness is on the side of the police, and the law has become a license for them to kill with impunity. He writes:

Police demilitarization, the decriminalization of working-class people, new policing models: these are all projects that could work in Ferguson and thousands of other American cities. Although none of these large-scale ideas is explicitly race-conscious, they would most likely tighten the severe racial disparities in policing violence that exist all over the country, more so than pouring more money into racial sensitivity training for cops. These big-picture reforms are fundamentally political solutions that will require long-term effort, coalition politics that spans race, ethnicity and political affiliation—a challenge, but also a necessity. As police and prosecutors assume more and more power in the United States—regulating immigration (formerly a matter of administrative law), meting out school discipline, and other spheres of everyday life where criminal law was almost unknown even a generation ago—getting law enforcement on a tight leash is a national imperative. In the meantime, the constant stream of news reports of unarmed, mostly black and Latino civilians killed by police demands bigger, bolder approaches. They are the only available paths to getting the police under control.[15]

As this suggests, the question of police brutality has to be addressed far beyond the discourse of liberal reforms. But the questions being asked must also do more than focus solely on police violence. All of the cases mentioned above should raise questions about what kind of society produces such lawless institutions. In totalitarian regimes, the mass psychology of authoritarianism runs amok as indiscriminate acts of state violence are followed by the language of demonization, racism, cruelty, and mad utterances of hate. We can see this happening in the United States when black men are called dangerous criminals, drug addicts, or thugs—even by a black president in Baltimore. Or when Donald Trump in his presidential campaign announcement speech stated that most Mexican immigrants were rapists, criminals, and drug runners.[16] This is a discourse of abusive certainty, unmoved even by an awareness of its ignorance, and determined to legitimate massive extremes of inequality, material deprivation, and human misery as it produces widening zones of violence and abandonment.

Lawlessness in the authoritarian state thrives on the purported existence of a "culture of criminality" much like the one invoked by Giuliani's and

Trump's comments above. The culture of criminality thesis has taken on a new register in the American context as the punishing state increases the range of social behaviors it now criminalizes. If somebody is poor, unable to pay their debts, violates a trivial rule in school, is homeless, or viewed as the Other, they are prime targets for the criminal justice system. As the police become more militarized and the culture of cruelty becomes more pervasive, the senseless harassment of black men is followed by a spate of racist killings. Under such circumstances, the criminal justice system is not noted for its respect for justice but for how it has "become criminal in its lack of justice."[17] Unfortunately, there is not only a fabricated culture of criminality in the United States but a real one—it resides in the mega-banks, the ultra-rich hedge funds, and other apparatuses of the finance state. On this issue there is nothing but silence from alleged reformers.

The darkest side of the authoritarian state feeds and legitimizes not only state violence, the violation of civil liberties, a punishing state, and a culture of cruelty, but also a culture in which violence becomes the only mediating force available to address major social problems. America is awash in a culture of cruelty reinforced everyday by the mainstream media, popular culture, and an entertainment industry that trades in violence. Under such circumstances, a culture of violence erupts and punishes the innocent, the marginalized, and the demonized individuals who become victims of both hate crimes and state terrorism. The killings in South Carolina of nine black parishioners in Charleston's Emanuel African Methodist Episcopal Church by a twenty-one-year-old white man, Dylann Roof, who claimed he wanted "to start a civil war," once again register the lethal combination of racism, lawlessness, and a culture that sanitizes violence, rendering it so totally safe that the American public does not recognize it as violence anymore.

The institutional violence that now seeps into practically every sphere of American life has lost its ability to shock, move people to bear witness, and address the conditions that produce it. Violence is now both an American ideal celebrated in the production of war, soldiers, and the highly publicized workings of the surveillance state. Most important, it fuels an entertainment and news industry that uses violence as a way to produce pleasure, indulge voyeurism, and mobilize humanity's darkest instincts. At the same time, American culture is saturated in myriad forms of material and symbolic violence that weaken public values while contributing to a hardening of the culture and a self-righteous coldness that takes delight in the suffering of others.

Under such circumstances, politics becomes corrupt and supports both the ideological conditions that sanction racist violence and the militarized institutional culture that celebrates rather than scorns such brutality. Should anyone be surprised by these senseless killings in South Carolina where the Confederate battle flag, the flag of white supremacy, "the flag of Dylann Roof—[flew until recently] on the Capitol grounds in Columbia,"[18] and where the roads are named after Confederate generals, and where hate crimes are not reported? South Carolina is only the most obvious example of a racist legacy that refuses to die throughout the United States.

This deep-seated legacy has its political apologists as can be seen in the initial unwillingness of conservatives such as Ted Cruz, Rand Paul, and others to call for the removal of a flag on the grounds of the state capitol "that stands for slavery, racism, and treason."[19] As former *New York Times* columnist Frank Rich points out, this type of moral cowardice is symptomatic of a party that not only refuses to stand up to racism and the unreconstructed bigots that are part of the party's base, but also registers the deep-seated racism that is fundamental to the party and its embrace of a species of racial hatred endemic to totalitarian politics in general:

Not even the slaughter of nine people in a church could stir the consciences of the Republican presidential contenders. They came out against the flag only after the previously hedging Governor Haley came around. No doubt she spent a long weekend calculating how failing to do so would inflict economic retribution on her state much as the "religious liberty" law had threatened to bring corporate and convention boycotts to Indiana. Before Haley finally spoke up on Monday, the only major Republican figure to unequivocally call for the flag's banishment was Mitt Romney, who isn't facing GOP primary voters in 2016. After Haley joined him, we were treated to the embarrassing spectacle of Bush, Rubio, and Walker—by most reckonings, the GOP's three leading candidates—all asserting that they had agreed with Haley all along. This combination of disingenuousness and spinelessness on a no-brainer issue should disqualify all of them from the White House.[20]

While the controversy over the Confederate flag is not unimportant given the violent history and racist propaganda to which it points—all a matter of moral witnessing and the reclaiming of public memory—the debate ultimately is a diversion and buries the burning issue of an unregulated gun culture and its murderous consequences, the attempts to turn back voting rights, the rise of the racist mass incarceration state, the para-militarization of the police, the rise of the surveillance state, the proliferation of homicidal police violence, and the increasing impoverishment of black communities. Taking down the flag in South Carolina and other states is not a sign of racial progress if these issues do not figure prominently in any debate about the proliferation of violence and racism in American society.

Violence has become like an out-of-control firestorm rampaging unchecked through American society. And it will continue until a broken and corrupt political, cultural, and market-driven system, now controlled largely by ideological, educational, economic, and religious fundamentalists, can be broken. Until then the bloodshed will continue, along with the spectacle of violence which will fill America's screen culture, and the militarization of American society will continue. Neither Orwell nor Huxley could have imagined such a violent dystopian society.

What drives the increasing brutalization and killing of innocent people in the United States is a form of terrorism untethered from democratic oversight or any sense of social responsibility, guilt, and morality. This is a form of state violence and domestic terrorism fed by a culture obsessed with guns, the criminalization of poverty, the militarization of the lives of low-income and poor minorities, and the misery spawned by neoliberal slash-and-burn policies aimed mainly at the poor and the welfare state. It is also fueled by a racism that refuses to be acknowledged in an alleged post-racial society in which the election of an African American president serves to wipe any acknowledgment of either the legacy of racism or its persistent and poisonous influence on America society. Calls for reform of one or more parts of the system do not challenge the totalitarian politics and financial forces that rule American society; they simply give the system a veil of legitimacy suggesting it can be fixed. It can't be fixed. This is not to suggest that it is better for cops to carry military-grade weapons rather than carry cameras, or that there is no point in creating new policing models. But these are short-term solutions and do not address the larger structural violence and racism built into the neoliberal financial state. It is a death-dealing system ruled by political and moral zombies, and it has to be transformed through the development of nonviolent social movements that can imagine a democracy that is real, substantive, and radical in its calls for justice, equality, and freedom. The dark possibilities of our times are everywhere.

The killing of Freddie Gray, Walter Scott, Samuel DuBose, and others serve as flashpoints that have mobilized people all over the country. Some people, especially black youth, are beginning to realize that the ongoing killing of black people is attributable not only to a persistent racism but also to the existence of the militarized finance state—a police and punishing state that operates as the repressive apparatuses of the financial elite. The demonstrations must continue full force, and, as a first step, criminal charges must be brought against rogue cops and lawless police departments that believe it is permissible for them to engage in racist repression and brutalize black neighborhoods by treating them as war zones.

In a country in which militarism is viewed as an ideal and the police and soldiers are treated like heroes, violence has morphed into the primary modality for solving problems. One consequence is that state violence is either ignored, rendered trivial, or is shamelessly legitimated in the name of the law, security, or self-defense. State violence fueled by the merging of the war on terror, the militarization of all aspects of society, and a deep-seated and increasingly ruthless and unapologetic racism is now ubiquitous and should be labeled as a form of domestic terrorism.[21] Terrorism, torture, and state violence are no longer simply part of our history; they have become the nervous system of an increasingly authoritarian state. Eric Garner told the police as he was being choked to death that he could not breathe. His words now apply to democracy itself, which has lost the civic oxygen that gives it life and is on its death bed. America has become a place where democracy cannot breathe.

The mainstream press seems especially interested in such stories when the victims can be viewed as assailants, as in the case of Trayvon Martin and Michael Brown, but are less interested when the old stereotypes about crime and black culture cannot be invoked. When the victims of police violence cannot be tarred with labels such as super-predators or thugs,[22] as in the case of Tamir Rice, who was only twelve when shot to death by a policeman—who in his previous police assignment in another city was labeled as unstable—demonizing discourse becomes useless and such acts of state terrorism simply fade out of view.

Why is it that there was almost no public outcry over the case of Kalief Browder, a young black man who was arrested for a crime he did not commit and incarcerated at the notorious Rikers Island and spent more than a thousand days, two years, in solitary confinement, waiting for a trial that never happened? Shortly after being released he committed suicide.[23] Would this have happened if he were white, middle-class, and had access to a lawyer? How is what happened to him different than the egregious torture inflicted on innocent children at Abu Ghraib prison? What has the United States become in the age of domestic terrorism?

Not surprisingly, the discourse of terrorism once again is only used when someone is engaged in a plot to commit violence against the government but not when the state commits violence unjustly against its own citizens. What needs to be recognized, as historian Robin D. G. Kelley has pointed out, is that the killing of unarmed African Americans by the police is not simply a matter that speaks to the need for reforming the police and the culture that shapes it, but also for massive organized resistance to a war against black youth that is being waged on American soil.[24] Ending police misconduct is certainly acceptable as a short-term goal to save lives, but if we are going to prevent the United States from becoming a full-fledged police state serving the interests of the rich who ensconce themselves in their gated and guarded communities the vicious neoliberal financial and police state has to be dismantled. Such resistance is beginning with the emergence of the Black Lives Matter movement, along with youth movements such as the Black Youth Project, Millennial Activists United, We Charge Genocide, and other groups.[25]

Black youth are safe neither in their own neighborhoods nor on public streets, highways, schools, or any other areas in which the police can be found. A new brutalism haunts America, drenched in the ever-increasing flood of intolerable police and state violence.[26] More and more people are being locked up, jailed, beaten, harassed, and violated by the police and other security forces because they are poor, vulnerable, viewed as disposable, or simply are marginalized by being black, brown, young, and poor.[27] Let's hope this scourge of domestic terrorism, especially aimed at poor black youth, signals the further development of a civil rights movement that confronts the horrors of the authoritarian state.

Under such circumstances, the reinvention of racist ideologies, institutions, and language under the new authoritarianism must be seen as part of a larger, systemic project of disposability, harassment, and expulsion. This project is supported in the United States by a culture that increasingly treats minority groups as potential "enemy combatants"[28]—a premise that lays the moral foundation for the brutalizing treatment, and in some cases killing, of young black men and others with impunity. A fundamental transformation of this culture of cruelty will only begin when political formations at every level of government dismantle the barbarous system run by financial looters and backed up by rogue paramilitary forces. The political left and other progressives need a cause that speaks to multiple instances of oppression, and that cause is the promise and struggle for a radical democracy. Let's hope the endless array of racist harassment, shootings, and killings of innocent and unarmed African Americans by right-wing vigilantes, a militarized police force, and paramilitary security forces propel the beginning of a political and social movement to fight what has become a dark and gruesome form of governance in the United States.

6

The Fire This Time: Black Youth and the Spectacle of Post-Racial Violence

Let's hope it isn't too late to listen, listen intently, carefully, minds open, hearts full. Let's hope.—JAMES BALDWIN

IN 1963, JAMES BALDWIN PUBLISHED an essay entitled "The Negro Child—His Self-Image," in *The Saturday Review*. Later celebrated as "A Talk to Teachers," his prescient opening paragraph unfolds with the following observation:

> Let's begin by saying that we are living through a very dangerous time. Everyone in this room is in one way or another aware of that. We are in a revolutionary situation, no matter how unpopular that word has become in this country. The society in which we live is desperately menaced . . . from within. To any citizen of this country who figures himself as responsible—and particularly those of you who deal with the minds and hearts of young people—must be prepared to "go for broke."[1]

Signaling the existential crisis engendered by a profound political crisis, Baldwin's first title resonates more powerfully with the current historical moment, especially as black youth are increasingly assaulted, even killed, by white policemen in alarming numbers. His essay also points to both the need for resistance and the hazardous price one might have to pay by engaging in open defiance. Baldwin was right then, but his words are even more relevant today as we are truly living in "dangerous times." As I have mentioned in previous chapters, the killings of young black men such as twelve-year-old Tamir Rice, sixteen-year-old Kimani Gray, eighteen-year-old Michael Brown, twenty-two-year-old James Crawford III, and twenty-five-year-old Freddie Gray, among others, are part of a historical pattern of racist terror in which African American populations have been contained and controlled by so-called legitimate mechanisms of state violence.[2] Today, this pattern is being reenacted with a vengeance. Not only is an African American killed by the police "every three or four days," but "the rate of police killings of black Americans is nearly the same as the rate of lynchings in the early decades of the 20th century."[3]

Racist brutality in the United States is abetted and legitimated through a discourse of demonization, stereotypes, and objectification. For example, Frank Rich observed in relation to the 2015 Baltimore uprisings that "the right has so far blamed the crisis on unions, welfare, single-parent families, Democrats, the 'animalism' of Baltimore residents and President Obama."[4] Fox News commentators blamed the Baltimore uprisings on gangs, schools, and the welfare system, and in some cases called for the use of deadly force against the participants. Though the racist implications of this discourse are partially blunted through deploying language that focuses on social disorder and alleged cultures of criminality, the messages supporting and justifying the use of violence within and against communities of color come through loud and clear. John Nolte, a conservative news pundit, stated in response to the uprisings that in his home of rural North Carolina, "The residents don't riot. We shoot rioters."[5] Such comments reveal more than the racist sensibilities that fuel them, they also exhibit the intellectual and symbolic violence aimed at poor black youth and the communities in which they live.

Rather than being seen as victims, black youth are vilified—viewed as suspicious, delinquent, or dangerous by the mass media—with often devastating consequences. They signify the most recent population once again regarded as the "wretched of the earth," considered disposable and treated as human refuse, preyed upon by the criminal justice system, private probationary companies, and the financial elite who have brought back the debtors' prison.[6] Though violence waged against black people in the United States is nothing new, we have witnessed the appearance of new death-dealing military weapons and the militarizing of entire police forces. In addition, there is the more recent neoliberal economic destruction of entire cities, and the collapse of the welfare state, the war on terror, and the rise of the punishing state, all of which add a new and more capacious register to a long history of such racist violence.[7]

Vicious forms of militarized repression have always been visible to black communities. More recently, assaults have aired almost weekly as another African American is killed for walking through the wrong neighborhood, playing music too loud, for taking umbrage at police harassment, or for simply holding an unloaded air rifle in a Walmart store.[8] The killings play in the mainstream media as a spectacle, which by definition offers little or no critical commentary about the long legacy of racist violence in the United States. Nor does the mainstream media examine the myriad conditions that both produce and normalize such violence. After decades of political inaction and retrenchment abetted by a compliant media, the United States has dissolved into a racist, militarized, and corrupt financial state. Award-winning journalist Isabel Wilkerson goes so far as to argue that the killing of black men has surpassed the spectacle of lynching associated with the country's segregated past. She writes:

Lynchings were spectacles with hundreds if not thousands of witnesses and were often photographed extensively. Now, much of the recent police violence has been recorded as well. The chokehold killing of Eric Garner on Staten Island, New York, the beating of great-grandmother Marlene Pinnock on a Los Angeles freeway and the gut-wrenching case of 17-year-old Victor Steen, tasered while riding his bicycle and then run over by the police officer in Pensacola, Florida, were all caught on videotape and have reached hundreds of thousands of watchers on YouTube—a form of public witness to brutality beyond anything possible in the age of lynching.[9]

Indeed, as I mentioned in the last chapter, such images play nightly in the mainstream media. The death of Eric Garner and countless others serve less as a mode of public witnessing than as fodder for right-wing and conservative pundits to condemn an alleged black culture of criminality and for the networks to increase their ratings. We know what such images mean for many black youth who view the police as responsible, in part, for their precarious existence. Black youth, especially those who are mobilizing across the country against police violence, refuse to be titillated by these images that both demonize them and reinforce the forms of domestic terrorism directed against them. Inoculated against the perception of the police as public servants whose job is to protect and serve their communities, young people, especially poor people of color, experience the police as a dangerous and violent paramilitarized force, an arm of state terrorism.

Young people have watched as their peers have been accosted by the police, harassed, beaten, and too often killed. As entire cities are transformed into zones of lawlessness, the police appear not only more violent but more brazen, routinely violating the law rather than upholding it—their own video cameras be damned. They also inflict abuse and violence with impunity because lawlessness is on their side, safely secured by the absence of effective civilian oversight systems.[10] Hence, it should not be surprising that many black and brown youth both fear for their lives and view their neighborhoods as occupied territory. But it has been surprising nonetheless, especially for those who bought into the post-racial mythology of the Obama era.

When journalist Amy Goodman asked Aniya, a thirteen-year-old African American girl in Staten Island, why she was marching to protest the death of Eric Garner she replied: "I want to live until I'm 18. . . . You want to get older. You want to experience life. You don't want to die in a matter of seconds because of cops."[11] Democracy for this thirteen-year-old has not only receded but its civil institutions have also become toxic for those marginalized by class and race. Manufacturing threats of fear and violence fails to create what Tariq Ali has called "sleepwalking citizens," among these populations.[12] Rather, the undiminished presence of violence and suffering has produced new modes of politics for young people of color. The older myths that upheld a more liberal form of color-blind multiculturalism are no longer operable against the massive contradictions that have come to characterize a more fully realized corporate statehood and form of market fundamentalism.

The so-called American dream has been emptied of its mythical status, relegated to a form of nostalgia fit only for the *Mad Men* fans and right-wing pundits who inhabit that imaginary calling for a return to a time when women knew their "place," privileged whites and corporations ruled society with an iron grip, and blacks were largely restricted to hidden enclaves of poverty or contained and disciplined by local police forces. Replacing this world—reflected in the rags to riches stories of Horatio Alger, the soothing conformity produced in *Reader's Digest*, and the 1950s television series *Leave It to Beaver*, with its suffocating, white, middle-class notion of the heterosexual family, is a dystopian social order in which "violence . . . operates not on the periphery of society but at its center as an organizing idea and serves as a primary form of mediation in addressing major social problems."[13]

As the traditional social welfare state is transformed into the corporate state, those democratic public spheres that support public goods are under attack. As the social contract and the democratic values and ideals that uphold it are replaced by a regime of neoliberalism that celebrates privatization, commodification, and self-interest, inequality in wealth and power grows exponentially, destroying the healthy social structures necessary for a democracy and the requisites for embracing citizenship as a matter of political, ethical, and social responsibility. Citizenship is now reduced to consumerism and politics is emptied of any wider sense of community and respect for the common good.

A ruthless form of state control, a culture of fear, pedagogies of repression, an expanding incarceration Panopticon, and an all–embracing surveillance state now define the politics of governance.[14] No longer restricted to military battlefields or the world of "underground" crime, state and corporate violence are now the default solutions for a society that views social problems as a threat to state security. At the same time, the misery and suffering caused by a failed state are viewed as form of criminalized behavior, relegated to the repressive disciplinary practices of the criminal legal system. One consequence is a hardening of the culture that gives credence to state repression and its most visible form of domestic brutality, unchecked police violence, which targets the most vulnerable populations, particularly poor black people.

Police violence is the most obvious form of state terrorism and has been fueled by the transformation of local police units into SWAT teams that adopt what the ACLU has called "warrior-like mind sets."[15] Since the early 1990s, an entrenched militarism and "culture of war"[16] has seeped into civil society as the Department of Defense, under a stratagem known as the 1033 program, provided "tens of thousands of pieces of military equipment to local police departments for free."[17] Weapons no longer used on foreign battlefields found their way into police precincts across the country and included "machine guns, magazines, night vision equipment, aircraft and armored vehicles."[18] Overall it has been estimated that the DOD program has provided over $4.3 billion in free military supplies to local police. Military grade weapons do more than provoke fear and hostility in black communities; they also produce among the police modes of repressive behavior shaped by the notion that war, not trust, is the modality for dealing with those populations considered dangerous and disposable. Military aggression in this case becomes the organizing principle that not only informs police strategies in dealing with poor black and brown communities; it also becomes a generalized rule of governance, reinforcing a culture of violence and lawlessness. In the aftermath of the tragic terrorist attack on 9/11, state militarization was intensified by a culture of fear and surveillance presented to the American public as the war on terror. The culture of war, joined with a ruthless form of market fundamentalism, put in place a new authoritarianism that was now complete.[19]

Pervasive police abuse and violence have become the foci of emerging social movements, from Black Lives Matter to a growing number of rap groups and young black militants.[20] And rightly so. As more and more unarmed black men and youth are shot by white police officers, the cries for an indictment of perpetrators and broad-based reform have been superseded by a more general cry for justice.[21] Lawlessness functions both to abuse the innocent and protect the guilty. And too many local police departments have bought into this dreadful logic, indulging with impunity the notion that war and policing have merged. Andrew Kolin argues that as the police become more aggressive, they begin to "look increasingly like a civilian branch of the military."[22] One indication of the emerging police state is not only evident in the transition of the police into a civilian branch of the military, but also in the transformation of the police into paramilitarized SWAT teams, which are used disproportionately against people of color. The report *War Comes Home* states that "50% of the people impacted by SWAT deployments from 2011 to 2012 are black or Latino [whereas] whites account for 20%."[23] Inexplicably, although SWAT teams are used overwhelmingly to investigate incidents in which people are "suspected of committing nonviolent consensual crimes," too many encounters prove deadly.[24]

Consider the following deeply revealing and tragic incidents:

Tarika Wilson, a 26-year-old mother who was shot and killed holding her 14-month-old son and Eurie Stamp, a 68-year-old grandfather . . . shot while watching baseball in his pajamas during a SWAT invasion. [In addition] Bounkham Phonesavanh, a 19-month-old baby, was in a medically induced coma after paramilitary squads unwittingly threw a flash grenade into his crib, piercing a hole in his cheek, chest and scarring his body with third-degree burns. None of the victims were suspects.[25]

As a result of their warrior mentality and their increasing willingness to use aggressive, belligerent methods, SWAT teams function largely to produce rather than prevent violence, as author and journalist Radley Balko points out:

> Because these raids often involve forced entry into homes, often at night, they're actually *creating* violence and confrontation where there was none before. . . . In short, we have police departments that are increasingly using violent, confrontational tactics to break into private homes for increasingly low-level crimes, and they seem to believe that the public has no right to know the specifics of when, how and why those tactics are being used.[26]

The registers of state violence now appear even to seep into every compassionate institution in American society. The tentacles of the police state extend from criminalizing those who seek social services to students who, as John Whitehead points out, are routinely "being photographed, fingerprinted, scanned, x-rayed, sniffed and snooped on. Between metal detectors at the entrances, drug-sniffing dogs in the hallways and surveillance cameras in the classrooms and elsewhere, many of America's schools look more like prisons than learning facilities."[27] Mosques are regarded as terrorist organizations. The institutions of higher education are stripped of democratic values and turned into training centers for the financial elite, centers for military research, and recruiting spaces for the national intelligence agencies.[28] Youthful peaceful protesters are beaten and arrested for holding power accountable. Ruthless politicians exhibiting a loathing for social welfare programs slash $8.6 billion for food stamp recipients, half of whom are children, insisting that, even for low-income children, "there is no such thing as a free lunch."[29] Georgia Representative Jack Kingston, exhibiting one vicious register of the neoliberal culture of cruelty, argues that low-income and poor school kids should be required to "sweep the floor of the cafeteria."[30] In this instance, the pain of others, particularly those considered disposable, becomes the subject of scorn and ridicule, rather than compassion.

On a national level, the most visible and visceral expressions of the expanding surveillance-security state include: the erosion of civil liberties, the crackdown on dissent, the war on whistleblowers, the legal illegalities of drone warfare, the unapologetic existence of a White House kill list, and a war on terror, all of which reveal an abandonment of any respect for democratic values. Any revitalization of democracy fades as governance and politics begin to take on the disturbing characteristics of a broken society marked by the making of a war culture in which rampant violence and unchecked levels of human suffering become common currency. As the state descends into what Alex Honneth has called an "abyss of failed sociality,"[31] it produces a mode of governance legitimated through a state of emergency that unleashes a politics of lawlessness as well as unchecked state and corporate violence. But none of these reveals the anti-democratic and authoritarian tendencies fueling these initiatives more than the forty-year-old racist experiment of mass imprisonment.[32]

While the killing of unarmed blacks may represent police violence in one of its most lethal forms, these killings are part of a larger structure of violence aimed at destroying the promise of a democracy in the "post-racial" era, which includes a mass incarceration system in which even young children are now arrested for minor infractions. The stories are legion. In one such revealing and symptomatic incident, a five-year-old Stockton, California, "student was handcuffed with zip ties on his hands and feet, forced to go to the hospital for a psychiatric evaluation and was charged with battery on a police officer."[33] An equally disturbing event took place in a Baltimore City Detention Center in which juveniles awaiting trial for adult crimes were illegally kept in solitary confinement—one youngster was confined under such conditions for 143 days.[34] Not only is this practice, performed on young people, reminiscent of the torture methods used by the United States on prisoners at Guántanamo, it also "violates article 7 of the International Covenant on Civil and Political Rights and article 16 of the UN Convention against Torture."[35]

The war on African American youth, in particular, has culminated in a simple morally repugnant statistic: by "age 23, almost a third of African Americans have been arrested for a crime."[36] As Michelle Alexander indicates, the racist nature of such violence is clear, given that "there are more African American adults under correctional control today—in prison or jail, on probation or parole—than were enslaved in 1850, a decade before the Civil War began."[37]

Moreover, the use of the police state to crush democratic aspirations is increasingly expanding not only to include the ongoing jailing of immigrants and their families[38] and the use of violence against youthful protesters, but also incorporates expanding populations of the poor by the arduous demands of debt and survival. Since the 1980s, the war on poverty has been transformed into an assault on the poor. Increased impoverishment is the net result of policies aimed at harassing poor people of color in racial profiling, the school-to-prison pipeline, practices that mandate "drug testing for eligibility to receive welfare assistance,"[39] and jailing the underprivileged because they cannot provide bail.[40] The criminalization of poverty has become clear, especially in the Department of Justice Report investigation of the Ferguson Police Department and municipal court. According to Karen Dolan, a Fellow at the Institute for Policy Studies, the report includes practices that result in the arrest of the poor, especially people of color, for such minor offenses as "a broken taillight, an unpaid parking ticket, a minor drug offense, sitting on a sidewalk, or sleeping in a park," all of which can result not only in "excessive fines imposed by the courts and outside debt collectors, but also in jail time."[41]

The DOJ report revealed that many African Americans, young and old, were targeted, arrested, incarcerated, and sometimes killed not because they had committed a crime, but due to racial and economic profiling. According to numerous accounts, municipalities all over the United States were imposing exorbitant fees and court costs for transgressions as minor as "putting one's feet up on a subway seat," expired parking meters, walking in the street, and in "some cases jail time when someone was unable to pay court fines and probation fees for misdemeanor offenses such as a speeding ticket."[42] In short, criminalizing poverty, especially in communities of color, has gone hand-in-hand with the return of the debtors' prison. All of these incidents add up to a shakedown scheme used to fund local police departments and municipalities. The Ferguson example is perhaps the most shocking since "the city of Ferguson collected $2.6 million in such fines and fees in 2013, most of them for traffic violations and other low-level offenses. This collection of fines and fees was Ferguson's second-largest source of income."[43] David Graeber argues that the institutionalized racism uncovered by the DOJ report was the criminalization of an entire city:

> More damning is this: in a major American city, the criminal justice system perceives a large part of that city's population not as citizens to be protected, but as potential targets for what can only be described as a shake-down operation designed to wring money out of the poorest and most vulnerable by any means they could.[44]

What these revelations amount to is that Ferguson ran an "offender-funded criminal justice service . . . effectively turning this city into an occupied territory, with a 95 percent white police force supporting itself by forcibly preying on a nearly 70 percent black population."[45] Subject to pervasive low-level but high-cost harassment, African Americans "experienced 85 percent of all traffic stops, 90 percent of citations, 88 percent of incidents in which an officer used force, and 93 percent of all arrests. They received almost all of the citations for petty crimes like jaywalking. Black drivers were twice as likely to have their cars searched as whites, yet significantly less likely to actually have drugs or other contraband. Of the people who spent two or more days in the city jail, 95 percent were black."[46] In Ferguson, predatory finance practices merged with police violence and an utterly corrupt and unjust criminal justice system to produce a deadly brew of police brutality in conjunction with the ongoing criminalization of the minor transgressions that defined the fabric of everyday life for most African Americans.[47] Drawing from the DOJ report, Marion Wright Edelman, founder of the Children's Defense Fund, mentions one particular case in Ferguson that would seem incomprehensible in meaningful democratic society:

> In one case a woman who parked her car illegally in 2007 and couldn't pay the initial $151 fee has since been arrested twice, spent six days in jail, paid $550 to a city court, and as of 2014 still owed the city $541 in fines, all as a result of the unpaid parking ticket. . . . And Ferguson isn't alone. The criminalization of poverty is a growing trend in states and localities across the country.[48]

Crucial to recognize is that the criminalization of poverty is a national trend and not an unusual practice that only took place in Ferguson.[49] As Dolan observed, such practices are pervasive throughout the United States.[50] When the profit motive becomes a reason to arrest people, not only do such practices lead to massive inequities in the justice system, disproportionally targeting poor minorities, they also enact a substantive transformation of the police and the criminal justice system from "a public safety organization to a for-profit corporation that has the legal backing of the government and the ability to coerce the public with the threat of force." Moreover, because the poor, immigrants, and blacks "are targeted disproportionately by the police and are the least able to defend themselves in court, these vulnerable groups are fleeced for their money and often forced into virtual debt servitude."[51] As anthropologist David Graeber states, another consequence of such targeted abuses is that

> citizens who had never been found guilty—indeed, never even been accused—of an actual crime were rounded up, jailed, threatened with "indefinite" incarceration in fetid cells, risking disease and serious injury, until their destitute families could assemble hundreds if not thousands of dollars in fines, fees, and penalties to pay their jail-

ers. As a result of such practices, over three-quarters of the population had warrants out for their arrest at any given time. [52]

There is a certain unmistakable irony here in that as neoliberal policies strip all public services of their resources, the institutions that the state relies upon to maintain control of the 99 percent adopt criminal behavior themselves, simply to be able to function. That criminality is then projected onto victims of such privatizing schemes, mimicking all the while the central values and corruption of the failed neoliberal mode of governance. This is clearly a prescription for the authoritarian state, which serves as a grim reminder of how the police and the criminal legal system more generally function to engage in massive shakedowns not only designed to get revenue to support their repressive institutions, but also to implant fear in the most vulnerable by crippling their sense of individual and collective agency and decimating any sense of organization and challenge. This is domestic terrorism operating under the mantle of neoliberalism.

Hundreds of miles from Ferguson, the Baltimore community in which Freddie Gray grew up is typical of abandoned poor neighborhoods throughout the United States. These economically depressed and deprived communities suffer from the violence of willful neglect, the willingness of the neoliberal state to proliferate zones of social abandonment and terminal exclusion marked by deep poverty, few job opportunities, hopelessness, drug use, a culture constrained by the relentless struggle to survive, and a suppressed rage that often turns inward, dissipating any notion of collective resistance and struggle.

West Baltimore, along with hundreds of neighborhoods just like it, represents not only zones of desperation and social abandonment, it stands as a stark reminder of how the most vulnerable—children and young adults—are saddled with a life scarred by police brutality, corrupt corporate practices, and a criminal justice system that produces crime rather than protects its citizens. This is the face of domestic terrorism, one that far exceeds the violence enacted by police brutality, as shocking as that is in an allegedly post-racial era. Freddie Gray had his spine severed and voice box crushed for making eye contact with a cop. This case is not exceptional.

In Los Angeles County alone between 2007 and 2013, the police killed "41 people each year."[53] In one particularly gruesome act of police brutality, Aiyana Jones, a seven-year-old black grade-school girl from Detroit, "was shot to death during a raid on her home."[54] How is it possible for a police officer to shoot a seven-year-old, regardless of the circumstances? It gets worse. As I mentioned in the last chapter, Tamir Rice, a twelve-year-old, was shot dead in a Cleveland park within seconds of the police arriving. His crime was that he was playing with a toy BB gun. Tamir Rice was killed by Officer Timothy Loehmann, who was deemed psychologically "unfit for service" by his previous employer, Deputy Chief Polak of the Independence, Ohio, police department.[55] He was eventually hired by the Cleveland Police Department.

Such unhinged brutality points to a degree of lawlessness fed by a mixture of racism and administrative incompetency that could only exist in a society in which police violence has become normalized. Too typically, the mainstream media begin with the question of whether the shooting of children such as Jones and Rice is justified, bypassing altogether essential questions such as: Does the real threat in poor black communities come primarily from the police? Given the generally minor or nonexistent offenses residents are charged with, why are the police in these communities in the first place and who is responsible for sending them?[56] These questions become all the more critical in a city such as Baltimore— CBS News reported on May 12, 2015, that the city paid out over $5.7 million between 2011 and 2014 in more than 100 police abuse lawsuits.

Even worse, between June 2012 and April 2015, 700 detainees were turned away from Central Booking in Baltimore because they suffered from a variety of injuries, including fractures, head wounds, and severe swelling, suggesting that police violence and abuse is rampant throughout the city. And Baltimore is only one of the cities in which the police have clearly broken the law. Police violence in this instance only becomes understandable within the larger context of a failed state in which low-income black and brown youth are considered excess, disposable, and a threat to be either contained or killed.

Under such circumstances, the enemy abroad becomes indistinguishable from the "dangerous classes" at home.[57] Recent killings offer up flashpoints that are increasingly more visible and incendiary, fueling modes of resistance that are focused rightfully on the most brutal and visible elements of state terrorism and violence. Yet, as important as such growing resistance to the emerging police state and state terrorism might be, it is crucial that the incipient protest movements embrace and address the broader context of state violence, a problem that plagued protest movements in the last few decades. Borrowing a phrase from law professor Constance Backouse, a number of protest movements in the past seized upon issues that "enshrine the defining moments of their time," but undercut a discourse of reform by refusing to engage the more radical call for structural change.[58] This was especially true for certain liberal elements in the environmental movement, feminist movement, and in the call for university reforms. Fortunately, there are current anti-racist youth movements that refuse to be limited to short-term reforms and are mobilizing young people and others in a concerted effort to make structural reforms central to their demands. For instance, Alicia Garza, cofounder of #BlackLivesMatter and special project director for the National Domestic Workers Alliance, makes this clear in a recent interview:

> First, I'll say that changing Black Lives Matter to All Lives Matter is not an act of solidarity. What it is, is a demonstration of how we don't actually understand structural racism in this country. When we say All Lives Matter, that's a given. Of course, we're all human beings—we all bleed red—but the fact of the matter is some human lives are valued more than others, and that's a problem. The other thing that we've seen is replacing Black with other things. I saw Animal Lives Matter one time and I just threw up a little bit in my mouth, actually. In this country, we commodify things, and we commodify movements. We see people like Ford doing commercials

that say the American Revolution, right? What I think is important here is that we've been pushing people to really talk about what does structural racism look like in this country. It's not about people being mean to each other.[59]

Under the auspices of a militarized neoliberal agenda with its assault on the welfare state, public goods, and a range of populations now considered disposable, the call to simply reform police behavior does not address the fundamental issue of brute force as the default mechanism for addressing all manner of civil unrest. Writing in *The Atlantic*, Ta-Nehisi Coates insists that "the idea of police reform [is] a symptom of something larger. The idea that all social problems can, and should, be resolved by sheer power is not limited to the police. In Atlanta, a problem that began with the poor state of public schools has now [ended] by feeding more people into the maw of the carceral state."[60] Whether at the federal, state, or municipal level, legitimate authority has given way to the force of power and the machinery of repression in dealing with social problems.[61] All of the major public services in the United States share a common element in that they operate through active practices championed for their efficiency, cost-effectiveness, and standardization that punish rather than serve people.

The examples have become legion: corporations lay off millions to fill the coffers of their exorbitantly overpaid CEOs; the Veterans Administration refuses to provide needed care to wounded and mentally unstable soldiers; millions of dollars are cut from federal and state programs that largely serve poor children; young people cannot find jobs consistent with their talents because the government refuses to fund a decent jobs program through a modern-day Marshall Plan; mega-corporations either pay no taxes or have them reduced while the nation's infrastructure is underfunded despite putting American lives at risk; prison construction bypasses the cost of investing in higher education and so it goes. As the channels of exclusion and expulsion proliferate, the conditions of misery, poverty, homelessness, and despair deepen with no end in sight.[62]

To reiterate a central argument of this chapter, reforming police policies and practices, however meaningful and well-intentioned, will not bring about justice if larger structural conditions continue to go unchanged or worsen. Under a racist, militarized neoliberal state, the police embrace violence as central to their mission because the only interests they now protect are those of the corporate and financial elites. Moreover, when political and civil society are transformed under a militarized corporate state, not only does the definition of what constitutes state terrorism and violence expand, but so do the conditions, if not the meaning of politics itself, which has to be addressed by those who resist domestic terrorism if such violence is to be challenged in a meaningful and emancipatory way. When the police are treated as warriors and war becomes an extension of politics, the police are primed for battle and violence rather than the kind of police work that employs dialogue, close community relations, and an attentiveness to the problems that often serve as a petri dish for crime.

Yet, mass violence, only partially understood in all of its ramifications, has provoked young people throughout the United States to "break the silence," in the spirit of sustained and peaceful resistance once employed by Martin Luther King, Jr.[63] The reality of the terrorist state has been exposed through the increasing levels of repression and assaults waged against young people. Not only have young people recognized that orthodox liberal reforms are anemic and ineffective, they are increasingly challenging such reforms, such as their demand for a $15-an-hour minimum wage, which though limited, has opened up a space to address deeper structural conditions and the necessity for new political formations outside the established political parties. This is not to suggest that calls for community control of the police, independent prosecutors, curbing inequality, regulating corporations, creating stronger unions, and a progressive tax system are not useful.

All of these reforms, including the call to end mass unemployment and the failed war on drugs, should be addressed.[64] But they should be viewed only as necessary short-term corrections in the service of struggling for those deeper structural and political changes that would reject the existing form of neoliberalism and, in the end, capitalism itself and the political, social, economic, and ideological structures through which it is reproduced. What is needed are not liberal reforms but the transformation of a political and economic system that is not merely broken but has developed into a bold authoritarianism. Providing one argument, Professor Peter Bloom argues that focusing on isolated incidents such as police violence often functions to prevent "radical challenges to the existing order."[65] Condemning state and corporate violence is not enough and can serve to reproduce a larger ideology of containment. Although some commentators responding to the wave of police violence against African American youth and the subsequent Ferguson and Baltimore uprisings have attempted to put such violence in a larger context, they have not gone far enough. Bloom is exceptional in this regard, offering an astute meta-analysis:

> But mere contextualizations of the riots are not enough. They simply keep the discussion fixated in a place of reaction rather than transformation. It is imperative that arising from this unrest is a more forward-thinking politics that actively acknowledges the unacceptability of present conditions and continuously demands that they be radically changed. By focusing on the deeper factors underpinning this violence, both from police and protesters, new possibilities for solidarity can emerge: allowing law enforcement and citizens to recognize that they are victims, though to different degrees, of the same unfair economic policies that under develop communities while asking police to "preserve the peace." . . . The current reactive approach only produces a reactionary politics of containment.[66]

Poor youth in the United States live in the belly of a predatory system that has been depriving them of economic and cultural resources while criminalizing their behavior for quite some time. These youth are the objects of a low-intensity war waged by a rapidly consolidating authoritarian state. Rather than being nurtured, even respected, by the commanding institutions they come in contact with every day, they are humiliated, harassed, and often brutalized and imprisoned. Sociologist Elijah Anderson underscores the structural contradictions and the psychic consequences on youth and recapitulates those of Baldwin, written over fifty years ago:

> As children, they see police officers walk the hallways of their schools like in a prison. When black boys are involved in an altercation or disruption, instead of being sent to the principal's office, they are too often handcuffed on the spot and given a criminal record. Experience teaches [them] that police officers exist not to protect them, but to criminalize and humiliate them. Few black boys get through adolescence without a story of police harassment, and with age, their stories proliferate. Aggressive police tactics turn black males into subjects of suspicion and skeptical scrutiny. This makes them vulnerable to harassment, whether their crime is real or imagined. . . . With each negative encounter…they develop defense mechanisms and toughen up to protect their pride and perceived respectability. With this built-up hostility, interactions over minor offenses, like suspicion of selling loose cigarettes, become quickly charged.[67]

If young people are protesting, sometimes violently, it is not because they are "thugs" and "looters" as conservatives label them, but because they are too frequently treated as potential criminals, harassed daily, deprived of a decent future, and cast aside as an excess population that represents a threat rather than a crucial social investment. Moreover, a culture of racism, lawlessness, cruelty, and criminalization runs deep in American society and points to the need to dismantle and transform those cultural apparatuses that play a major role in disseminating hate, legitimating state violence, and reproducing a culture that disdains compassion, justice, civil rights, and economic equity. When young black boys and girls see people in their neighborhood killed by the police for making eye contact, holding a toy gun, walking in a stairway, or as in Eric Garner's case for selling cigarettes while "the financial elite go free for a bookmaking operation that almost brought the country to economic ruin," not only do the police lose their legitimacy, but so do established norms of conduct and modes of governance.[68]

Resistance in the name of liberal reform is not enough. Power is too concentrated, the power elite too removed and unaccountable to have any respect for democracy, and the intellectual servants of the financial power brokers are too cowardly to speak truth to power. At the same time, it is not enough to simply call for placing checks on corporate power or for renouncing power in general. Any political strategy that matters will have to merge a notion of democratic authority based on consent, dialogue, trust, and support for economic justice with a notion of power that represents the antithesis of repressive authority. Any collective struggle today must include an understanding of how to use power in the interest of democratic authority and values. Power in the service of democracy is antithetical to a political culture organized by the rule of force; it is the exercise of the polity to create the conditions in which critical agency and democracy flourish. It is the merging of democratic authority with the power of the people to ensure the mutually determining conditions of freedom and justice.

Philosopher Richard Bernstein captures the democratic nature of power in his analysis of the work of Hannah Arendt: "Power, which she distinguishes from strength, force, authority, and violence, arises and grows spontaneously through participation of citizens. Power is not to be understood in a vertical fashion, where power means control or domination *over* some individual or group. It is a *horizontal* concept—power springs up when individuals act together."[69] And it is precisely this horizontal notion of power that must be part of any collective struggle to overturn the authoritarian nightmare that currently engulfs American society.

The problems of Ferguson, Baltimore, and elsewhere are not limited to those cities; they are America's problems and demand a "transition from protest politics to long-term, strategic movement building."[70] Recently black youth and other concerned Americans are making real strides in moving beyond sporadic protests, short-lived demonstrations, and non-

violent street actions in the hopes of building sustained political movements. As I mentioned in chapter 5, groups such as Black Lives Matter,
Black Youth Project, We Charge Genocide, Drear Defenders, and others
represent a new and growing political force. These groups are not only
connecting police violence to larger structures of militarism throughout
society, they are also reclaiming public memory in establishing a direct link
"between the establishment of professional police systems in the United
States with the patrolling systems that maintained the business of human
bondage in chattel slavery."[71] Young people in America, especially poor
people of color, are faced with a sense of hopelessness in the future that is
almost unparalleled in recent history and is a script for despair and reckless
violence. But when hopelessness moves beyond itself and embraces the
need to reclaim public memory, history, and empowering forms of civic literacy, there is a space for developing new modes of understanding, insight,
and an alternative sense of the future. Page May, one of the organizers
of We Charge Genocide, makes a strong, and in my mind essential, argument for defining community organizers as public intellectuals and pedagogy as central to politics itself. She insists that any notion of leadership
must be charged with the task of making knowledge and skills available
to oppressed groups so they can not only reclaim their sense of history,
understand the current forms of oppression and how they work, but also
reclaim a sense of self and social agency. She writes:

> One of the things I am most excited about right now is the Radical
> Ed Project. I think this is so essential because people are outraged,
> and they're ready, but we need the skills. If we don't do this work
> with the knowledge that is out there and exists, we can wind up
> making vulnerable people even more vulnerable. I think we have a
> responsibility as organizers to be sharing this knowledge, and build-
> ing up the knowledge of others in our communities, so they feel
> equipped to be the leaders of their own events, and the sharers of
> their own skills. To build a network of people who can share these
> skills—I think that's so critical.[72]

It is within such critical and energizing spaces that new pedagogical and analytical frameworks emerge in which it becomes possible to imagine a new and more comprehensive understanding of politics, one that is right for a new historical conjuncture. It is also a space in which to rethink the tactics, strategies, and tools necessary to turn this newly discovered truth into an event, one in which hope merges with indignation, the ethical imagination, and new political formations as part of a broader struggle to create a radical democracy. That is the challenge young people face today, but it is certainly not only their challenge. As Baldwin once stated, it is "time to go for broke."

7

Higher Education under Siege and the Promise of Insurgent Public Memory

What happens to the memory of history when it ceases to be testimony?
—JAMES YOUNG

AT A TIME WHEN BOTH POLITICAL PARTIES, anti-public intellectual pundits, and mainstream news sources view the purpose of higher education almost exclusively as a way station for training a global workforce and generating capital for the financial elite, it becomes more difficult to reclaim a history in which the culture of business is not the culture of higher education.[1] This is certainly not meant to suggest that higher education once existed in an ideal past in which it functioned only as a public good by providing a public service in the interest of developing a democratic polity. Higher education has always been fraught with notable inequities and anti-democratic tendencies. But it also once demonstrated a much needed awareness of both its own limitations and the potential role it might play in attacking social problems and deepening the promise of a democracy to come. As difficult as it may seem to believe, John Dewey's insistence that "democracy needs to be reborn in each generation, and education is its midwife" was taken seriously by many academic leaders.[2]

Today, it is fair to say that Dewey's once vaunted claim has been willfully ignored, forgotten, or made an object of scorn.[3]

Throughout the twentieth century, there have been flashpoints in which the struggle to shape the university in the interest of a more substantive democracy was highly visible. Those of us who lived through the 1960s—when higher education was perceived as a significant threat to the power of the military, corrupt governments and corporations, and the ultra-rich—remember a different image of the university than the one we see today. Rather than narrow its focus to training potential MBAs, define education through the lens of mathematical utility, indoctrinate young people into the culture of capitalism, decimate the power of faculty, and turn students into mindless consumers, the university was under pressure to define itself as a place that educated people to be well-rounded workers, citizens, and critical agents. That is, it served, in part, as a crucial public sphere that held power accountable, produced a vast array of critical intellectuals, joined hands with the anti-war and civil rights movements, and robustly challenged what Mario Savio once called "the machine"—an operating structure infused by the rising strength of the financial elite that posed a threat to the principles of critique, dissent, critical exchange, and a never-ending struggle for inclusivity. The once vibrant spirit of resistance that refused to turn the university over to corporate and military interests is captured in Savio's moving and impassioned speech on December 2, 1964, on the steps of Sproul Hall at the University of California, Berkeley:

> There is a time when the operation of the machine becomes so odious, makes you so sick at heart, that you can't take part, you can't even tacitly take part. And you've got to put your bodies upon the gears, upon the wheels, upon the levers, upon all the apparatus and you've got to indicate to the people who run it, to the people who own it, that unless you're free the machine will be prevented from working at all.[4]

The 1960s may have been the high point of the period in American
education in which the merging of politics, justice, civil rights, and the
search for truth made clear what it meant to consider higher education as
a democratic public sphere. Not everyone was pleased or supported this
explosion of dissent, resistance to the Vietnam War, and struggle to make
campuses across the United States more inclusive and emancipatory. Conservatives were deeply disturbed by the campus revolts and viewed them
as a threat to their dream worlds of privatization, deregulation, militarization, capital accumulation, and commodification. What soon emerged was
an intense struggle for the control of higher education. For instance, the
Powell Memo released on August 23, 1971, and authored for the Chamber
of Commerce by Lewis F. Powell, Jr., identified the American college campus "as the single most dynamic source" for producing and housing intellectuals "who are unsympathetic to the [free] enterprise system."[5] Powell,
who would later be appointed to the U.S. Supreme Court, recognized that
one crucial strategy in changing the political composition of higher education was to convince university administrators and boards of trustees that
the most fundamental problem facing universities was the lack of conservative educators, or what he labeled the "imbalance of many faculties."[6]

The Powell Memo was designed to develop a broad-based strategy
not only to counter dissent but also to develop a material and ideological
infrastructure with the capability to transform the American public consciousness through a conservative pedagogical commitment to reproduce
the knowledge, values, ideology, and social relations of the corporate state.
Not only did the Powell Memo understand and take seriously the educative
nature of politics. Powell also realized it was possible to reproduce a society
in which conformity could be bought off through the swindle of a neoliberal mantra that used the discourse of freedom, individuality, mobility, and
security to serve the interests of the rich and powerful. The Powell Memo
was the most influential of a number of ideological interventions in the
1970s that developed political road maps to crush dissent, eliminate tenure,
and transform the university into an adjunct of free-market fundamentalism. Powell recognized how culture could deploy power and how educa-

tion could be used in a variety of spheres as a form of public pedagogy with its own institutions, intellectuals, and ideas to further the interest of market fundamentalism. But it certainly was not the first shot fired as part of a larger conservative struggle to shape American higher education.[7]

Conservatives have a long history of viewing higher education as a cradle of left-wing thought and radicalism. As early as the 1920s, conservatives were waging an ideological war against liberal education and the intellectuals who viewed higher education as a site of critical dialogue and a public sphere engaged in the pursuit of truth and in developing a space where students learned to read both the word and the world critically. Conservatives were horrified by the growing popularity of critical views of education and modes of pedagogy that connected what students were taught both to their own development as critical agents and to the need to address important social problems, a theme taken up by many academic novels of which Bernard Malamud's *A New Life* was especially insightful. During the McCarthy era, criticism of the university and its dissenting intellectuals cast a dark cloud over the exercise of academic freedom, and many academics were either fired or harassed out of their jobs because of their political activities outside the classroom or their alleged communist fervor or left-wing affiliations. In 1953, the Intercollegiate Studies Institute (ISI) was founded by Frank Chodorov in order to assert right-wing influence and control over universities. ISI was but a precursor to the present era of politicized and paranoid assaults on academics. In fact, the first president of ISI was William F. Buckley, Jr., who catapulted to fame among conservatives in the early 1950s with the publication of *God and Man at Yale*, in which he railed against secularism at Yale University and called for the firing of socialist professors. Another former president of ISI, T. Kenneth Cribb, Jr., delivered the following speech to the Heritage Foundation in 1989, one that perfectly captures the elitist spirit and ruling-class ideology behind ISI's view of higher education:

We must . . . provide resources and guidance to an elite which can take up anew the task of enculturation. Through its journals, lectures, seminars, books and fellowships, this is what ISI has done successfully for 36 years. The coming of age of such elites has provided the current leadership of the conservative revival. But we should add a major new component to our strategy: the conservative movement is now mature enough to sustain a counteroffensive on that last Leftist redoubt, the college campus. . . . We are now strong enough to establish a contemporary presence for conservatism on campus, and contest the Left on its own turf. We plan to do this greatly by expanding the ISI field effort, its network of campus-based programming.[8]

ISI was an early effort on the part of conservatives to "'take back' the universities from scholars and academic programs regarded either as too hostile to free markets or too critical of the values and history of Western civilization."[9] As part of a larger project to influence future generations to adopt conservative ideology and leadership roles in "battling the radicals and PC types on campus," the ISI now counts as one among many right-wing foundations and institutes to have emerged since the 1980s that target college students and campuses by providing numerous scholarships, summer programs, and fellowships.[10]

In the 1980s, the idea of higher education flourishing as a democratic public space in which a new multiethnic, middle-class generation of students might be educated was viewed as a dire threat to many conservatives. The most famous advocate of the position against accessible and inclusive higher education was the conservative academic Allan Bloom.[11] Bloom responded to this alleged threat with a discourse that was as hysterical as it was racist. In *The Closing of the American Mind*, Bloom was clear in his claim that admitting people of color to Ivy League schools was an insult to white elites whom he considered the only constituents qualified to manage and lead American society. The hidden structure of politics was quite visible in Bloom's work and revealed unapologetically his deeply held belief that the commanding institutions of the economy, culture, and government should be headed by mostly white, ruling-class males who were privileged and eager to do their best to maintain the classist and racist structure that defined the United States at that particular historical moment. This was an era in which left-wing academics and critical academic fields were under siege. A battle over the terrain of higher education was being aggressively waged under the political and academic leadership of right-wing reactionaries, such as Governor Ronald Reagan (who began his career by attacking leftists like Angela Davis at the University of California, Berkeley) and the former president of Boston University, John Silber (who prided himself on firing and denying tenure to numerous left educators, including myself).[12] These attacks took place at the same time in which there was a growing movement to define colleges as workplaces, with teachers subject to the same Tayloristic managerial techniques used in industry.[13] In fact, right-wing governors in states such as Florida, Texas, and Wisconsin have intensified this type of assault on higher education.

The culture wars of the 1980s and 1990s then gave way to the new McCarthyism of the post-9/11 era, which took a dangerous turn that far exceeded the attacks marked by the culture wars of the earlier period. In the aftermath of 9/11, the university was once again under attack by a number of right-wing organizations emboldened by a growing culture of fear and unflinching display of jingoistic patriotism. This was particularly exemplified by the American Council of Trustees and Alumni, which issued a report shortly after the attacks accusing an allegedly unpatriotic academy of being the "weak link in America's response to the attack."[14] The legacy of a full-fledged new style McCarthyism was resuscitated as academics and others who looked critically at the imperialistic registers of American foreign policy were routinely dismissed from their jobs or made the object of public shaming. Some universities in Ohio, California, and other states started requiring job applicants to sign statements confirming they did not belong to any terrorist groups. Academics who criticized the war in Iraq or questioned the Bush administration's use of torture often found their names on blacklists posted on the Internet by right-wing groups such as Campus Watch and Target of Opportunity.

The culture wars and the post-9/11 attacks on higher education under the reign of the new McCarthyism were followed by the hollowing out of the social state and the defunding of higher education. The more overt political attacks gave way to an economic war waged against higher education, of which one current example is the attempt by billionaires such as the Koch brothers to turn higher education into nothing more than an ideological factory for neoliberal capitalism. In desperate need of money, more and more universities are selling off naming rights to their buildings, accepting gifts from hedge fund managers, and caving in to the demands of big donors to influence what is taught, what programs deserve to be sustained, and what faculty should be rewarded. At the same time as higher education is being defunded, corporatized, and managed by an expanding class of administrators wedded to a neoliberal model of leadership, permanent faculty has been downsized, creating an exploited and invisible class of underpaid, part-time workers. Many faculty members are now consigned to employment conditions that seem more aligned with Walmart policies: they are stripped of full-time positions; relegated to the status of "stoop laborers";[15] lack power, security, a living wage; and are largely devoid of any hope for a full-time position in the academy in the future. According to the American Association of University Professors, at the present moment, over 70 percent of faculty are now adjuncts barely able to pay their rents, let alone conduct research or exercise any influence over the increasing corporatization and militarization of higher education. Many part-time faculty make less than $21,000 annually, and as journalist Colman McCarthy points out, "slog like migrant workers from campus to campus."[16] A record number of adjuncts are now on food stamps and receive some form of public assistance. Given how little they are paid, this should not come as a surprise though that does not make it any less shameful.[17]

These throwaway academics are the new invisible poor fighting for better wages, job security, benefits, and full-time positions. The status and exploitation of the labor of part-time workers is reprehensible and is indicative of the degree to which neoliberalism's culture of cruelty, brutality, and iniquitous power now shapes higher education.[18] And though there are a number of serious movements among adjuncts and others to fight against this new form of exploited labor, it is fair to say that such resistance will face an uphill battle.[19] The corporatized university will not only fight such efforts in the courts with their bands of lawyers and anti-union thugs, they will also use, as we have seen recently on a number of campuses, the police and other repressive state apparatuses to impose their will on dissenting students and faculty. But if this growing group of what Kate Jenkins calls the "hyper-educated poor"[20] joins with other social movements fighting against the war on public goods, militarization, public servants, and full-time workers, then it increases the chance that a new political formation may emerge and succeed in turning the momentum around in this ongoing battle over academic labor and the fate of higher education in the future.

The concerted post-9/11 attacks on higher education suggest it is still a site of intense struggle, and it is fair to say the right wing is winning. The success of the financial elite in waging its war and expanding the influence of a military-industrial-academic complex to serve its own ends is suggested by the elimination of full-time tenured jobs for faculty, the dumbing down of the curriculum, the view of students as customers, the incursion of for-profit businesses on campuses, and the growing stranglehold of neoliberal policies over higher education. It is also suggested in the erasing of public memory. Memory is no longer insurgent; that is, memory's role as critical educational and political optic for moral witnessing, testimony, and civic courage has been all but obliterated. The new apologists for the status quo instead urge people to "love America," which means giving up any sense of counter-memory, interrogation of dominant narratives, or retrieval of lost histories of struggle.

The current call to "love America" is a call to cleanse history in the name of facile patriotism. It does more than celebrate a new form of political illiteracy. Loving America is a discourse of anti-memory, a willful attempt at forgetting the past in the manufactured fog of historical amnesia. This is particularly true when it comes to erasing the work of a number of critical intellectuals who have written about higher education as the practice of freedom, including John Dewey, George S. Counts, W. E. B. Du Bois, the Social Reconstructionists, and others, all of whom viewed higher education as integral to the development of engaged, critical citizens and the university as a democratic public sphere.[21]

Under the reign of neoliberalism, with few exceptions, higher education appears to be increasingly decoupling itself from its historical legacy as a crucial public sphere, responsible for both educating students for the workplace and providing them with the modes of critical discourse, interpretation, judgment, imagination, and experiences that deepen and expand democracy. As universities adopt the ideology of the transnational corporation and become subordinated to the needs of capital, the war industries, and the Pentagon, they are less concerned about how they might educate students in terms of the ideology and civic practices of democratic governance and the necessity of using knowledge to address the challenges of public life.[22] Instead, as part of the post-9/11 military-industrial-academic complex, higher education even more conjoins military interests and market values, identities, and social relations. The role of the university as a public good, a site of critical dialogue, and a place that calls students to think, question, learn how to take risks, and act with compassion and conviction is dismissed as impractical or, indeed, uncomfortably subversive.[23]

The corporatization, militarization, and dumbing down of rigorous scholarship and the devaluing of the critical capacities of young people mark a sharp break from a once influential educational tradition in the United States, extending from Thomas Jefferson to John Dewey to Maxine Greene. These important thinkers held that freedom flourishes in the worldly space of the public realm only through the work of educated, critical citizens. Within this democratic tradition, education was not confused with training; instead, its critical function was propelled by the need to provide students with capacities that enable them to acquire any knowledge or skills needed to form a "politically interested and mobilized citizenry, one that has certain solidarities, is capable of acting on its own behalf, and anticipates a future of ever greater social equality across lines of race, gender, and class."[24] Other prominent educators and theorists such as Hannah

Arendt, James B. Conant, and Cornelius Castoriadis have long believed and rightly argued that we should not allow education to be modeled after the business world. Dewey, along with Thorstein Veblen in particular, warned about the growing influence of the "corporate mentality" and the threat that the business model posed to public spaces, higher education, and democracy. Dewey argued:

> The business mind, having its own conversation and language, its own interests, its own intimate groupings in which men of this mind, in their collective capacity, determine the tone of society at large as well as the government of industrial society. . . . We now have, although without formal or legal status, a mental and moral corporateness for which history affords no parallel.[25]

Dewey and the other public intellectuals mentioned shared a common vision and project of rethinking what role education might play in providing students with the habits of mind and ways of acting that would enable them to "identify and probe the most serious threats and dangers that democracy faces in a global world dominated by instrumental and technological thinking."[26] James B. Conant, a former president of Harvard University, and no progressive, argued that higher education should create a class of "American radicals" who could fight for equality, support public education, elevate human needs over property rights, and challenge "groups which have attained too much power."[27] Conant's views seem so mutinous today that it is hard to imagine him being hired as a university president at Harvard or any other institution of higher learning. All of these intellectuals offered a notion of the university as a bastion of democratic learning and values, a notion that provided a crucial referent for exploring the more specific question regarding the form of the relationship between corporations and higher education in the twenty-first century. It now seems naive to assume that corporations, left to their own devices, would view higher education as more than merely a training center for future business employees, a franchise for generating profits, or a space in which corporate culture and education merge in order to produce literate consumers.

What has also emerged in this particular historical moment is the way in which increasing numbers of young people are excluded from higher education. As tuition skyrockets, they are being locked out of higher education so as to reinforce the two-tier system that Bloom and others once celebrated. The steep rise in tuition fees, the defunding and corporatization of higher education, and the increasing burden of student debt, along with the widening gap in wealth and income across the entire society, have left many low-income and poor minority youth inhabiting sites of terminal exclusion, ranging from struggling public schools to prisons. As a result, American higher education is increasingly more divided into those institutions educating the elite to rule the world in the twenty-first century and second- and third-tier institutions that largely train students for low-paid positions in the capitalist world economy.

It is more and more apparent that the university in America has become a social institution that not only fails to address inequality in society, but also contributes to a growing division between social classes. In essence, it has become a class and racial sorting machine constructing impenetrable financial and policy boundaries that serve updated forms of economic and racial Darwinism. As tuition exceeds the budgets of most Americans, quality education at public and private universities becomes a privilege reserved for the children of the rich and powerful. While researchers attempt to reform a "broken" federal student financial aid system, there is "growing evidence . . . that the United States is slipping (to 10th now among industrialized countries) in the proportion of young adults who attain some post-secondary education."[28]

Higher education has a responsibility not only to be available and accessible to all youth, but also to educate young people to make authority politically and morally accountable. This means expanding academic freedom and the possibility and promise of the university as a bastion of democratic inquiry, values, and politics, even as these are necessarily refashioned at the beginning of the new millennium. Questions regarding whether the university should serve public rather than private interests no longer carry the weight of forceful criticism as they once did when raised by Dewey, Veblen, Robert Lynd, and C. Wright Mills in the first part of the twentieth century. Yet such questions are still crucial in addressing the reality of higher education and what it might mean to imagine the university's full participation in public life as the protector and promoter of democratic values among the next generation. This is especially important at a time when the meaning and purpose of higher education is under assault by a phalanx of right-wing forces attempting to slander, even vilify, liberal and left-oriented professors, cut already meager federal funding for higher education, and place control of what is taught and said in classrooms under legislative oversight.[29]

Currently the American university faces a growing number of problems that range from the increasing loss of federal and state funding to the incursion of corporate power, a galloping commercialization, and the growing influence of the national security state. It is also currently being targeted by conservative political forces that have hijacked political power and waged a focused campaign against the principles of academic freedom, sacrificing the quality of education made available to youth in the name of patriotic correctness, and dismantling the university as a site of critical pedagogical practice, autonomous scholarship, independent thought, and uncorrupted inquiry. For instance, right-wing politicians such as Republican Wisconsin Governor Scott Walker unapologetically denounce the university as a threat to the success of market forces and go out of their way to defund its operating budget. In Walker's case, he recently announced that he was slashing $300 million from the state university budget over a two-year period. At the same time, he announced that he is requesting $220 million to build the Milwaukee Bucks a new basketball arena.[30] It gets worse: Walker's disempowering view of higher education was made crystal clear in his attempt to sneak into his new budget an attempt to rewrite the purpose and mission of the university system, one that clearly was aimed at sabotaging the university as a public good. As journalists Mary Bottari and Jonas Persson pointed out:

Buried in his proposed budget bill—on page 546 out of a whopping 1,839—Walker scratched out "the search for truth" and took an ax to Wisconsin Idea, the guiding philosophy that the university is created to solve problems and improve people's lives beyond the boundaries of the campus. Instead he wanted the university to "meet the state's workforce needs." For extra measure, he scratched out "the legislature finds it in the public interest" to provide a system of higher education; he instead made it a "constitutional obligation."[31]

Under the current regime of neoliberal savagery and its cruel austerity policies, Walker is not a political exception: he is the rule. The extremist wing of the Republican Party hates the notion that the university might function primarily to address important social issues in the name of the public good. Couple this particular fear and ideological fundamentalism with the rampant idiocy and anti-intellectualism that has become an organizing principle of the new extremists at all levels of government and it becomes clear that public and higher education are prime targets in the struggle to create a fundamentalist-driven culture that supports those identifications, desires, and modes of agency receptive to the rise of an authoritarian society. Their vision for the future of the United States falls only steps short of a police state in which criticism is viewed as a form of treason and even the mildest of liberal rhetoric is vilified or deemed cause for censorship.

In another example, this time in Oklahoma, the state's politicians and lawmakers have introduced a bill that eliminates the teaching of Advanced Placement U.S. History courses in public high schools.[32] The reason behind the bill defies logic and reflects the new stupidity and religious fundamentalism that are at the heart of the conservative suppression of reason and critical thinking. According to Judd Legum, "Oklahoma Rep. Dan Fisher (R) has introduced 'emergency' legislation 'prohibiting the expenditure of funds on the Advanced Placement United States History course.' Fisher is part of a group called the 'Black Robe Regiment' which argues that 'the church and God himself has been under assault, marginalized, and diminished by the progressives and secularists.'"[33] Ben Carson, a potential GOP presidential candidate and pediatric neurosurgeon, stated that the students who finished the course would be "ready to sign up for ISIS."[34] The disparagement of the AP U.S. History course was echoed by the Republican National Committee in a resolution claiming that its lessons were too negative, and reflected "a radically revisionist view of American history that emphasizes negative aspects of our nation's history while omitting or minimizing positive aspects."[35] What at first glance appears to be a case of egregious ignorance is in reality a religious fundamentalist attack on any viable notion of historical consciousness and public memory.[36] These politicians are the ground troops for the new authoritarianism that rewards and revels in thoughtlessness and despises any criticism of American domestic and foreign policy. Truly the Brownshirts of our time, they are a new breed of ideological muggers whose minds are unburdened by complicated thought, who choke on their own ignorance and sutured political certainties. They represent another one of the forces, in addition to the apostles of a savage neoliberalism and the hedge fund criminals, that are out to destroy public and higher education in the United States, even the weakest liberal version of it in the institutions' history.

Yet another example of this type of fundamentalism being used as an engine of conformity wrapped in the mantle of American exceptionalism can be found in comments by former New York City mayor Rudy Giuliani when he challenged President Obama's loyalty to the United States for what Giuliani construed as weak foreign policy decisions. Giuliani claimed unapologetically at a fundraiser supporting Governor Scott Walker's bid for the presidency that Obama did not "love America," and oddly enough that he "doesn't love you. And he doesn't love me. He wasn't brought up through love of his country."[37] For Giuliani and others of his warmongering ilk, patriotism is the lifeblood of empire and any attempt to offer up constructive criticism in which U.S. policies are interrogated is disparaged as an act of negativism, at best, and as un-American or even treasonous at worst.

This poisonous ideology has a long history in the United States and is gaining ground once again with the emergence of a creeping authoritarianism. Moreover, it is an ideology that promotes a deep-seated anti-intellectualism and a climate of fear that crosses over into criticisms of higher education. Giuliani's comments are not merely idiotic and stupid; they are infused with a racism and militant nationalism reminiscent of the rise of totalitarian ideologies and regimes in the1930s.[38] Moreover, they are suggestive of the degree to which all vestiges of democracy, liberty, dissent, and equality have become a liability in a society that is now ruled by the financial elite and ideological barbarians who support this shameful anti-democratic rhetoric and policies that reinforce it. This is the discourse of totalitarianism, and its endpoint is a recapitulation of the worst horrors that history has produced.

Higher education is not going to save the United States from becoming more authoritarian, but its destruction as a democratic public sphere is a crucial signpost as to how far we have tipped over into the nightmare of authoritarianism. The shutting down of higher education as a democratic public sphere is not a definitive marker of defeat. On the contrary, it suggests the need for a new understanding of politics, one in which the university has a crucial role to play in defending radical democracy as the new commons and education as central to a politics that takes it seriously. The winds are changing, and a democratic horizon is coming once again into view. We see it in Europe with the rise of radical political parties in Spain and Greece that connect the struggle over economic power with the struggle to create new modes of agency, culture, education, and ideology, all of which now encourage the linking of politics to larger social movements.

What the current state of higher education suggests is that the left in its various registers has to create its own public intellectuals in sites ranging from universities, schools, and online media to any alternative spaces where meaning circulates. I completely agree with the late Pierre Bourdieu when he insists that it is of enormous political importance "to defend the possibility and necessity of the intellectual" as one who is tirelessly critical of the existing state of affairs.[39] Intellectuals have a responsibility to connect their work to important social issues, collaborate with popular movements, and engage in the shaping of policies that benefit all people and not simply a few. At the heart of this suggestion is the need to recognize that ideas matter in the battle against authoritarianism, and that pedagogy must be central to any viable notion of politics and collective struggle. Public intellectuals have an obligation to work for global peace, individual freedom, care of others, economic justice, and democratic participation, especially at a time of legitimized violence and tyranny. There is no genuine democracy without a genuine critique of power. The very notion of being an engaged public intellectual is neither foreign to, nor a violation of, what it means to be an academic scholar—it is central to its very definition. Put simply, academics have a duty to enter into the public sphere unafraid to take positions and generate controversy, function as moral witnesses, raise political awareness, and make connections to those elements of power and politics often hidden from public view. They also have a duty to engage in pedagogical practices that renounce the notion that teaching is an impartial act or practice. As Paulo Freire pointed out, pedagogy is rooted in the ethical responsibility to create the conditions for students to be self-reflective, knowledgeable, and able to connect learning to individual and social change.[40] The critical educator's role is to address important social problems, encourage human agency rather than to mold it, and to promote critical consciousness, which means educating the subject to be a critical and engaged individual and social agent. Pedagogy in this instance is an ethical and political practice that urges students to see beyond themselves, to transcend the call to privilege and self-interest, and to become a subject in the shaping of power, modes of governance, equality, and justice.

Higher education must be widely understood as a democratic public sphere—a space in which education enables students to develop a keen sense of prophetic justice, claim their moral and political agency, utilize critical analytical skills, and cultivate an ethical sensibility through which they learn to respect the rights of others. What is at stake here is for students to create alternative public spheres, particularly with the use of the new media to articulate their voices and make visible ideologies and modes of critical knowledge central to their own struggles. They can fight for unions, create alternative study groups, connect with social movements outside of the university, and work with neighboring communities to unite around struggles that they both have an interest in such as preventing the corporatization of public services, public goods, and the growing paramilitarization of police forces in the United States. They can also produce their own public intellectuals willing to write for alternative media outlets, give interviews on radio stations, and work with journals and book publishers to produce material that inspires and energizes their generation and others struggling to redefine the meaning of democracy.

Higher education has a responsibility not only to search for the truth regardless of where it may lead, but also to educate students to make authority and power politically and morally accountable. Higher education is one of the few public spheres left with the potential to sustain a democratic formative culture. When it is engaged in communicating critical knowledge, values, and learning, it offers a glimpse of the promise of education for nurturing public values, educated hope, and a substantive democracy. Democracy places civic demands upon its citizens, and such demands point to the necessity of an education that is broad-based, critical, and supportive of meaningful civic values, participation in self-governance, and democratic leadership. Only through such a formative and critical educational culture can students learn how to become individual and social agents rather than merely disengaged spectators. It is imperative that current and future generations be able to think independently and to act upon civic commitments that demand a reordering of basic power arrangements fundamental to promoting the common good and producing a meaningful democracy.

Anyone with an interest in democracy's survival should be aware of education's political role as it shapes how people think, desire, and dream, and must struggle to make education central to a new politics. As a number of theorists from Antonio Gramsci and Raymond Williams to Paulo Freire, Maxine Greene, and Stanley Aronowitz have argued for the last fifty years, education is a crucial to the development of any radical political formation. To challenge the neoliberal stranglehold on all cultural and education institutions in the United States, such a formation would need to envision and develop new educational programs—extending from the creation of online journals and magazines to the development of alternative schools—as well as launch a comprehensive defense of those formal educational institutions that have historically acted as a safeguard for democracy.

In this struggle for democratic renewal, there is a need to reclaim an insurgent public memory and the lost or suppressed narratives of older progressive battles in order both to learn from them and to build upon their insights. This is necessary to enable educators and others to rethink the meaning of politics, reclaim the radical imagination, launch a comprehensive education program that speaks to the concrete issues bearing down on people's lives, and develop new political formations capable of merging the various struggles together under the wide banner of a post-capitalist democracy that "serves people over corporations."[41] If education does not become the center of politics, democracy as an ideal and site of struggle will fail to inspire and energize a new generation of young people. Surely, then, what awaits is a new wave of domestic terrorism that will descend on the United States, and which is already becoming visible in the signs of an emerging police and surveillance state. At stake here is the need to take seriously Pierre Bourdieu's insistence that "the most important forms of domination are not only economic but also intellectual and pedagogical, and lie on the side of belief and persuasion."[42] As Professor Tariq Ali has mentioned in a different context, the history of the struggles and suppression of the American working class, Communist Party, and other progressive movements have been all but erased: "This is a history that is not emphasized. This wretched neoliberalism has downgraded the teaching of history. It is the one subject they really hate."[43] It is well worth remembering that politics undermines its pedagogical functions and democratic goals when it underestimates "the symbolic and pedagogical dimensions of struggle."[44]

Such a failure on the part of progressive movements to engage the educative nature of politics generally produces not only the tactics of vanguardism but also strategies that overlook the challenge of getting people to think differently and to invest something of themselves in an insurgent politics in which they can recognize hope and their own future. Not only is there a need to challenge, disrupt, and interrogate the market imaginaries, visions, and vocabularies that undermine the great ideals that a range of social movements have fought for in the past, there is also the need to combine the educative task of changing hearts and minds with sustained efforts to build robust, large-scale organizations and what sociologist Nancy Fraser calls "large-scale public powers."[45] The Occupy movement taught us that "emancipatory ideas [should] not be confined to separate enclaved arenas where only those who already believe in them are exposed to arguments for them."[46] Occupy created a large umbrella movement under the call to eliminate inequality in a wide range of areas extending from the economic realm to a variety of spheres that included all manner of exclusions based on race, sexual orientation, and the destruction of the environment. At the same time, however, Occupy failed to create a strong presence because it lacked the capacity for large-scale coordination and long-term organization. That is, it failed to develop and sustain a public space in which a broad-based movement could be mobilized in the interest of creating sustainable counter-publics. Tariq Ali captures this failure perfectly in his comment:

> I was sympathetic to the Occupy movement, but not to the business of not having any demands. . . . They should have had a charter demanding a free health service, an end to the pharmaceuticals and insurance companies' control of the health service, a free education at every level for all Americans. The notion, promoted by anarchists such as John Holloway, that you can change the world without taking power is useless. I have a lot of respect for the anarchists that mobilize and fight for immigrant rights. But I am critical of those who theorize a politics that is not political. You have to have a political program.[47]

Surely any movement that wants to challenge neoliberal capitalism should have the courage to put forth an agenda with radical demands.

These might include a call to break up big banks; a tax on trading; free education for all; free health care; a guaranteed basic income; drastic reductions in the military budget to create a jobs program; investing in crucial infrastructure; expanding public transportation; and a high tax rate on big corporations and the salaries of the ultra-rich job destroyers such as the CEOs who run banks, hedge funds, and other rogue financial institutions. Economist Salvatore Babones has put forth a number of additional reforms including extending Medicare to everyone, refinancing social security, ending the incarceration state, making it easy to join a union, setting a minimum living wage, and making it easy for people to vote.[48] Bernie Sanders's economic agenda includes a number of what might be considered radical demands such as reversing climate change, ending the disastrous trade polices such as NAFTA and TPP, creating a single-payer health care system for all, and the breaking up of big banks.[49]

Such demands would constitute a disruptive political formation in the service of producing social movements that could seriously challenge market fundamentalism rather than accommodate it. Hopefully, such an attempt to create a new radical sensibility would challenge the ways in which people see things, allowing people to invest in issues in which they can see reflected their own values, hopes, and sense of agency. Offering the American public new modes of identification has the potential not only to change "public consciousness, the conventional wisdom about what is possible, [but also to] shift and open up the space for changes in policy."[50] Resistance to oppressive power structures demands a politics, public pedagogy, and political formation that embrace struggle as part of developing a political program on national and international scales that can inspire, energize, and produce a collective show of sustained solidarity. But it also demands a struggle that goes right to the core of how neoliberal power and its repressive machineries work.

What is particularly crucial is that such a struggle takes seriously the pedagogical power of neoliberalism to persuade those over whom it rules that its political and economic apparatuses are inevitable, its organizing principles universal, and the social relations it produces unquestionable.

Michael D. Yates is right in claiming that any strategy that resorts to compromising with neoliberalism's death-dealing machinery in order to get "a few crumbs from its table is a strategy guaranteed to fail."[51] Instead, Yates argues for broad set of related disruptive strategies that confront directly those who hold power along with the institutions they control. He writes:

> Initially, we could get as many organizations and individuals as possible to sign on to a list of general principles, formulated as a set of demands and commitments. The demands might include much shorter working hours, early and secure retirement, free universal health care, an end to the link between work and income, an end to all corporate subsidies, bans on fracking and other profit-driven environmental despoliations, an end to the war on terror and the closing of U.S. military bases in other countries, the abolition of the prison system, free schooling at all levels, open borders combined with the termination of U.S. financial support for oppressive governments, community-based policing, and the transfer of abandoned buildings and land to communities and groups who will put them to socially useful purposes. The commitments could embrace as many forms of collective self-help as imaginable (Cuban-style urban organic farming, cooperatives dedicated to education, child care, health, food provision, the establishment of worker-controlled enterprises), a shedding of unnecessary possessions, a willingness to offer material support to local struggles aimed at empowering those without voice, a refusal to join the military or participate in the mindless and dangerous patriotism so prevalent in the United States, and a promise to educate ourselves and others about the nature of the system in whatever venues present themselves to us.[52]

The current historical moment calls for a politics that is as bold as it is courageous. Moreover, such a politics must be transnational in its scope, global in its sense of responsibility, and capable of creating new democratic public spheres in which it becomes possible to show that private troubles can be linked to larger social issues, and that modes of connection and solidarity can be sustained beyond the private sphere. Only then will the promise and possibility of creating a global commons in the service of a radical democracy come into view.[53] Under such circumstances, education becomes a central feature of politics, because, as renowned anthropologist David Price rightly argues, public consciousness of historical memory is one of the primary weapons to be used against the abuse of power and that is why "those who have power create a 'desert of organized forgetting.'" [54]

History is open, and the possibility of producing counternarratives, public memories, and forms of moral witnessing is crucial at a time rife with unrest accompanied by new levels of state terrorism. The emergence of state terrorism and the increasing militarization of society, legitimated through the war on terrorism, require new ways to subvert the theater of cruelty and class consolidation that has the globe in a stranglehold. Neoliberalism in its many punitive forms has exhausted its credibility and now threatens the entirety of human life and the planet itself. Hope is in the air, but it won't succeed in creating the promise of a new democratic future unless it first recognizes and grapples with the depth of the American nightmare and the collective death wish that lies at its core. We are seeing the beginning of such a struggle among youth of color, especially the Black Lives Matter movement, which emerged after the killing of Trayvon Martin.[55] Whether this movement will develop into a powerful political formation remains to be seen, but one thing is certain: it is time for fresh and inspiring visions, radical imagination, workable tactics, new political formations, and sustained, coordinated international struggles. It is time to march into a future that sheds once and for all the dark authoritarianism haunting the present.

8

Academic Terrorism, Exile, and
the Possibility of Classroom Grace

IDEOLOGICAL FUNDAMENTALISM AND political purity appear to have a strong grip on society in both the United States and Canada.[1] This can be seen in the endless attacks on reason, truth, critical thinking, informed exchange, and dissent itself. The endpoint of such attacks can be grasped in comments in which an academic at West Point publishes a paper claiming, without irony, that dissident intellectuals should be the subject of drone attacks.[2] As bizarre as this appears, the ideology that informs it was on full display when Wesley Clark, a liberal and former presidential candidate, called for internment camps for "radicalized Americans."[3] While such comments appear extreme, there is an element of truth in these extremes that points to the dark side of American politics and culture. Paraphrasing Theodor Adorno, there is always some truth to be found in such exaggerations. Such attacks are not just endemic to the United States. Canada's prime minister, Stephen Harper, routinely attacks intellectuals and journalists whom he says are "committing sociology" by including critical analysis in their communication of facts and statistics—in other words, critics who are intelligent enough to value context, brave enough to hold power accountable and take seriously their role as engaged public intellectuals. Insinuating that sociological analysis is tantamount to "committing" an egregious sin, if not a criminal act, becomes a way for Harper and his conservative cronies to argue for the condemnation and removal of critical thought from both the university and public discourse. His disdain for any form of scientific evidence proving that climate-warming trends are due to human activities has resulted in the Canadian government banning federal scientists from sharing their findings with their colleagues and the public. For fear that scientists might provide evidence that climate change is the result of human activity over the past century, the government has banned them from releasing their research or talking publicly about their work.[4] The Canadian government's defense of dirty oil has become synonymous with an act of brazen censorship.

Comments like Canada's prime minister's provide only a glimpse of a wholesale ideological and policy shift by the Canadian federal government under his conservative leadership. A number of scientists and academics have indicted the Harper government for what increasingly appears to be its systematic suppression of ideas that challenge Harper's views on climate change. They have pointed to "a pattern that has seen the . . . government reduce media access to scientists and cut funding and programs."[5] In this instance, scientists are being censored because they have provided evidence for the destructive effects of climate change, among other social and environmental research that might put into question a lack of government response and proper oversight regarding corporate power, industrial development, and financial markets.

In the United States political illiteracy seems to be the one qualification, besides great wealth, that gets one elected to political office. For example, prominent Republican Party politicians from Marco Rubio to Scott Walker deny that climate change is produced by human activity while Louisiana Governor Bobby Jindal rejects evolutionism and supports teaching creationism in the public schools.[6] At the same time, American mass culture, especially its obsession with celebrities, mind-deadening reality TV, and game shows smother the American public with a rampant idiocy that reinforces a prevalent anti-intellectualism that often serves to legitimate the normalized view that there is nothing wrong with experiencing vio-

lence primarily as entertainment. All this provides the foundation for paralyzing most forms of critical and engaged agency. Censorship, state secrecy,
a sustained attack against whistleblowers, and violations of civil liberties
are now matched by the increased use of censorship in public schools, the
rewriting of textbooks to remove progressive ideas and struggles, and the
reduction of mainstream media to a combination of entertainment and
the elimination of any form of critical analyses.[7] The search for the truth
has been transformed into an attack on the truth. In part, this is evident
with the ongoing manufacture of lies, hate, and misrepresentation that
takes place daily on conservative and religious radio stations, Fox News,
and other corporate-controlled media.[8]

Ideological fundamentalism might be expected in a society that has
become increasingly anti-intellectual and displays a growing commitment to commodities, violence, privatization, the death of the social, and
the bare-bones relations of commerce. But it is more surprising when it
appears in universities, especially among so-called liberals and progressives. This is a moralism marked by an inability or reluctance to imagine
what others are thinking. This type of ideological self-righteousness by
so-called progressives and elements of the orthodox left is especially dispiriting because it makes a mockery of academic freedom, and often condemns other positions even before they are heard or are available to be
discussed and analyzed.

Rather than open up conversations, this type of pedagogical terrorism closes them down and then collapses into a kind of comedy of
intellectual boasting while assuming the moral high ground. Hubris
becomes more than shameful in this instance; it becomes toxic, blind-
ing the ideological warriors to their own militant ignorance and anti-
democratic rhetoric while shutting down any notion of the university
as a democratic public sphere. What is lost here is how a pedagogy of
repression assumes a revolutionary stance when in fact everything about
it is counterrevolutionary. In the end, this suggests a kind of theoretical
helplessness, a replacing of careful analysis with the inability to think, a
discourse of denunciation, and a language overflowing with binarisms of

good and evil. What is at risk here is both the moral collapse of politics and the undermining of the very nature of critical thought and agency. Of course, this raises the question of how one survives in the university without being in exile, or at the very best existing with one foot inside and one foot outside the institution.

Attacks from both the left and the right have been waged against critics who speak outside the box of normalized political positions, though the right has had far more power in waging and sustaining such attacks. Historically, these would include figures ranging from Scott Nearing, Paul Sweezy, and I. F. Stone to more recent radicals such as Ward Churchill, Norman Finkelstein, and Steven Salaita. One can hear echoes of such attacks on women who criticize some versions of what might be called a lingering "all boys" club in administration; critics of Israel's state policy and its government; anyone who calls for overcoming political fragmentation among the left; and theorists who speak of the need for emancipatory forms of leadership and authority while refusing the anarchist-inspired so-called leaderless revolution in favor of long-term organizations and political strategies. And so it goes.

And then there are those academics who write and talk about pedagogy in the tradition of Raymond Williams, Stuart Hall, and Paulo Freire. Such academics, already tainted by their association with education and pedagogy, are often viewed as not being abstract enough or are relegated to the garbage can of "theory" because they believe that matters of agency and culture are as important as economic and political structures. Any attempt to connect theory to important social issues is often dismissed as antitheoretical or, even worse, anti-intellectual. What the fundamentalists cannot understand is that the call for lifting ideas into public life supports the assumption that theory is crucial but that it should also be accessible and address important social issues. In this instance, matters of politics, morality, and connection are not stripped from theory, but give it life, room to breathe, and provide a connection with the rhythms of everyday life.

In other cases, intellectual capacity and insight collapse into biology as certain individuals and groups are excluded from voicing a position because they are deemed not authentic enough. When Paulo Freire was alive, there was a group of ideologically orthodox feminist editors at the *Harvard Educational Review* who argued that he should not be published in the journal because he was considered a white male voice expounding critical pedagogy. Under such circumstances, the poisonous embrace of a deadening essentialism and paralyzing binaries turned critical pedagogy into the alleged enemy of feminists and minorities. In this instance, a zeal for political purity drove an embrace of a version of intellectual moralism in which all that was left politically was what the writer Richard Rodriguez calls "an astonishing vacancy."[9]

How can one not be in exile working in academia, especially if one refuses the cliques, mediocrity, hysterical forms of resentment, backbiting, and endless production of irrelevant research? The spaces of retreat from public life in the academy have become dead zones of the imagination mixed with a kind of brutalizing defense of their own decaying postures and search for status. Leadership in too many academic departments is empty, disempowering, and utterly rudderless, lacking any vision or sense of social responsibility. Students are constantly being told that they should feel good instead of working hard and focusing. Too many academics no longer ask students what they think, but how they feel. Everyone wants to be a happy consumer. When students are told that all that matters for them is feeling good and that feeling uncomfortable is alien to learning itself, the critical nature of teaching and learning is compromised.

This is an academic version of the *Dr. Phil* TV show, and often results in modes of infantilizing pedagogy that are as demeaning to students as they are to professors, who now take on the role of therapists speaking in terms of comfort zones but rarely offer support in the interest of empowering students to confront difficult problems and risk feeling "unsafe" if it means examining hard truths or their own prejudices and those of others—in other words, learning to think for themselves. This is not to suggest that students should feel lousy about themselves, that they shouldn't feel good, or that educators shouldn't care about their students. To the contrary, caring in the most productive sense means providing students with the knowledge, skills, and theoretical rigor that offer them the kinds of challenges that engage them and help them, in turn, feel good about what they accomplish through developing their capacity to grow intellectually, emotionally, and ethically. As Victoria Harper puts it, a longer lasting and more productive sense of well-being emerges when students have "learned to grapple with difficult material, understand critical ideas, and even start to engage in real dialogue."[10]

In the neoliberal university, there seems to be a pathological disdain for community, trust, and collaboration. As the bounds of sociality and social responsibility are undermined, all that is left is a kind of sordid careerism and the quest for status and some financial crumbs from corporations and defense contractors. What remains is the insufferable cultural capital of academics driven by self-interest and bounded by the private orbits in which they live. These are academics who have surrendered to a regime of conformity and instrumental rationality while reducing politics to something done during one's leisure time. At their most cartoonish moment, these academics appear to inhabit a kind of cultural capital made visible by their desire to tattoo an Oxford degree on their foreheads and speak with a British ruling-class accent.

Academia is now characterized by a withdrawal into the private and the irrelevant. Solidarity, rigor, public scholarship, and integrity are in short supply in most departments. So is sanity. Under such circumstances, exile seems less like a refuge than a revitalized kind of public space where a new language, a new understanding of politics, and new forms of solidarity can be nurtured among the displaced and those viewed as the threatening other—that is, among those who refuse the neoliberal machinery of social and political death that now defines education solely as a source of profit and mode of commerce. The renowned sociologist Zygmunt Bauman's comments on his notion of welcoming exile under certain circumstances should not therefore surprise us, especially in light of his own experience of marginality in American scholarship. But what must be understood is that his position does not constitute a celebration of marginality; rather, it is an affirmation to keep going in the midst of what sometimes appears as a form of academic madness driven by forces that undermine the university as a democratic public sphere. Bauman writes:

> I need to admit, however, that my view of the sociologists' vocation does not necessarily overlap with the consensus of the profession. Dennis Smith has described me as an "outsider through and through." It would be dishonest of me to deny that denomination. Indeed, throughout my academic life I did not truly "belong" to any school, monastic order, intellectual camaraderie, political caucus, or interest clique. I did not apply for admission to any of them, let alone did much to deserve an invitation; nor would I be listed by any of them—at least unqualifiedly—as "one of us." I guess my claustrophobia—feeling as I do ill at ease in closed rooms, tempted to find out what is on the other side of the door—is incurable; I am doomed to remain an outsider to the end, lacking as I [do] the indispensable qualities of an academic insider: school loyalty, conformity to the procedure, and readiness to abide by the school-endorsed criteria of cohesion and consistency. And, frankly, I don't mind.[11]

Although I don't want to romanticize positions of marginality, they may represent the only spaces left in the university where one can develop a comprehensive vision of politics and social change. Such spaces are well placed in producing interdisciplinary work, more than willing to challenge the often deadening silos of some versions of identity politics, and make connections with social movements outside the university. Maybe the space of exile is one of the few spaces left in neoliberal societies where one can cultivate a sense of meaningful connection, solidarity, and engaged citizenship that goes beyond allegiance to interest groups and an immersion in a deadly conformism and culture of mediocrity. Exile might be the space where a kind of double consciousness can be cultivated that points beyond the structures of domination and repression to what the poet Claudia Rankine calls a new understanding of community, politics, and citizenship in which the social contract is revived as a kind of truce in which we allow ourselves to be flawed together. She writes:

> You want to belong, you want to be here. In interactions with others you're constantly waiting to see that they recognize that you're a human being. That they can feel your heartbeat and you can feel theirs. And that together you will live—you will live together. The truce is that. You forgive all of these moments because you're constantly waiting for the moment when you will be *seen*. As an equal. As just another person. As another *first* person. There's a letting go that comes with it. I don't know about forgiving, but it's an "I'm still here." And it's not just because I have nowhere else to go. It's because I believe in the possibility. I believe in the possibility of another way of being. Let's make other kinds of mistakes; let's be flawed differently.[12]

To be "flawed differently" works against a selfish desire for power and a sense of belonging as a given as well as the narrowed circles of certainty that define fundamentalisms of all ideological stripes. It suggests the need to provide room for the emergence of new democratic public spheres, noisy conversations, and a kind of alternative third space informed by compassion and a respect for the Other. Under such circumstances, critical exchange matters not as a self-indulgent performance in which the self simply interviews itself but as public act, a reaching out, a willingness to experience the Other within the space of exile that heralds a democracy to come. This would be a democracy where intellectual thought informs critique, embodies a sense of integrity, and reclaims agency in the service of justice and equality.

What might it mean to imagine the university as containing spaces in which the metaphor of exile provides a theoretical resource in which to engage in political and pedagogical work that is disruptive, transformative, and emancipatory? Such work would both challenge the mainstream notion of higher education as a kind of neoliberal factory as well as the ideological fundamentalism that has emerged among some alleged progressive voices. What might it mean to address the work we do in the university, especially with regard to teaching as a form of classroom grace?[13] In what follows, I address this issue against the backdrop of ideological fundamentalism I have mentioned above.

Today, the purpose of higher education functions largely to prepare students for what is often called the new global economy. Hence, it is not surprising that many of the advocates of higher education as a training ground for the global workforce also view the more progressive ideals of higher education as a threat to the power of the surveillance state, the ultra-rich, and religious fundamentalists. Under such circumstances, it becomes more difficult to reclaim a history in which higher education views its mission as not only pushing forward the frontiers of knowledge, truth, teaching, and service, but also educates students as engaged critical citizens willing to deepen and expand the ideals of a democratic society. This is certainly not meant to overlook a history of higher education marked by racism and the suppression of dissent. Higher education never existed in an idyllic past in which it only functioned as a public good and provided a public service in the interest of developing a democratic polity. At the same time, its understanding as a public good, however compromised, largely defined its mission.

At a time when the public good is under attack and there seems to be a growing apathy toward the social contract, or any other civic-minded investment in public values and the larger common good, education should be seen as more than a credential or a pathway to a job. It should be viewed as a crucial public sphere for understanding and overcoming the current crisis of agency, politics, and democracy faced by many young people today. One of the challenges facing the current generation of educators and students is the need to reclaim the role that education has historically played in developing critical literacies and civic capacities. At the heart of such a challenge is the question of what education should accomplish in a democracy. What work do educators have to do to create the economic, political, and ethical conditions necessary to endow young people with the capacities to think, question, doubt, imagine the unimaginable, and defend education as essential for inspiring and energizing the citizens necessary for the existence of a robust democracy? In a world in which there is an increasing abandonment of egalitarian and democratic impulses, what will it take to educate young people to challenge authority and, in the words of James Baldwin, "rob history of its tyrannical power, and illuminate that darkness, blaze roads through that vast forest, so that we will not, in all our doing, lose sight of its purpose, which is after all, to make the world a more human dwelling place."[14]

I have been writing about the relationship among education, pedagogy, and democracy in the United States for over forty years. I have done so because I believe that democracy has become ever more fraught, ever more at risk in the past several decades. If educational institutions choose not to nurture and develop generations of young people who are multi-literate, take on the role of border crossers, embrace civic courage, embrace the practice of being socially responsible, and display compassion for others, it is possible that the democratic mission of higher education will disappear. I believe that any talk about democracy, justice, and freedom has to begin with the issue of education, which plays a central role in producing the identities, values, desires, dreams, and commitments that shape a society's obligations to the future. Education in this instance provides the intellectual, moral, and political referents for how we both imagine and construct a future better than the one previous generations inherited. Within such a critical project, education is defined not by test scores, or draconian zero-tolerance regimes, but by how it expands the capacities of students to be creative, question authority, and think carefully about a world in which justice and freedom prevail and the common good is reaffirmed. Once students leave the university, their actions and choices should be informed by a broader sense of ethical and social responsibilities and a developing sense of who they are and what kind of world they want to make for themselves and future generations.

Under the current regime of market fundamentalism, education is often narrowed to the teaching of pre-specified subject matter and stripped-down skills that can be assessed through standardized testing. This constitutes a pedagogy of repression, one that kills the imagination, and produces what might be called an "embodied incapacity." Increasingly, the administration of education suffers a similar fate. It, too, is often defined by a business culture, a rigid embrace of bureaucracy, and corporate strategies rooted in a view of schooling that reduces it to a private act of consumption and an endless search for capital.[15] Lost here is the creation of the thinking, speaking, acting human being "competent in matters of truth and good-ness and beauty . . . [equipped] for choices and the crucibles of private and public life."[16] In opposition to the instrumental reduction of education to an adjunct of corporate and neoliberal interests that offer no language for relating the self to public life, social responsibility, or the demands of citi-zenship—young people should address the challenge of developing critical approaches to education that illuminate how knowledge, values, desire, and social relations are always implicated in power and related to the obli-gations of engaged citizenship.

Critical education matters because it questions everything and compli-cates one's relationship to oneself, others, and the larger world. It also func-tions to "keep historical memory alive, to give witness to the truth of the past so that the politics of today is vibrantly democratic."[17] Education has always been part of a broader political, social, and cultural struggle over knowledge, subjectivities, values, and the future. Today, however, public and higher education are under a massive assault in a growing number of countries, including the United States and the United Kingdom, because they represent one of the few democratic public spheres that are capable of teaching young people to be critical, thoughtful, and engaged citizens who are willing to take risks, stretch their imaginations, and, most impor-tant, hold power accountable.

The attack on education is now matched by a war on youth. Conse-quently, the current generation confronts a number of serious challenges. They live at a time in which civil liberties, long-term social investments, political integrity, and public values are under assault from a number of fundamentalist groups who exercise power from a wide range of spaces and cultural apparatuses in an age marked by a politics of disposability.[18] This is an age defined by a rising number of homeless, a growing army of debt-ridden students, whole populations deprived of basic necessities amid widening income disparities, swelling refugee camps and detention centers housing millions of economic migrants, political refugees and those displaced by ecological catastrophes. And in addition to these millions, more are contained in prisons and jails, mostly nonviolent, mostly poor, and mostly uneducated. The current generation lives at a time in which local police forces are militarized, and drone strikes miss terrorists and wipe out wedding parties. The surveillance state threatens to erase any sense of privacy along with personal and political freedoms, and consuming appears to be the only obligation of citizenship. Legal lawlessness and a politics of disposability are the antidemocratic methods for dealing with those who are unable to pay their debts, violate a trivial rule in school, are unhoused from mental hospitals, or caught jaywalking in poor neighborhoods that make them a prime target for the criminal justice system. The politics of disposability has gone mainstream as more and more individuals and groups are now considered without social value and vulnerable, consigned to zones of abandonment, surveillance, and incarceration.

The culture of fear now drives the major national narratives and in doing so has replaced a concern with social and economic injustice with an obsession regarding the violation of law and order. Fear now propels the mainstream representations, discourses, and stories that define social relations and legitimize dominant forms of power freed from any sense of moral and political responsibility, if not accountability. These conditions raise challenges for existing and future generations, which they will have to address. These might include questions such as: What conditions need to be put in place that will enable young people to develop their critical capacities to be agents of change? What will it take to dismantle the school-to-prison pipeline? How will the mechanisms be dismantled that attempt to turn all black men into criminals in the schools and on the streets? How will the widespread anti-intellectualism that enables a culture of thoughtlessness and violence be stopped? What role might education play in putting limits on the growing atomization and isolation of everyday life and the ludicrous assumption that shopping is the highest expression of citizenship?

Education should prepare students to enter a society that badly needs to be reimagined against the ideals of a substantive democracy. Such a task is both a political as well as a pedagogical. Politically, it suggests defining higher education as a democratic public sphere and rejecting the notion that the culture of education is defined solely by the lure of commercial advantage and a crude form of instrumental rationality. Pedagogically, this suggests modes of teaching and learning that take on the task of producing an informed public, enacting and sustaining a culture of questioning, and enabling a critical formative culture that advances not only the power of the imagination but also what Professor Kristen Case calls "moments of classroom grace."[19] Pedagogies of classroom grace allow students to reflect critically on commonsense understandings of the world, and begin to question, however troubling, their sense of agency, relationship to others, and their relationship to the larger world. This is a pedagogy that asks why we have wars, massive inequality, a surveillance state, the commodification of everything that matters, and the collapse of the public into the private. This is not merely a methodological consideration but also a moral and political practice because it presupposes the creation of critically engaged students who can imagine a future in which justice, equality, freedom, and democracy matter.

Taking seriously the role of higher education as a democratic public sphere also poses the challenge of teaching students to become agents of social change. Another is to teach them the skills, knowledge, and values that they can use to organize political movements capable of stopping the destruction of the environment, ending the vast inequalities in our society, and building a world based on love and generosity rather than on selfishness and materialism. In this instance, the classroom should be a space of grace—a place to think critically, ask troubling questions, and take risks, even though that may mean transgressing established norms and bureaucratic procedures. At the same time, it is important to remember that schools are not going to change one classroom at a time. Faculty need to organize not just for better pay, but also to once again gain control over their classrooms by altering the modes of governance that are concentrating power in the hands of administrators and reducing most faculty to the part-time status of Walmart workers. That means building a movement to create a different kind of educational system and a more democratic society. It also suggests that academics need to do more than teach behind the safety of their classroom doors. They should also make an effort to be involved in politics, run for local school boards, become publicly engaged citizens, use the power of ideas to move their peers and others, and work to develop the institutions that allow everybody to participate in the creation of a world in which justice matters, the environment matters, and living lives of decency and dignity matters. In short, they can become public intellectuals willing to create the pedagogical, political, and economic conditions that connect learning to social change and pedagogy to the pressing problems facing both the United States and the rest of the globe.

There are many issues that academics in their capacity as public intellectuals can take up and address, of which I will suggest three. First, they can define higher education as a public good and write for multiple audiences, address a range of important social issues, and lend their voices and analyses to the plethora of alternative public spheres opening up online. One important issue they could highlight is that in any democratic society, education should be viewed as a right, not an entitlement, and such a position suggests a reordering of state and federal priorities to make that happen. More specifically, high quality public and higher education should be free, viewed as a crucial social investment. There are a number of countries such as Germany and Mexico in which this is already happening. Funding for free quality education could come from cutting back on military spending and using what is left over to finance higher education costs, implementing what Bernie Sanders calls the Robin Hood tax on stock trading and putting that money into education, jettisoning federal funding for for-profit colleges, and eliminating tuition costs while providing grants and scholarships, especially to poor students.[20]

Second, academics need to fight for the rights of students to have some say in the development of their education. They are not customers but students who should have the right to a formidable and critical education not dominated by corporate values; moreover, they should have a say in the shaping of their education and what it means to expand and deepen the practice of freedom and democracy. Young people have been left out of the discourse of democracy. They are the new disposables who lack jobs, a decent education, hope, and any semblance of a future better than the one their parents inherited. They are a reminder of how finance capital has abandoned any viable vision of the future, including one that would support future generations. This is a mode of politics and capital that eats its own children and throws their fate to the vagaries of the market. If any society is in part judged by how it views and treats its children, American society by all accounts has truly failed in a colossal way and in doing so provides a glimpse of the heartlessness at the core of the new authoritarianism.

Finally, though far from least, there is a need to oppose the ongoing shift in power relations between faculty and the managerial class. Central to this view of higher education in the United States is a market-driven paradigm that seeks to eliminate tenure, turn the humanities into a job preparation service, and transform most faculties into an army of temporary subaltern labor. For instance, in the United States, out of 1.5 million faculty members 1 million are "adjuncts who are earning, on average, $20K a year gross, with no benefits or health care, and no unemployment insurance when they are out of work."[21] The indentured service status of such faculty is put on full display as some colleges have resorted to using "temporary service agencies to do their formal hiring."[22] A record number of adjuncts are now on food stamps and receive some form of public assistance. Given how little they are paid this should not come as a surprise, though that does not make it any less shameful.[23] As Noam Chomsky has argued, this reduction of faculty to the status of subaltern labor is "part of a corporate business model designed to reduce labor costs and to increase labor servility."[24] Too many faculty are now removed from the governing structure of higher education and as a result have been abandoned to the misery of impoverished wages, excessive classes, no health care, and few, if any, social benefits. This is shameful and not merely an education issue but a deeply political matter, one that must address how neoliberal ideology and policy has imposed on higher education an antidemocratic governing structure that mimics the broader authoritarian forces now threatening the United States.

Americans live under the shadow of the corporate state, a culture of fear, and an ongoing spectacle of violence, but the future is still open. The time has come for the public to defend and develop forms of education in which civic values and social responsibility become central to invigorating and fortifying a new era of civic engagement, a renewed sense of social agency, and an impassioned vision, organization, and set of strategies capable of once again making higher education central to the meaning and ongoing struggle to embrace and live out the promise of a substantive democracy. What must be avoided is isolating such reforms by limiting them to particular institutional struggles. It is crucial for educators and others to extend the struggle over workplace governance to faculty in other colleges and universities and to build alliances so that such struggles can be transformed into national and international movements for all workers.

9

Barbarians at the Gates: Authoritarianism and the Assault on Public Education

BOTH THE UNITED STATES SENATE and House of Representatives are now controlled by a Republican Party that is exhibiting some of the most extremist political views in U.S. history.[1] Coupled with the empty centrism of the Democratic Party, the Republican ascendency does not bode well for public education and a host of other important social issues. Nor does it bode well for democracy. If we conjured up George Orwell and his fear of state surveillance; or the philosopher Hannah Arendt and her claim that thoughtlessness was the foundation of totalitarianism; or Franz Kafka, whose characters embodied the death of agency and the "helplessness of the living,"[2] then it would be difficult for these authors and their imaginary dystopias to compete in terms of grimness with the real assault on public education and public values that materialized in the United States at the beginning of the twenty-first century.

These are ominous times. Compromise and compassion are now viewed as pathological behaviors, a blight on the very meaning of politics. Moreover, in a society controlled by financial monsters, the political order is no longer sustained by faith in critical thought and care for the Other. As any vestige of critical education, analysis, and dissent is disparaged, the assault on reason gives way to a crisis in both agency and politics. The right-wing

Republican Party, their Democratic Party counterparts, and their corporate supporters despise public schools as much as they disdain taxation, institutions that enable critical thinking, and any call for providing social provisions that would benefit the public good. Not only are both parties attempting to privatize much of public education in order to make schools vehicles for increasing the profits of investors, they are also destroying the critical foundations that sustain schools as democratic public spheres in which learning actually takes place.[3]

The rights of children become more difficult to protect when the rights of teachers and teacher unions are either dismantled or weakened by the apostles of privatization. Teachers are being de-skilled. Losing much of their autonomy to be creative in the classroom, they have been relegated to the role of technicians whose sole objective appears to be the enforcement of a deadening instrumental rationality in which "teaching to the test" becomes the primary purpose of schooling. Moreover, teachers are being demonized by the claim that the major problem with public education is a lack of teacher accountability. In the hidden order of politics here, larger political and economic considerations such as crushing poverty, mammoth inequality, a brutalizing racism, and iniquitous modes of financing public education all disappear from the list of problems facing schools in the United States.[4] Teachers also serve as easy targets for the (un)reformers to weaken unions, bash organized labor, discredit public servants, and "argue that education can be improved if taxpayer money is funneled away from the public school system's priorities (hiring qualified teachers, implementing quality teaching, reducing class size, etc.) and into the private sector (replacing teachers with computers, eliminating teacher job protections, replacing public schools with privately run charter schools, etc.)."[5] Under the reign of a savage neoliberalism, teachers, like other public servants, are losing control of their workplaces as they are subject to more and more state-imposed objectives that mimic an audit culture with its obsession with empiricism and the testing of every aspect of the educational encounter.[6] Not only are students treated as good for nothing more than taking tests, but teachers are subject to modes of empirical evaluation based on test scores that determine if they should be fired, rewarded, or reprimanded and denied salary raises—and in some cases their jobs. What is clear is that the attack on teachers makes it easier to attack other workers.[7]

These policies and practices echo the principles of neoliberal casino capitalism and are designed to enforce a pedagogy of repression—one that kills the imagination, sanctions a deadening mode of memorization, and instills in students only what is necessary in order for them to accommodate existing power relations—at the expense of developing a capacity to be critical and engaged agents. The aim of this pedagogy of repression mimics Hannah Arendt's claim that "the aim of totalitarian education has never been to instill convictions but to destroy the capacity to form any."[8] Public schools are also being defunded as states increasingly develop policies that drain state budgets by giving corporations substantial tax breaks. Educational theorist Diane Ravitch elaborates on the right-wing agenda to destroy public education, which is being led by groups ranging from right-wing politicians to shadowy organizations such as the American Legislative Exchange Council (ALEC). She is worth quoting in full:

> Since the 2010 elections, when Republicans took control of many states, there has been an explosion of legislation advancing privatization of public schools and stripping teachers of job protections and collective bargaining rights. Even some Democratic governors, seeing the strong rightward drift of our politics, have jumped on the right-wing bandwagon, seeking to remove any protection for academic freedom from public school teachers. This outburst of anti-public school, anti-teacher legislation is no accident. It is the work of a shadowy group called the American Legislative Exchange Council, or ALEC. Founded in 1973, ALEC is an organization of nearly 2,000 conservative state legislators. Its hallmark is promotion of privatization and corporate interests in every sphere, not only education, but health care, the environment, the economy, voting laws, public safety, etc. It drafts model legislation that conservative legislators take back to their states and introduce as their own "reform" ideas.

ALEC is the guiding force behind state-level efforts to privatize public education and to turn teachers into at-will employees who may
be fired for any reason. The ALEC agenda is today the "reform"
agenda for education.[9]

The educational needs of students for many Republican and Democratic Party members, pundits, lobbying groups, and politicians rank low
next to the financial needs of hedge fund managers, the ultra-rich such as
Bill Gates, the Walton family, and the Koch brothers, as well as the legisla-
tors who make up ALEC, and any number of major corporations. Individual achievement is invoked to justify education as a private right rather
than a public good. The discourses of empiricism and standardized testing
become the ultimate measures of achievement just as pedagogical matters
concerning civic responsibility, engaged citizenship, thoughtfulness, and
critical thought disappear from the vocabulary of educational reform.

Under the regime of neoliberalism, a sense of community and working
together are viewed as burdens because they are at odds with the neoliberal
celebration of a survival-of-the-fittest ethos. Paul Buchheit goes even further, arguing that "privatizers believe that any form of working together
as a community is anti-American."[10] In this instance, the labeling of community and caring for others as anti-American has deeper political roots. As
Robert Hunziker observes, "As for neoliberalism, its dictate of 'survival of
the fittest economics' is really 'bottom-feeder economics' whereby the rich
accumulate more and more and more at the expense of lower and lower
and lower wages, less benefits, and crushed self-esteem. What could be
worse?"[11] As market economies are transformed into market societies, the
investment in young people has been replaced by an overarching emphasis on investing in economic capital. In this context, public education and
its mission are divorced from equality, justice, and the search for truth.
Indeed, economic policies that benefit the bankers, corporations, and the
financial elite result in massive inequities in wealth, income, and power
that increasingly determine how the American policymakers view both
public education and the needs of young people. Unchecked market fun-

damentalism now eats its own children while destroying any viable hope they may have for being included in the social and political infrastructure of democracy and a future that benefits them.[12]

The defunding of public education has gotten so out of control that, as freelance writer Aaron Kase reports, one public school in Phila-delphia asked parents to "chip in $613 per student just so they can open with adequate services."[13] Kase rightly adds, if this "becomes the norm, [it] effectively defeats the purpose of equitable public education, and is entirely unreasonable to expect from the city's poorer neighborhoods."[14] Quality education is no longer a right but an entitlement designed mostly to benefit the children of the rich, who flee from public schools to attend wealthy private schools or to attend public schools in wealthy commun-ities, which more often than not resemble private schools in terms of how they are segregated in class and racial terms, cater to the whims of the rich, and enshrine values that are consistent with the market. Schooling for poor minorities of class and color has come to represent an appendage of the carceral state, as part of a system that has been called the school-to-prison pipeline.[15] This is not only an attack on public education, but an attack on democracy itself. The infrastructure of education has been under assault since the 1980s with the advent of market fundamentalism in America and the growing disdain for the welfare state, the public good, and public val-ues. By educational infrastructure, I am referring to the material, finan-cial, and intellectual resources necessary for public schools to be able to function in ways that protect teacher autonomy, encourage viable unions, create curricula that are both critical and relevant, and produce modes of critical pedagogy that truly embrace education as the practice of freedom and young people as critical agents and engaged citizens necessary for making democracy meaningful and substantive.

The shadow of Orwell now haunts public education and democracy itself, as the political defenders of torture and state surveillance exert control over the U.S. Congress. Lawlessness and moral depravity infect all modes of governance. This is seen as the push toward treating public schools as prisons, and their students as objects of surveillance and control, becomes more widespread.[16] The presence of police, security guards, cameras, and a host of surveillance apparatuses have turned schools into incubators for creating students willing to surrender their freedoms to the national security state. As a police culture replaces an educational culture in schools, more student behaviors are criminalized. Students learn quickly that harsh punitive measures are the administration's primary reaction to any disciplinary infraction, however trivial, and that the threat of incarceration quickly becomes the default response to any disciplinary problem they face as students.

The ghost of Kafka disturbs any vision of democratic education as fear becomes the operative principle in organizing public education, especially for schools in low-income neighborhoods inhabited by minorities of color. For the underserved, education is not designed to inspire and energize. Nor is it designed to get students to think, reflect, or question. On the contrary, such schools disable the capacities of students to become knowledgeable, informed speaking agents. They focus instead on the dreary pedagogical tasks of mastering low-level skills such as memorization, a willingness to conform, and a refusal to question authority. This is more than a pedagogy of repression: it is a pedagogy of helplessness that infantilizes students while undermining any relationship between learning and social change.[17]

Too many schools have become punishing factories, subjecting students to zero-tolerance policies that three decades ago were only tolerated in prisons.[18] Under such circumstances, the notion of "safety" becomes a rationale for treating students like criminals and modelling schools after prisons. What young people need are the institutional, educational, and pedagogical conditions that provide them with safe and supportive environments. Such environments do not exist in school climates dominated by fear, distrust, and acts of brutality. Schools no longer are viewed as places that create dreams of greatness, extend the horizons of the imagination, or point to a future that refuses to mimic the present. On the contrary, they are increasingly held hostage both to the market values embraced by the corporate and financial elite and the fundamentalist ideologies of religious conservatives. And all of this is not the worst of it.

Orwell's premonition about state-enforced surveillance and Kafka's understanding of the danger of powerlessness encouraged by regimes of fear are now matched by Arendt's warning that any threat to critical thought is a threat to the foundation of politics itself, especially in a culture that directs people to desire the most trivial of pursuits and anti-intellectual modes of learning. Diminishing the citizenry's capacity to think and act as autonomous subjects is as dangerous to democracy as the heavy hand of state repression. While Arendt did not use the phrase "radical imagination" to bring home her warning about the crisis and death of critical agency, this is exactly what is being destroyed in the testing factories and penal warehouses that have replaced public education. When the imagination is no longer considered the subject and object of learning, thoughtlessness expands, as does the prospect of shaping students who are better suited for a totalitarian regime than for a struggling democracy. Totalitarian governments believe that thinking is dangerous, and rightly so.[19] As Arendt points out:

> Everything which happens in thinking is subject to a critical examination of whatever there is. That is, there are no dangerous thoughts for the simple reason that thinking itself is such a dangerous enterprise. . . . I think, nonthinking is even more dangerous. I don't deny that thinking is dangerous, but I would say not thinking, *ne pas reflechir c'est plus dangereux encore* [not thinking is even more dangerous].[20]

In the new Gilded Age with its growing economic divisions, vast punishing state, criminalization of social behaviors, and war on youth and minorities of class and race, public education is being destroyed. Against the prevailing antidemocratic reforms of the economic and religious fundamentalists, the noble belief in schools as democratic public spheres and in schooling as the center of critical thinking and learning needs to be reclaimed, struggled over, and taken up as part of a larger social movement for the defense of the public good, public values, and the democratic commons. It is precisely the concept of education as a building block for both critically engaged youth and a broader democratic public sphere that inspires a great deal of fear in the billionaire, anti-public (un)reformers.[21]

Within the next decade, the new extremists who now control the commanding institutions of culture, politics, and economics will do everything they can to replace a weak ideal of democracy with the economic and social principles of a ruthless mode of casino capitalism that is part of a broader effort to replace permanently any vestige of radical politics with a new form of authoritarianism. Public spheres that currently provide a challenge to market-driven fundamentalisms that "promote selfishness and thereby corrode both society and the moral character of individuals" will be under further assault and run the risk of disappearing altogether.[22] As selfishness and the amassing of great wealth and power are transformed by the new extremists into a civic virtue, agency itself withers, trapped within the orbits of an inward-looking privatized world.

But there is more at stake than the collapse of public values and the destruction of a comprehensive vision of politics, largely under assault by the ongoing predatory market forces of commodification, privatization, and an unchecked celebration of self-interest as the cornerstone of human agency. Antidemocratic practices in American society now manifest in rampant xenophobia and racist killings, the rise of the militarized surveillance state, and the loss of privacy, growing poverty and widening inequality, the increasing corporatization of public goods, and the depletion of resources that serve the commons. This all points to something more than the privatization and atomization of everyday life. What must be acknowledged is that a mounting pedagogy of fear and repression now leaks into every sphere to stifle dissent and punish those who speak out, including those such as academic Steven Salaita who lost his job because he dared speak against what he viewed as an injustice by the Israeli government or attorneys Stanley Cohen and Lynn Stewart who have been incarcerated for speaking in defense of the those who resist repression and are demonized by the government. In this instance, the ghosts of Orwell, Kafka, and

Arendt all intimate an approaching attack not just on education and the formative cultures that support dissent, critical thought, and engaged civic action, but on democracy itself. What unites all of these seemingly disparate issues is a growing threat of authoritarianism—or what might be otherwise called totalitarianism with elections. Neoliberal societies embrace elections because they "exclude and alienate most people from political power," and thus provide a kind of magical defense for the authoritarian project of depoliticizing the public while curtailing objections to their efforts to enshrine massive inequities in power, wealth, and the accumulation of capital.[23] It is impossible to understand the current assault on public education without coming to grips with the project of neoliberalism and its devaluation of the social, critical agency, and informed thinking as part of its attempt to consolidate class power in the hands of a largely white financial and corporate elite.

The struggle for public education as a crucial civic resource and public good must continue through the large-scale organizing of teachers and labor unions, students, and groups outside of education that are also struggling against a range of injustices. The struggle over public education cannot be removed from wider struggles against student debt, funding for public goods, the elimination of massive inequalities in wealth and power, the dismantling of the military-industrial-security state, the abolition of police brutality, and the eradication of the punishing, mass incarceration state, among other struggles. These struggles all share underlying values and the goal of restoring and reclaiming a notion of radical democracy that puts power in the hands of the people rather than in the hands of the ruling elite. They also intersect around the need to elevate social needs over the narrow interests of the market and those factions that benefit from the privatization and financialization of society.

As the ruthlessness and misery produced by neoliberalism is made clear, the state resorts to increased levels of violence, often with impunity, particularly when it comes to attacking peaceful student protesters and assaulting and sometimes killing unarmed black men.[24] In response, large-scale protests have taken place throughout the United States, making it clear that the public will no longer tolerate the indiscriminate kill-ing of black men, the enforcement of racist policies across a wide social landscape, unrestrained police brutality, and the continuing of widespread lawlessness that corrupts every institution—and schools in particular—that has been reorganized according to the narrow, if not savage and anti-democratic, interests of the market.

The ongoing protests in response to the failures to indict the police offi-cers who killed Michael Brown in Ferguson, Missouri, Eric Garner in New York City, and twelve-year-old Tamir Rice in Cleveland must intersect with protests over the defunding of public schools and movements to defend welfare state institutions and services, the environment, nuclear disarma-ment, and a host of other struggles now being waged in the United States. These movements need to join together in a new political formation capa-ble of challenging the financial elite who have taken over the U.S. govern-ment and all the commanding institutions of American society. The "Black Lives Matter," "Hands Up Don't Shoot," and "I Can't Breathe" protests must overlap and connect with the struggle over public and higher educa-tion and the broader struggle for reclaiming a democracy that fulfills both its most radical ideals and its commitment to the common good, public values, and a capacious notion of justice.

The best hope for reforming public education resides in the emer-gence of what Stanley Aronowitz calls "disruptive social movements that operate outside of the two-party system."[25] Young people, single women, LGBT organizations, students, union members, and other constituencies and socially progressive groups no longer believe in either the Democratic Party or the two-party system. How else to explain their massive refusal to vote in the 2014 elections, which had the lowest voter turnout since 1943? As Aronowitz points out, for the last few decades, the Democratic Party has been particularly beholden to big money, wealthy donors, and the Pen-tagon, pursuing "centrist politics that allow them to follow the Republi-cans ever further to the right."[26] Obama all but personifies the political and moral cowardice of the Democratic Party, given his violation of civil liberties and civil institutions, his support for the development of a foreign policy that amounts to a doctrine of perpetual war, and his backing of "corporate-friendly economic policies."[27] Moreover, the Obama administration's educational policies have been even more conservative than those of his predecessor, George W. Bush, and are based on accountability schemes that reproduce the worst of the testing craze along with an aggressive approach to promoting charter schools, attacking unions, and privatizing public education.

The "disruptive social movements" emerging all over the United States, especially among black youth, have opened up a national conversation about police brutality. They have also challenged the "conventional wisdom about what is possible" politically, and if they continue they could produce more far-reaching changes.[28] Both the Black Lives Matter and other movements against police brutality and the now largely defunct Occupy movement have provided new discursive signposts for acknowledging important social issues such as racially based police brutality and massive inequality in wealth, income, and power.[29] Central to these movements is the recognition of the educative nature of politics and the need to harness the rage of the public to points of identification that move people and indicate to them that they have the power collectively to challenge and transform the current corrupt regime of neoliberal capitalism.

These movements have created new ideological and affective spaces in which to assert the radical imagination and develop a project and politics of educated hope. Making education and the symbols of culture central to their tactics, they have engaged in a war in which representation, affect, struggle, and the need to produce new desires, identities, and modes of consciousness and agency matter. But they have done something more. These emerging movements are taking risks in not only confronting the raw power of state repression, but also putting forth bold new and controversial issues such as the call for a social wage, free education, gay marriage, the legalization of marijuana, single-payer universal health care, a shorter work week, the dismantling of the surveillance state, a new Marshall Plan for job development, subsidized child care, and racial justice. Rabbi Michael Lerner has offered a number of reforms to address such problem, including what he calls the Domestic and Global Marshall Plan (GMP). He writes that the GMP

> calls upon the US to take the leadership by example in convincing all the top 20 industrial powers to dedicate 1–2% of their gdp each year for the next twenty to eliminate (not reduce or ameliorate, as the Millennium goals and other UN summits aim at) poverty, homelessness, hunger, inadequate education, inadequate health care, and to repair the environmental damage caused by 150 years of irresponsible forms of industrialization pursued by self-described capitalist, socialist and communist societies.[30]

Some progressives believe that one response to the extremism of the Republican Party can be found in pushing the Democratic Party to embrace more radical reforms such as gay marriage and raising the minimum wage. I'm afraid the notion that real political, economic, and social reform can be realized within the Democratic Party is more than pure fantasy and suffers from a form of historical amnesia regarding the fact that the only "reform the Democratic Party has implemented is to move more and more to the right, all in the name of a safe centrism that has marked its legacy for the last fifty years."[31]

What Orwell, Arendt, and Kafka have taught us is that when power is decoupled from accountability and responsibility, then thoughtlessness prevails, repression increases, and fear becomes the organizing principle of a society, regardless of the form of totalitarianism it may take. The legacy of fear and the lawlessness it inspires run deep in America, and their destructive effects are spreading into every public sphere capable of recognizing them and offering critical reflection on the nature of power in a society. The collapse of education into training, the loss of autonomy by teachers, and the removal of the conditions that enable students to be critical and engaged citizens all speak to the character of a society in which independent thought is debased, creativity stifled, and dissent squelched.

We live in an age dominated by financial barbarians who are more than willing to place the vast majority of Americans in strangulating debt, low-paying jobs, devastating poverty, class-based health care opportunities, and spheres of life-threatening abjection, or, even worse, in "criminogenic ghettoes" and penal gulags. Under such circumstances, the rich commit crimes with impunity while the poor are put in jail in record numbers. Depravity and illegality feed each other as torture is defended by the political leadership as a reasonable tactic to extract crucial information from prisoners. All that stands between state terrorism and mass-induced fear are informed citizens, critically educated agents, and political formations willing to act with the courage necessary to refuse the new authoritarianism and think politics anew, while developing innovative strategies, institutions, and organizations that will make radical democracy actually possible. Such struggles will not happen in the name of reform alone. Liberal reforms constitute a form of political regression and lack a powerful vision for challenging the corrupt and lifeless political vision produced by the regime of neoliberalism. Mass resistance to the authoritarian financial state must take place, and its goal must be the dismantling of the current corrupt political system that has little to do with democracy and a great deal to do with the values, practices, and policies of authoritarianism.

In the current historical conjuncture, the democratic institutions in which education has been historically defined as the practice of freedom, critical learning, and civic responsibility are under siege by lobbyists, hedge fund managers, and the billionaires' club. Yet the radical spirit of education is too powerful to be contained under state and corporate repression. The promise of educated citizens—along with the enduring character of critical reflection and the search for economic, political, and racial justice—lives on in the demonstrations of workers, unions, and young people all across America. These are the groups of concerned citizens who are not just protesting police brutality but also marching in order to have their voices heard as part of the promise of a radical democracy along with the arrangements that give it and them a meaningful and just life. At its best, civic education is dangerous because it offers young people and other actors the possibility of racial and economic justice, a future in which democracy becomes inclusive, and a world in which all lives matter. Renowned writer Ursula K. Le Guin, who was honored at the National Book Awards in 2014, spoke about the power of books, words, and artists who believe in and imagine freedom. I think her words also apply to critical educators and other public intellectuals:

> Books, you know, they're not just commodities. The profit motive often is in conflict with the aims of art. We live in capitalism. Its power seems inescapable. So did the divine right of kings. Any human power can be resisted and changed by human beings. Resistance and change often begin in art, and very often in our art—the art of words. I think hard times are coming when we will be wanting the voices of writers who can see alternatives to how we live now and can see through our fear-stricken society and its obsessive technologies to other ways of being, and even imagine some real grounds for hope. We will need writers who can remember freedom. Poets, visionaries—the realists of a larger reality.[32]

Le Guin's words remind us of the agency that comes from critical education—the power to envision realities other than what we now live—and suggest indirectly the need to resist all forms of miseducation that suppress our capacities for thought, hope, and imagination. Miseducation in the contemporary moment breeds isolation, consumerism, ignorance, militarism, a hatred of the Other, and indifference to the public good. It feeds a logic of disposability embraced by those who view justice and democracy as a liberal burden, if not a pathology. At its best, the critical and humane spirit of public education lives on in the social movements and militant labor unions willing to unify into a third party, create a new language of politics, defend those civic principles that are incompatible with casino capitalism, and recognize that the most important investment a country can make is in its youth and educational institutions. The assault on public education is part of the war on democracy—both are, in part, born of the legitimate fear that the emergence of larger, more effective social movements in the future depends on the present vitality of a formative educational culture and its imparting of modes of subjectivity that will develop agents to sustain and strengthen such movements. For those of us who hope for freedom, this apprehension is one worth nurturing, and fighting for a more democratic future is a struggle worth waging, but time is running out.

— 10 —

Hollywood Heroism in the Age of Empire:
From *Citizenfour* and *Selma* to *American Sniper*

UNDER THE REGIME OF NEOLIBERALISM with its warlike view of competition, its unmitigated celebration of self-interest, and its disdain for democratic values and shared compassion for others, the notions of unity and solidarity have lost their democratic value. Contaminated by the fog of misguided patriotism, a hatred of the Other now denigrated as an enemy combatant, and an insular retreat into mindless consumerism and the faux safety of gated communities, unity has been transformed into a militarized concept in the service of a neoliberal order. With the merging of militarism, the culture of surveillance, and a neoliberal culture of cruelty, solidarity and public trust have morphed into an endless display of violence and the ongoing militarization of visual culture and public space.[1]

America's addiction to violence is especially evident in the heroes it chooses to glorify. Within the last few years three important films appeared that offer role models, however flawed, to young people while legitimating particular notions of civic courage, patriotism, and a broader understanding of injustice. I am less concerned in this inquiry with the historical accuracy or artistic merits of the films than with the identifications they mobilize and the narratives they unfold about valor—in Hollywood still a solely masculine trait. *Citizenfour* is a deeply moving film about the former NSA intelligence analyst and whistleblower Edward Snowden and his admirable willingness to sacrifice his freedom and life in order to reveal the dangerous workings of an authoritarian surveillance state. It also points to the role of intrepid journalists such as Glenn Greenwald, Laura Poitras, and Julian Assange. These are some of the brave journalists and cultural workers who work in the alternative media, refusing to become embedded within the safe and whitewashed parameters of established powers. These are the journalists who also fiercely challenge the death-dealing war-surveillance machine Snowden reveals both in the film and in later revelations published by the *Guardian, Salon, Washington Post*, and summed up in Greenwald's book *No Place to Hide.*[2]

At one point in *Citizenfour* Snowden makes clear that his revelations carry extraordinary political value, particularly when he states that the United States is "building the biggest weapon for oppression in the history of mankind"—this despite the lies and denials of the government and politicians on both sides of the ideological isle. Snowden's sense of political and moral indignation is captured in his belief that the United States had crossed over into a totalitarian politics that it now shares with the infamous Stasi, the ruthless and feared official state security service of the former German Democratic Republic. According to Snowden, the United States has morphed into a colossal digital update of the Stasi, and has fully retreated from any notion of democratic values and social responsibility. As the surveillance state grows, the United States is increasingly obsessed "by a creepy intoxication with what is now technically possible, combined with politicians' age-old infatuation with bullying, snooping and creating mountains of bureaucratic prestige for themselves at the expense of the snooped-upon taxpayer."[3]

In the documentary, Snowden comes across as a remarkable young man who shines like a bright meteor racing across the darkness. He is calm, unpossessing, articulate, and almost nerdy in his demeanor, appearing utterly reasonable and believable. In many ways, despite some political shortcomings and omissions in the film, Snowden embodies the best of what any viable notion of leadership has to offer given his selflessness, moral integrity, and fierce commitment to both renounce injustice and to do something about it. But the film is not without its flaws. By omission it leaves out the countless additional acts of heroism of other whistle-blowers such as Thomas Drake, William Binney, and Kirk Wiebe. More-over, the film erases the crucial role that WikiLeaks, Julian Assange, and Sarah Harrison played in providing the conditions for Snowden's eventual escape to a safe haven. The film comes close to decontextualizing Snow-den's actions in light of the erasure of the mounting acts of resistance against government surveillance and state violence that have been intensi-fied since the end of the Vietnam War.[4] Snowden comes across as a nice guy, a poster boy for the liberal press when in actuality he is a radical in the best sense of the term and is far from interested in simply reforming the empire. Moreover, the film adds to its own depoliticization by focus-ing exclusively on the whistleblower and not situating Snowden's behavior within a broader context of struggle. Snowden's eventual development in the film comes a bit too close to grooming him as a potential celebrity. Indeed, Douglas Valentine goes so far as to argue that Glenn Greenwald is more concerned about Snowden's potential celebrity status than anything else, writing:

> And that's how the fable of Ed Snowden unfolds in *Citizenfour*. His handlers at GG Industries Inc. embrace him as cannon fodder for their careers, and happily turn him into a Hollywood star, a celebrity and perpetual money-making myth for the faux gauche, in the mold of Dan Ellsberg. . . . All this focus on celebrities distracts the Ameri-can public from the real issues, like the fact that they live in a police state that controls every thought they think.[5]

I think Valentine's critique might serve as a cautionary tale, but overall it borders on *ad hominem* and is too harsh. At the same time, as mentioned, there is no reference to the crucial role of Jeremy Scahill, Julian Assange, and WikiLeaks in revealing and challenging the various acts of spying, vio-lence, widespread illegal surveillance, and ruthless militarism at the heart of authoritarian regimes, not to mention the corruption and crimes committed by the financial elite in many countries. Nor is there any sense that what Snowden is revealing has less to do with the state's violation of civil liberties and privacy rights than with the existence of an emerging police state. At the same time, as important as these omissions are, what is compelling for me, despite the film's shortcomings, is the incredible courage and commitment of a young man who is willing to risk his life in exposing the dark secrets of the deep state. Moral and political courage are in short supply these days and rarely represented in any form in the Hollywood celluloid universe.

Selma focuses on a three-month period in 1965 when Dr. Martin Luther King, Jr., and others organized and planned to challenge the racist power structure in Alabama by eventually marching from Selma to Montgomery as a nonviolent act of civil defiance in order to secure equal voting rights. The strength of the film lies in its attempts to reveal not only the moral and civic courage of Martin Luther King, Jr. in his fight against poverty and racial oppression but also the courage and deep ethical and political commitments of the incredibly brave men and women unwilling to live in a racist society and willing to put their bodies against the death-dealing machine of militarized state force (eerily anticipating Ferguson) to bring it to a halt. It is this representation, however limited, of civic courage, collective struggle, and the violence at the heart of American history that redeems *Selma*. The film offers up not only a much needed form of moral witnessing, but also a politics of confrontation that serves as a counterpoint to the weak and compromising model of racial politics offered currently by the Obama administration. It is in this representation of collective courage, popular struggle, and daring resistance against the exercise of visceral racist violence that *Selma*'s oppositional narrative, however imperfect, offers the possibility for a more complete understanding of valor and heroism in the interest of justice. The film also demonstrates how important education was as part of the civil rights movement and the role it played in highlighting the interrelated elements of nonviolence and vast social movements struggling for radical democratic change. *Selma* may have buried important historical and political truths, but there is a kernel of visionary politics in the film waiting to be rescued.

Selma represents Hollywood's attempt to rescue public memory, albeit, as dozens of critics have already revealed, a deeply flawed attempt. While the film provides a historical snapshot of a particular moment in the civil rights movement that offers a horrifyingly visceral portrayal of a vicious and brutalizing racism, it compromises itself by distorting and underplaying the crucial role of SNCC.[6] Not only does it downplay the important role of James Foreman in the movement, it also infantilizes his role in the events of Selma by depicting him as a petulant and immature young boy, when at the time he was older than King. As is well known, the film also constructs a self-serving and disparaging image of President Johnson's relationship with Dr. King, one that is allegedly at odds with the historical record. The film "depicts Johnson authorizing FBI Director J. Edgar Hoover to smear King and—as King himself suspected—try to drive him to suicide. It is a profoundly ugly moment."[7] This is more than a gross distortion. As Glen Ford makes clear, it was "the Kennedy brothers who were the ones who authorized the bugging of Dr. King's phones and office and hotel rooms."[8]

The liberal retreat into the fog of low-intensity battles, a quick willingness to compromise rather than fight, and the habit of ignoring embarrassing truths are also evident in the way in which *Selma* whitewashes history not only with regard to the role of SNCC and President Johnson in the civil rights movement, but in the way in which King is portrayed as a kind of compromising liberal, surely a nod to legitimize the politics of President Barack Obama. This might best be viewed as a capitulation to the false purity of liberal political intentions, if not obsessions. Omissions of this sort add up to a kind of liberal amnesia evident in the fact that the actual journey of a more radical Dr. Martin Luther King, Jr. is undermined by portraying him in the film as a pragmatist intent on compromising with the white power structure in order to get black people the right to vote and ensure them a place in the electoral process. King was not a liberal and that may be why he was assassinated. Near the end of his life, King had developed into a full-fledged democratic socialist who was more than willing to connect the violence of war, militarism, poverty, inequality, and racism with the scourge of a ruthless, punishing, and dehumanizing capitalism.[9] I think that the movie critic Steven Rea is partly right in insisting that "*Selma* may be flawed, even spurious at points. But in its larger portrait of a man of dignity, purpose, and courage" the film succeeds in making visible a courageous movement exhibiting the best of collective resistance and heroism in its quest for racial and economic justice.[10]

Though *Selma* makes clear the viciousness of racism during this moment in the civil rights movement, the film echoes the liberal ideology that structures its politics. More specifically, *Selma* echoes Oprah Winfrey's stripped-down liberal ideology, which can only focus on individual agency at the expense of larger structural dynamics rooted in the forces of a racist capitalist state. After all, *Selma* was produced by Oprah Winfrey, who plays, unsurprisingly, the role of one of the most militant characters in the film, which all but guarantees that any hint of a radical politics will constitute a present absence in the film. What most positive commentaries on the film fail to acknowledge is that any viable politics for addressing racism then and now in the United States will not come from Winfrey's brand of celebrity liberalism or Hollywood's version of *Selma* but from the lessons learned from Dr. King's eventual theoretical and political turn to repudiating a society bounded by militarism and racism on one side, and inequality and financial capital on the other. *Selma* offers no hint of such a struggle.

The third film to hit American theaters at about the same time as the other two is *American Sniper,* a war film about a young man who serves as a model for a kind of overconfident, unreflective patriotism and defense of an indefensible war. Chris Kyle, the subject of the film, is a Navy Seal who at the end of four tours of duty in Iraq is heralded a hero for killing more than 160 people there—the deadliest soldier in that military conflict. Out of that experience, he authored an autobiographical book, which bears a problematic relationship to the film. For some critics, Kyle is a decent guy caught up in a war he was not prepared for, a war that strained his marriage and later became representative of a narrative only too familiar for many vets who suffered a great deal of anguish and mental stress as a result of their wartime experiences. This is a made for a CNN narrative that deals in only partial truths. Other critics have labeled the film as a "piece of myth-making and nationalistic war porn."[11] A more convincing assessment and certainly one that has turned the film into a Hollywood blockbuster is that Kyle is portrayed as an unstoppable and unapologetic killing machine, a sniper who was proud of his exploits. Kyle is a product of the American Empire at its worst. This is an empire steeped in extreme violence, willing to trample over any country in the name of the war on terrorism, and leave in its path massive amounts of misery, suffering, dislocation, and hardship. It is also an empire built on the backs of young men and women—though only men are featured—who are relentlessly engaged in buying into the myths of American military masculinity. Chris Kyle was the quintessential "army of one," able to triumph over all enemies thrown in his way, including a former Olympic rifleman.

Yet it seems that this homage to hyper-masculinity hides a deeper structure of violence in American society, fueled by an omniscient war on terror and culture of fear in which violence and lawlessness become normalized. Within this grim survival-of-the-fittest landscape of violence, the only way in which any sense of agency can be activated is to be in a constant state of alertness, narrowly defined by the need to constantly protect oneself. At the same time, a condition of this form of servile agency is to be in awe of a state that claims to offer protection and personal safety but largely produces the violence that saturates everyday life and functions to legitimize the rise of the war machine and punishing state. I think Joseph E. Lowndes is on to something crucial about the film when he writes:

> One can see, in Eastwood's rendering of Chris Kyle, that his desire—his need—to be a killer of almost superhuman proportions makes him not sociopathic, but rather a "sheepdog," someone operating in a state of anxious alertness at all times against inevitable attack. His violence is justified in advance. . . . It is neither male bravado nor triumphant nationalism that compels viewers to sympathize with

Chris Kyle. But nor is it an antiwar film. It is rather an assertion of both the grim inevitability of certain kinds of violence, and of our obligation to those who wage violence for that very reason.[12]

Of the three films, *Citizenfour* and *Selma,* however flawed, invoke the courage of men and women who oppose the violence of the state in the interest of two distinct but intersecting forms of lawlessness, one marked by a brutalizing racism and the other marked by a suffocating practice of surveillance—though we see early histories of the surveillance state in *Selma,* and racism can hardly be detached from the war in Iraq. *American Sniper* is a film that erases history, spectacularizes violence, and reduces war and its aftermath to cheap entertainment, with an underexplained referent to the mental problems many vets live with when they return home from the war. In this case the aftermath of war becomes the main narrative, a diversionary tactic and story that erases any attempt to understand the lies, violence, corruption, and misdeeds that caused the war in the first place.

American Sniper hides the fact that behind the celebrated image of the heroic vigilante sniper lie elite killer squads and special operations teams formed, under the George W. Bush administration, as part of a Joint Special Operations Command. The JSOC includes elite troops from a variety of America's fighting units and has grown "from fewer than 2,000 troops before 9/11 to as many as 25,000 today."[13] In *Dirty Wars,* Jeremy Scahill describes JSOC as a global killing machine, running covert wars, and allowing its special operations units to function as unaccountable death squads.[14] JSOC has a budget of more than $8 billion annually and constitutes the infrastructure that suggests that *American Sniper* is less about a lone wolf vigilante than it is symptomatic of a much larger and secret killing machine.[15]

Of course, though it may be redemptive for Hollywood to link targeted assassinations with American heroism, what it erases is that the real global assassination campaign is not the stuff of military valor, of "man-to-man" combat, but is being waged daily in the drone wars that have become the defining feature of the Obama administration. Many critics, including Noam Chomsky, have commented on Chris Kyle's memoir in which he calls the enemy he has been fighting "savages." There is more here than a trace of unadulterated racism; there is also an indication of how violence becomes so palatable, if not comforting, to the American public through the widespread ideological and affective spaces of violence produced and circulated in America's key commanding cultural apparatuses.

This is not surprising since under a regime of neoliberalism, a persistent racism and politics of disposability are matched by a theater of cruelty in which more and more individuals and groups—such as immigrants, low-income whites, poor blacks, the unemployed, and the homeless—are considered throwaways. Within such a politics of disposability, an increasing number of groups are tarred with the label of being less than human and hence all the easier to evict from any sense of social responsibility or compassion. Extreme violence has become an American sport that promotes delight in inflicting suffering on others. But it does more. It also ups the pleasure quotient when the Other is entirely reified and demonized, making it easier for the American public to escape from any sense of ethical responsibility for wars that are as immoral as they are illegal. In the end, *American Sniper* is both symptomatic of and serves as a legitimation for the savage struggle-for-survival ethic that dominates American life and resonates throughout the film. Moreover, violence becomes a kind of safety valve to protect individuals against the alleged perils of a notion of solidarity based on care rather than fear of the Other. Politics becomes an extension of war. This becomes crystal clear in the dinner table scene when Kyle's father lectures his kids about how there are three types of people in the world "wolves, sheep and sheepdogs." In this pernicious worldview, wolves are brutal killers who threaten an innocent public both at home and abroad. Abroad they can be found in Yemen, Afghanistan, and Iraq, or wherever Muslims live. At home, the category is quite fluid and includes groups ranging from drug dealers and urban thugs to dangerous black youth and criminal street gangs. The sheep are a metaphor for God-loving, patriotic, innocent Americans, while the sheepdogs are those patriotic and vigilant Americans whose role is to protect the sheep from the wolves. The sheepdogs include everyone who inhabits the warrior culture and includes a wide range of groups that extend from the paramilitary police forces and vigilante super-patriots along the nation's borders to the gun- loving soldiers that protect American interests overseas.

The analogy is not just pernicious; it is also a transparent rationale for a hyper-masculine gun and militarized culture that feeds on fear and racist hysteria. It also offers a rationale for killing those dangerous racial others (wolves), who in light of the recent killings of unarmed black men by the police, appear to be fair game for the sheepdogs. I don't believe this analogy is far-fetched, evident as it is in the discourse of prominent politicians such as former New York City mayor Rudy Giuliani, who has argued that the white cops in black communities are necessary because of the high numbers of black-on-black crime.[16] This is more than a false equivalency since the blacks are not armed by the state and many go to jail for the crimes they commit (or increasingly for not committing any crime at all). But more important, the disproportionate rate at which the police kill blacks rather than whites speaks to a not so hidden order of racial aggression and violence. According to recent data collected by *Pro-Publica*, "Young black men are 21 times as likely as their white peers to be killed by police."[17] What this discourse evokes is one of the central principles of neoliberalism—a survival-of-the-fittest culture in which violence, unchecked self-interest, and a militant individualism merge.

At the same time, *American Sniper* evokes sympathy not for its millions of victims but for those largely poor youth who have to carry the burden of war for the dishonest politicians who send them into war zones that should never have existed in the first place. Amy Nelson at *Slate* gets it right in stating that "*American Sniper* convinces viewers that Chris Kyle is what heroism looks like: a great guy who shoots a lot of people and doesn't think twice about it."[18] But *American Sniper* does more than inject the horror of wartime violence into the instrumental logic of efficiency and skill, it also offers young people a form of entertainment that is really a species of right-wing public pedagogy, a kind of "teachable moment." Its decontextualization of war serves as a recruiting tool for the military and reinforces a sickening rite of passage that suggests that one has to go to war to be a real man. This is a death-dealing myth wrapped in the mantle of American heroism. Moreover, it is a myth that young, vulnerable, poor youth fall prey to, especially when their everyday existence is steeped in despair and precarity and their identities are shaped in an endless number of cultural apparatuses that thrive on the spectacle of violence. There is no context, truth, or history in this film, just the passion for violence and a hint at the anguish that leaves its subjects and objects in a nightmarish world of despair, suffering, and death. In that sense, as Dennis Trainor, Jr., points out, the film is dangerous pedagogically:

> History has borne that fact out, and that lack of context makes *American Sniper* a dangerous film. Dangerous because kids will sign up for the military because of this movie. Dangerous because our leaders have plans for those kids. Some will kill. Some will be killed. Or worse. There is no narrative existing outside the strict confines of *American Sniper*'s iron sights that allows for the war on terror to be over. It's like a broken record looping over and over: attack, blowback and attack. Repeat.[19]

Citizenfour and *Selma* made little money, were largely ignored by the public, and all but disappeared except for some paltry acknowledgments by the film industry. *American Sniper* is the most successful grossing war film of all time. *Selma* will be mentioned in the history books but will not get the attention it really deserves for the relevance it should have for a new generation of youth confronting new forms of racism and state violence. There will be no mention in the history books regarding the importance of Edward Snowden because his story not only instructs a larger public but indicts the myth of American democracy. Yet *American Sniper* resembles a familiar narrative of false heroism and state violence for which thousands of pages will be written as part of history texts that will provide the pedagogical context for imposing on young people a mode of hyper-masculinity.

Such pedagogies will be built on the false notion that violence is a sacred value and that war is an honorable ideal and the ultimate test of what it means to be a man. This is the stuff of Disney posing as pure Americana while beneath the pretense to innocence, bodies are tortured, children are murdered, villages are bombed into oblivion, and the beat goes on. In an age of short attention spans, an infatuation with speed, and the need for instant gratification it is not surprising that the flight from thoughtfulness and intellectual rigor has also produced a retreat from history and public memory. Hollywood thrives on this loss of historical consciousness while also producing it. The always informative *Toronto Star* writer Olivia Ward is correct in arguing: "It is not only personality that is digitally altered by films, but history itself. In an era of dwindling attention spans, and where reality shows are more celebrated than real events, few people bother to delve deeper into the historical records behind the biopics they see."[20]

The stories a society tells about itself are a measure of how it values itself, its children, the ideals of democracy, and its future. The stories that Hollywood tells represent a particularly powerful form of public pedagogy that is integral to how people imagine themselves, their relations to others, and their relationship to a larger global landscape. In this case, stories and the communal bonds that support them in their differences become integral to how people value life, social relations, and visions of the future. *American Sniper* tells a troubling story codified as a tragic-heroic truth and normalized through an entertainment industry that thrives on the spectacle of violence, one that is deeply indebted to the militarization of everyday life.

Courage in the morally paralyzing lexicon of American patriotism has become an extension of a gun culture both at home and abroad This is a war and survival-of-the-fittest culture that trades in indulgent spectacles of violence and a theater of cruelty symptomatic of the mad violence and unchecked misery that is both a by-product of and sustains the fog of historical amnesia, militarism, and the death of democracy itself. Maybe the spectacular success of *American Sniper* over the other two films should not be surprising to any one in a country in which the new normal for anointing a new generation of heroes goes to billionaires, politicians who sanction state torture, and other leaders of the corrupt institutions and bankrupt celebrity culture that now are driving the world into political, economic, and moral bankruptcy, made visible in the most venal vocabularies of stupidity and cruelty.

Michael Lerner has reminded me that the fog of political and moral illiteracy that many Americans inhabit may have less to do with the power of the cultural apparatuses and the deadening public pedagogies they produce than what I have argued. He suggests that it is not enough to argue that the American public be viewed as "hopelessly bamboozled by the existing entertainments."[21] I think it is crucial to make clear that power never collapses entirely into domination; we observe moments of resistance while trying to chart how powerlessness plays out in ways that damage any viable sense of individual and collective agency. At the same time, Rabbi Lerner is right to suggest that deeper psychological modes of oppression might be at work in oppressing people, given the power of the ideological and affective spaces of a society many people inhabit—spaces fiercely dominated by militarization, consumerism, and finance capital. It is crucial for any politics that matters to understand how subjectivity is inhabited and shaped in oppressive times, especially among those it victimizes. But it is also necessary to understand the way in which the crisis of agency is the by-product of a massive machinery of concentrated power that drives a public pedagogy that incessantly works to define agency in the interests of war, militarism, commercialism, and privatization. War machines, the mainstream corporate-controlled media, and the financial elite now construct the stories that America tells about itself and in this delusional denial of social and moral responsibility monsters are born, paving the way for the new authoritarianism.

At stake here is the need to be mobilized by an awareness of the dark times that beset us. This means not using the present as an excuse to fall into despair, to deny one's sense of agency and the possibility of individual and collective resistance, but to recognize fully how such a crisis of agency came into being and how it can be challenged, especially at a moment when the relations among cultural institutions, political power, and everyday life have taken on a new intensity and power. This is not merely a political issue, nor is it solved by acknowledging that people are not dupes. It is a deeply pedagogical issue that recognizes that matters of desire, value, identity, and hope are at the heart of any viable politics. If people's needs are being hijacked, the real issue is not to condemn them for succumbing to the swindle of fulfillment, but to ask ourselves how those needs can be understood and mobilized for emancipatory ends. Raising consciousness matters, but that is often too easily said. At issue here are central questions about how one makes theories, narratives, stories, and the discourse of critique and hope meaningful so as to make them critical and transformative. That may be one of the greatest pedagogical challenges any left movement faces. The educative nature of politics must be embraced by the left and other progressives so the realm of subjectivity can be taken seriously. The thrust of any viable strategy will have to engage what it means to change the way people understand their relationship to the world, see things, and become energized in order to act on their principles in the interest of building a better and more just society and world.

There is a subversive side to popular culture when it is used as a powerful resource to map and critically engage the politics of the everyday, mobilize alternative narratives to capitalism, and activate those needs vital to producing more critical and compassionate modes of subjectivity. Unfortunately, as Stuart Hall lamented, too few progressive thinkers have a "sense of politics being educative, of politics changing the way people see things."[22] Hall was pointing in part to a failure of the left to take seriously the political unconscious and the need to use alternative media, theater, online journals, news outlets, and other resources. Indeed, film, television, social media, and other instruments of culture can be used to make education central to a politics that is emancipatory and utterly committed to developing a democratic formative culture. There is enormous pedagogical value in bringing attention to the rare oppositional representations offered within the dominant media. At stake is the need for progressives not only to understand popular culture and its cultural apparatuses as modes of dominant ideology, but also to take popular culture seriously as a tool to revive the radical imagination.

To be effective in this struggle, educators and other progressives need a discourse of critique and hope, a discourse that does not simply provide what Naomi Klein calls "a catalogue of disempowerment."[23] What is also needed is a discourse that relates private troubles to larger issues, one that gives meaning in broader terms to people's problems and links them to the possibility of individual and collective emancipation. Stories help because they make the invisible visible and offer a new form of cultural and political literacy—a new way of reading both the word and the world. Such narratives are dangerous to the status quo and speak to historical and current struggles in which people both talked and pushed back. Howard Zinn and other historians made those narratives available by making visible how history was made from the bottom up. Such histories and struggle were also led by antiwar activists in the 1960s, the brave civil rights workers, and the feminist and gay rights movements.

Chronicling these struggles is not just about offering narratives of hope; it is also about inciting action. These are stories about the force of civic courage and the power of people who are no longer willing to live on their knees. Such struggles not only embrace the radical imagination, they also represent stories of organized courage and collective resistance. In the current historical moment, we see a myriad of battles taking place among "student-debt resisters, fast-food and Walmart workers fighting for a living wage, regional campaigns to raise the minimum wage to fifteen dollars an hour or the various creative attempts to organize vulnerable immigrant workers."[24] These are the voices of the marginalized, this generation's authors of dangerous memories whose stories are never likely to appear in the mainstream media.

I conclude by stressing once again that power is never completely on the side of domination; nevertheless, in these times, resistance is not a luxury but a necessity. Those who believe in the democratic promise of the future have to engage issues of economic inequality and overcome social fragmentation, develop an international social formation for radical democ-

racy and the defense of the public good, undertake ways to finance oppositional activities and avoid the corrupting influence of corporate power,
take seriously the educative nature of politics and the need to change the
way people think, and develop a comprehensive notion of politics and a
vision to match. Making good on the promise of democracy, of education
as a practice of freedom, and the demands of justice are the core challenges of the twenty-first century. It must be motivated by a faith in the
willingness of people to fight together for a future in which dignity, equality, and justice matter, and at the same time recognize the potency of the
repressive forces that bear down on such a struggle. What is crucial is that
the American public be educated so as to go beyond mere reformism. This
means developing a social and political movement that rejects the notion
that "there is no alternative," a movement willing to fight for more than
expanding social provisions and the redistribution of wealth. What needs
to be dismantled is capitalism itself because it only recognizes markets in
its transactions, results in the undoing of every vestige of democratic and
participatory politics, and concentrates power in very few hands.

—— 11 ——

Hiroshima, Intellectuals, and the Crisis
of Terrorism

*Lacking the truth, [we] will however find instants of truth, and those instants are in
fact all we have available to us to give some order to this chaos of horror.*
—HANNAH ARENDT

ON MONDAY AUGUST 6, 1945, the United States unleashed an atomic
bomb on Hiroshima, killing 70,000 people instantly and another 70,000
within five years—an opening volley in a nuclear campaign visited on
Nagasaki in the days that followed.[1] In the immediate aftermath, the
incineration of mostly innocent civilians was buried in official government pronouncements about the victory of the bombings of both Hiroshima and Nagasaki. The atomic bomb was celebrated by those who
argued that its use was responsible for concluding the war with Japan.
Also applauded was the power of the bomb and the wonder of science
in creating it, especially "the atmosphere of technological fanaticism" in
which scientists worked to create the most powerful weapon of destruction then known to the world.[2] Conventional justification for dropping
the atomic bombs held that "it was the most expedient measure to securing Japan's surrender [and] that the bomb was used to shorten the agony
of war and to save American lives."[3] Left out of that succinct legitimating

narrative were the growing objections to the use of atomic weaponry put forth by a number of top military leaders and politicians, including General Dwight D. Eisenhower, who was then the Supreme Allied Commander in Europe, former president Herbert Hoover, and General Douglas MacArthur, all of whom argued it was not necessary to end the war.[4] A position later proven to be correct.

Kenzaburo Oe, the Nobel Prize winner for literature, noted that in spite of attempts to justify the bombing "from the instant the atomic bomb exploded, it became the symbol of human evil, [embodying] the absolute evil of war."[5] What particularly troubled Oe was the scientific and intellectual complicity in the creation of the atomic bomb and in the lobbying for its use, with acute awareness that it would turn Hiroshima into a "vast ugly death chamber."[6] More pointedly, it revealed a new stage in the merging of military actions and scientific methods, indeed a new era in which the technology of destruction could destroy the earth in roughly the time it takes to boil an egg. The bombing of Hiroshima extended a new industrially enabled kind of violence and warfare in which the distinction between soldiers and civilians disappeared and the indiscriminate bombing of civilians was normalized. But more than this, the American government exhibited a "total embrace of the atom bomb," that signaled support for the first time of a "notion of unbounded annihilation" and "the totality of destruction."[7]

Hiroshima designated the beginning of the nuclear era in which, as Oh Jung points out, "Combatants were engaged on a path toward total war in which technological advances, coupled with the increasing effectiveness of an air strategy, began to undermine the ethical view that civilians should not be targeted. . . . This pattern of wholesale destruction blurred the distinction between military and civilian casualties."[8] The destructive power of the bomb and its use on civilians also marked a turning point in American self-identity in which the United States began to think of itself as a superpower, which as Robert Jay Lifton points out refers to "a national mindset—put forward strongly by a tight-knit leadership group—that takes on a sense of omnipotence, of unique standing in the world that grants it the right to hold sway over all other nations."[9] The power of the scientific imagination and its murderous deployment gave birth simultaneously to the American disimagination machine with its capacity to rewrite history in order to render it an irrelevant relic best forgotten.

Pondering what Hiroshima means for American history and consciousness proves as fraught an intellectual exercise as taking up this critical issue in the years and decades that followed this staggering inhumanity, albeit for vastly different reasons. Now that we are living in a 24/7 screen culture hawking incessant apocalypse, how we understand Foucault's pregnant observation that history is always a history of the present takes on a greater significance, especially in light of the fact that historical memory is not simply being rewritten but is disappearing.[10] Once an emancipatory pedagogical and political project predicated on the right to study and engage the past critically, history has receded into a depoliticizing culture of consumerism, a wholesale attack on science, the glorification of military ideals, an embrace of the punishing state, and a nostalgic invocation of the "greatest generation." Inscribed in insipid patriotic platitudes and decontextualized isolated facts, history under the reign of neoliberalism has been either cleansed of its most critical impulses and dangerous memories or it has been reduced to a contrived narrative that sustains the fictions and ideologies of the rich and powerful. History has not only become a site of collective amnesia but has also been appropriated so as to transform "the past into a container full of colourful or colourless, appetizing or insipid bits, all floating with the same specific gravity."[11] Consequently, what intellectuals now have to say about Hiroshima and history in general is not of the slightest interest to nine-tenths of the American population. While writers of fiction might find such a generalized, public indifference to their craft freeing, even "inebriating" as Philip Roth has written, it is for the chroniclers of history a cry in the wilderness.[12]

Memories of the horror of Hiroshima are now present not only in the existential anxieties and dread of nuclear annihilation that racked the early 1950s but also in a kind of fundamentalist fatalism embodied in collective uncertainty, a predilection for apocalyptic violence, a political economy of disposability, and an expanding culture of cruelty that has fused with the

entertainment industry. We've not produced a generation of war protesters or government agitators to be sure, but rather a generation of youth
who no longer believe they have a future that will be any different from the
present.[13] That such connections tying the past to the present are lost signal
not merely the emergence of a neoliberal public pedagogy that wages an
assault on historical memory, civic literacy, and civic agency. It also points
to a historical shift in which the perpetual disappearance of that atomic
moment signals a further deepening in our own national psychosis.

If "Hiroshima and Nagasaki had rendered actual the most extreme
fantasies of world destruction encountered in the insane or in the night-
mares of ordinary people," as Edward Glover once observed, the neoliberal disimagination machine has rendered such horrific reality a collective fantasy driven by the spectacle of violence and the theater of
entertainment.[14] It threatens democratic public life by devaluing social
agency, historical memory, and critical consciousness, and in doing so it
creates the conditions for people to be ethically compromised and politically infantilized. Returning to Hiroshima is not only necessary to break
out of the moral cocoon that puts reason and memory to sleep but also
to rediscover both our imaginative capacities for civic literacy on behalf
of the public good, especially if such action demands that we remember,
as Robert Jay Lifton and Greg Mitchell remarked: "Every small act of violence, then, has some connection with, if not sanction from, the violence
of Hiroshima and Nagasaki."[15]

The anniversary and poisonous legacy of the bombing of Hiroshima,
arguably one of the single largest terrorist acts in history, appears to be
increasingly infused with a celebration of militarism and an investment in
technological fanaticism, both of which lay bare a brazen disregard for the
possibility of nuclear warfare and planetary obliteration. Reflecting on the
tragic historical events of 1945, American intellectuals offer nothing more
than a tepid response to the birth of the atomic age, which cannot but
signify a moral failure and political retreat tantamount to a callous indifference toward human suffering. The threat of global nuclear annihilation appears to have dissolved into a domestication of the unimaginable.[16]

America's intellectuals have lost sight of the horror, fear, anxieties, and sense of doom that gripped both the American public and its intellectuals during the second half of the twentieth century, despite that such fears and anxieties—and the criticism and modes of resistance to nuclear technology that grew out of them—were not without reason and are even more relevant today. If this threat is more dangerous and imminent now than in the past, how does one explain the retreat of intellectuals in the twenty-first century from addressing the memory of Hiroshima and the danger that such amped-up nuclear destruction poses to the world at this historical moment?

Jacques Derrida identified the possibility of a nuclear catastrophe as a "non-event," a likelihood beset by a paradox caught between "the necessity and the impossibility of thinking the event."[17] In an age in which wars have become indiscriminately murderous, intellectuals find themselves confronting forms of symbolic and material violence that produce an endless series of crises. Yet these crises have been reduced to Hollywood spectacles, just as the notion of crisis now gives way to a "disimagination machine" that divorces critically engaged modes of individual and collective agency from an understanding of the conditions that threaten human beings with apocalyptic disasters.[18] Instead of addressing the dark shadow of extinction that extends from Hiroshima to Fukushima, American intellectuals appear to have become quiet, tamed by the forces of privatization, commodification, and militarism while constantly being bombarded by the celebration of popular powerlessness.

As the widely circulated videos of the horrific decapitations of James Foley and Steven Sotloff by Islamic extremists in September 2014 made clear, terrorism in the age of mass media and communications technology attaches itself to the spectacle of violence so as to open up a new space in which global politics is shaped by the regressive morality of ideological fundamentalism, one that willfully exhibits its degeneration into a totalitarian pathology. As shocking as these atrocious events are, they offer no guarantees of moral outrage or political action because the substantive nature of crisis itself has become frail, subject to colonization by a neoliberal pedagogical machine that thrives on an excess of representation and surrender to the political cynicism of apocalyptic despair.

In contrast to the postwar reactions to the monstrous violence wrought by the atomic bomb on Hiroshima and Nagasaki, violence, torture, and human suffering are now framed outside the realm of historical memory, readily dissolving into the nonstop production of Hollywood movies, media spectacles, and a screen culture that promises instant gratification. In a society in which our inner worlds are subject to the reign of the "death-haunted"[19] dictates of casino capitalism, with its endless series of environmental, political, financial, and social cataclysms, the apocalypse has become a spectacle. Moreover, it is a spectacle that produces political infantilism and civic illiteracy, while thriving on a plethora of excessive violence. This is all done in the name of entertainment, which remains safely removed from the work of many academics—even though its messages are widely viewed and accepted as common sense by the American public—as if the public pedagogy produced by the merchants of desire and entertainment only exists in the realm of fiction and functions exclusively as a form of harmless amusement.[20]

Too many academics and other intellectuals now live under the shadow of manufactured precarity, insecurity, and the fear of relentless catastrophes in the wake of endless disasters that have become an ongoing feature of everyday life. Massive hurricanes, tsunamis, earthquakes, floods, droughts, along with the rise of racism, mass violence, terrorism, xenophobia, nationalism, and an increase in war around the globe are ignored or explained away in trivial analyses offered by the corporate media. Thus removed from any understanding of the conditions that produce catastrophic events, media coverage provides an endless cycle of material for consumption by what has become a culture that feeds on disaster and aesthetic depravity and that turns everything into a cheap form of entertainment or simply a crude spectacle. Lured by neoliberal dream-machines into their theater of cruelty, there is a tendency on the part of both intellectuals and the general public to become indifferent to even extreme forms of violence, preferring to flirt with irrationality and withdraw into private obsessions, all the while becoming complicit with the withering of political life. The legacy of the strong opposition to the dropping of the atom bomb and the fear of a nuclear holocaust dissipated over time and morphed into the growing vacuity and cowardice of intellectuals. Politics for many on the left dissolved as the post-1960s generation that entered academia and benefited by its rewards increasingly indulged in modes of theorizing and producing research projects that removed their work from larger social considerations and urgent political problems. Protests over nuclear arms gave rise to a left absorbed in high theory and an array of diverse movements that fractured any sense of unity or collective opposition to a potential nuclear holocaust. As critique morphed into insipid forms of professionalism and theoreticism ensconced in what often appeared to be jargon that functioned like a firewall, many intellectuals chose security over conscience and, as the twenty-first century appeared, became irrelevant.

Violence has become normalized even as the scale of destruction appears overwhelming and seems beyond the control of neoliberal societies such as the United States, where all social problems are largely understood through the reductive registers of individual character, responsibility, and atomized resilience. Under such circumstances, wider public and political concerns dissolve into personal dilemmas. In the absence of conceptual or practical means to address the conditions of our collective existence, growing fear feeds a crisis of meaning for many intellectuals. Any sustained critique that could motivate political action gives way to a sense of despair and flight from responsibility. The overwhelming array and scope of disaster appear beyond any hope of being addressed through the efforts of isolated individuals. As Michael Levine and William Taylor write:

> People are left without the mental or physical abilities they need to cope. Government is absent or useless. We find ourselves in what amounts to what Naomi Zack describes as a Hobbesian second state of nature—where government is inoperative and chaos (moral, social, political, personal) reigns. . . . Genuine [crisis], for example war, undermines and dismantles the structures—material structures

to be sure but also those of justice, human kindness, and affectivity—that give us the wherewithal to function and that are shown to be inimical to catastrophe as such. Disaster dispenses with civilization while catastrophe displaces it.[21]

The horrors of crises such as Hiroshima were met in the past by many intellectuals with moral outrage, criticism, and collective resistance, informed by a sense of hope for the future rooted in the power of the radical imagination. Today, such a culture of thoughtful reasoning and insightful analyses has been corroded under the flood of made-for-the-screen catastrophes that drown the moral conscience and muddy political reflection. Derrida's call for the necessity of action in the face of a crisis such as Hiroshima and the dawn of the nuclear age becomes difficult, if not impossible, to understand and act upon at the present time as the meaning of "crisis"—with its underlying appeal to critique and action—gives way to a notion of catastrophe in which inconceivable disasters and terrors dissolve into what Susan Sontag called "the threat of unremitting banality."[22] As endless neoliberal spectacles of catastrophe move between the registers of transgressive excess and extreme violence, they exhaust their shock value and degenerate into escapist entertainment.

Under such circumstances, many intellectuals are no longer dealing with crises, which in the past were often met by thoughtful, responsible, and organized responses to the challenges produced by calamitous events such as the bombing of Hiroshima. Such a state of ethical tranquilization and political paralysis induced by catastrophic spectacles is further reinforced by the widespread cynicism that has become the *modus operandi* of the neoliberal machinery of misery and precarity. Rather than lift people out of the rubble of disaster, catastrophes serve to "distract us from terrors . . . by an escape into the exotic dangerous situations which have last-minute happy endings."[23]

Manufactured catastrophes—and with them a generalized sense of manufactured helplessness—now reign supreme in the new interregnum of late modernity, a kind of liminal space that serves to neutralize action, derail the challenges posed by real social and political problems such as the threat of nuclear annihilation, and substitute the escape into fantasy for any attempt to challenge the terrifying conditions that often accompany a serious crisis. Such retreats from reality blunt civic courage, dull the radical imagination, and dilute any sense of moral responsibility, plunging historical acts of violence such as Hiroshima into the abyss of political indifference, ethical insensitivity, and depoliticization. Catastrophe, as Brad Evans has observed, speaks to an era of late modernity marked by "a closing of the political."[24] Resignation and acceptance of catastrophe has taken root in the ground prepared by the neoliberal notion that "nothing can be done." If, as Zygmunt Bauman argues, crisis speaks to the need to address what exactly needs to be done,[25] then what has been lost in the age of catastrophe and its overwhelming sense of precarity and uncertainty is a properly political response in the face of a pending or existing disaster.

In the aftermath of the bombing of Hiroshima, the question emerged as what was to be done about such horror. Catastrophe, in contrast, tends to be so overpowering that the issue is no longer how might intellectuals address and rectify a crisis, but how they endure and survive it. The horror of the atomic bomb once inspired the Beat Generation, a literature of resistance, film documentaries, and a plethora of thoughtful criticism. As Howard Zinn pointed out, today's images of violence and "the statistics of death and suffering that figures in the millions leave us numb, and nothing but the personal testimonies of individuals—even if they only faintly represent the reality—are capable of shaking us out of that numbness."[26] Such horror now survives as a script, not for confronting dark truths about human civilization, but for incorporating and embellishing as part of a Hollywood blockbuster.

Neoliberal regimes locked into the orbits of privatization, commodification, disposability, and militarization elevate extreme violence and its effects into a cultural and pedagogical spectacle. The spectacle in this sense is part of a pedagogical apparatus in which historical, individual, and social modes of agency degenerate, presenting a serious challenge to intellectuals regarding the very possibility of addressing diverse crises. Instead of responding to crises with the desire to correct a wrong and to reimagine a different future, all that appears to be left among many intellectuals, especially in the academy, is the desire to merely survive in the face of endless representations of state and non-state violence and the ever-encroaching apocalypses produced by the neoliberal machinery of disposability. The mass public indifference to the nuclear arms race and the threat of human extinction; the use of state torture; the indiscriminate and mass killing of children; the rise of debtors' prisons; the war against women; the militarization of the totality of American society; and the state violence waged against nonviolent student protesters—is only a short list indicating how the looming shadows of apocalypse and experiences of actual suffering have moved out of the realm of political responsibility and moral sensibility into the black hole of a depoliticizing mode of entertainment and suppression of dangerous memories. At the same time, mass violence has become individualized in that real-life violence in both screen culture and the corporate-controlled media is reduced to representations of suffering and tortured individuals rather than masses of people. Under such circumstances, mass violence such as what happened at Hiroshima becomes faceless and invisible since only the individual body denotes a legitimate representation of suffering, violence, brutality, and death. This individualization of violence reinforces the logic of neoliberal misery and disposability, construing the individual's plight as a matter of fate removed from larger structural forces as the normal and acceptable state of affairs. Mass deaths make it harder to strip away the humanity of the victims and the horror of the violence and are not easily forgotten. Today, the traces of both memory and moral responsibility become more difficult for intellectuals to address and grasp as crises are abstracted from the broader social, economic, and political conditions of their production.

As crisis gives way to catastrophe, the quest to merely survive now misdirects moral and political outrage toward forms of entertainment that lull us into a moral coma. As violence becomes normalized, it becomes more difficult to conceive other kinds of social behavior, modes of mediation, and types of collective resistance, let alone a more just and democratic future. Hence, the spectacle of the catastrophe signals a society in which a collective sense of despair merges with the notion of a future that is no longer worth fighting for. The lesson to be drawn here, however tentative, is that under the reign of neoliberalism the roles and responsibilities of the intellectual are being devalued, reduced to a stance marked by a flight from moral and political responsibility, infused by an indifference to the unpleasant necessities of mass violence, and safely tamed within public spheres such as higher education that have given themselves over to a crude instrumental rationality and endorsement of market-based values, practices, and policies.[27]

Many Americans now inhabit modes of time and space in which violence and the logic of disposability mutually reinforce each other. For example, the unarmed African American youth Michael Brown, standing with his hands raised, was not only shot and killed by a white policeman in Ferguson, Missouri, but his body was left in the street for four hours—which was eerily reminiscent of the treatment given the low-income, largely African American inhabitants of New Orleans whose bodies, rendered worthless and undeserving of compassion, were also left in the streets after Hurricane Katrina swept through the city.

The logic of disposability has a long history in the United States and has spurned a number of resistance movements and a plethora of dissent among intellectuals. Unfortunately, times have changed for the worse. In the case of the killings of Michael Brown, Tamir Rice, and Freddie Gray, there was an enormous expression of outrage by many poor minorities of color and some white progressives, yet too little was heard from American intellectuals and academics. In the absence of such an outcry, public attitudes are reinforced in their acceptance of the neoliberal notion that disposable populations and individuals are the new living dead—legitimately made invisible and rightly relegated to zones of terminal exclusion and impoverishment. Such silence reinforces the notion that the disposable are by their own actions the unknowable, invisible, and powerless marginalized by class and race and living in ghettoes that serve as dumping grounds largely patrolled by armies of police dressed like soldiers inspecting a war zone.

The disposable people inhabiting these sites, or what João Biehl calls "zones of social abandonment,"[28] constitute a new form of underclass, an expanding group of the American population that extends from poor urban minorities to a collapsing middle class to the millions incarcerated by the punishing state, to an entire generation of young people whose lives have been short-circuited by a rogue financial class that has robbed them of a future and who now live in a constant state of uncertainty and precarity.[29] Made voiceless, and hence powerless, the subjectivity of the dispossessed becomes not just the locus of politics, but part of the machinery of social and political death. The logic of disposability has become all-encompassing in American society, extending its tentacles outward from the neighborhoods of the poor and destitute to the middle-class confines of the suburbs and outlying rural communities. The power and reach of neoliberal misery and disposability have created a new culture of hopelessness and conformity among the many intellectuals who are themselves feeling always on the brink of being thrust into the ranks of the disposable. Increasingly, they appear too afraid of losing their jobs or of a fate even worse—such as incarceration—if they speak out against the violence that is now embedded in the nervous system of American society. In the face of a state government that hardly shies away from surveillance, punishment, and mass incarceration—and in these respects appears far more harsh and powerful than the one that dropped the bomb on Hiroshima—many intellectuals fear for their futures, and in some cases their lives.[30] Abandoning all efforts to advocate for change and embracing the survivalist mode peddled by the neoliberal social order and a 24/7 nonstop consumerist culture, intellectuals retreat from dangerous memories, making it easier for the logic of disposability to become the norm rather than the exception.

As consumerism becomes the only obligation of citizenship and expression of agency left, the pleasure of passive spectatorship along with a sterile careerism blunt for many intellectuals any sense of political engagement and the need to address crucial social problems. At the same time, the machinery of commodification rolls on in its efforts to promote a cleansing of historical memory, removing any trace of social and political irresponsibility, if not willful indifference, for which past and current generations might be held accountable.[31] Any thoughts of challenging mass violence and apocalyptic crisis are now left to the superheroes that populate comics, video games, and Hollywood films, all of which testify to the ways in which the dominant cultural apparatuses of our time depoliticize intellectuals by rendering, as David Graeber points out, "any thought of changing the world seem [like] an idle fantasy."[32] The apocalypse has come home, and it has become a video game and reality TV show at once effectively dethroning the political while smothering the never-ending task of history to enable moral witnessing and provide a critique of the horrors that give rise to what seems like an endless series of crises. The disimagination machine, especially regarding the nightmare of Hiroshima and Nagasaki that ushered in the nuclear age, now controls all the commanding institutions that once preserved history, and serves largely to erase memory. As Tom Engelhardt observes:

> Seventy years later, the apocalypse is us. Yet in the United States, the only nuclear bomb you're likely to read about is Iran's (even though that country possesses no such weapon). For a serious discussion of the U.S. nuclear arsenal, those more than 4,800 increasingly ill-kept weapons that could incinerate several Earth-sized planets, you need to look not to the country's major newspapers or news programs.[33]

Yet there is more at stake here than the erasure of historical memory among American intellectuals. Across the whole culture, the machinery of entertainment and its various cultural apparatuses advance the celebration of what might be called an aesthetics of catastrophe that merges spectacles of violence, war, and brutality into forms of collective pleasure that constitute an important and new symbiosis among visual pleasure, violence, and suffering. The aesthetics of catastrophe revels in images of human suffering that are subordinated to the formal properties of beauty, design, and taste—thus serving in the main to "bleach out a moral response to what is shown."[34] For social critic Susan Sontag and many other critical theorists, the aesthetics of catastrophe is revealed when it takes as its object the misery of others, murderous displays of torture, mutilated bodies, and intense suffering while simultaneously erasing the names, histories, and voices of the victims of such brutal and horrible acts. The philosopher Paul Virilio, in a meditation on the extermination of bodies and the environment from Hiroshima and Auschwitz to Chernobyl, refers to this depraved form of art as an "aesthetics of disappearance that would come to characterize the whole fin-de-siècle" of the twentieth century.[35]

The spectacles of intense violence, hyper-masculinity, celebrity culture, and extreme sports fit neatly into a culture that celebrates the devastation wreaked by unchecked market forces and embraces a survival-of-the-fittest ethic. Conformity and forgetting increasingly give way to a heightened mode of cruelty that is pleasure-driven and infuses not only the video game and Hollywood film industries but also the military-industrial-surveillance complex. Tied to forms of pleasurable consumption and sensations that delight in images of suffering, the depravity of catastrophe functions to anesthetize the entire culture ethically and politically, prompting passivity or even joy in the midst of violence, suffering, and injustice. Embodied in the form of reality TV shows, video games, and escapist entertainment, neoliberal public pedagogy now suppresses concrete memories of the suffering and horror associated with war and events such as the bombing of Hiroshima. This marriage of pleasure and depravity should not be seen as the province of individual pathology or evil; to the contrary, it functions largely to produce a collective subject through an economy of affect and meaning that traps people in their own narcissistic desires and callous self-interests while promoting an endless spectacle of catastrophes. Drawing upon the work of writers Robert Jay Lifton and Greg Mitchell, I would argue that the aesthetics of catastrophe works in tandem with casino capitalism so as to produce a kind of "psychic numbing" both for intellectuals and the American public. Psychic numbing manifests itself most clearly in the total disregard, if not disdain, voiced in response to the suffering of others on the part of powerful conservative elites, anti-public intellectuals, mainstream politicians, and the financial ruling classes. This is a notion of catastrophe in which unrestrained self-interest and ruthless competitiveness become the only intellectual and ethical values that matter.[36]

Surely it is possible to reinvigorate society so that there is a collective understanding that the problems people suffer individually should only be understood within a wider set of economic, social, and political considerations. There is no other choice, as a social order that has become a breeding ground for violence against those considered excess, disposable, and other is set on a course for self-destruction.[37] As material and symbolic forms of violence merge with the sadistic discourse of hate radio and right-wing politicians, a new and more intense culture of cruelty emerges that targets increasing numbers of people for disposal rather than compassion, trust, and empathy. Humane interventions and public values wane while the celebration of war-like values, militarism, a friend/enemy divide, and even the murder of children, as we have seen in Gaza, is sanctioned by the ruthless logic of military necessity.[38]

We now live in a time of administered lawlessness that not only fabricates legal illegalities, but also suggests that any impending crisis *demands* lawlessness and preemptive violence, which, while defining itself as an exception, becomes normalized as an expected facet of everyday behavior—if not also a source of cheap sensationalism and entertainment. Lawlessness is not only justified as a military imperative; it becomes part of the workings of corrupt politics and financial power. How else to explain that President Obama refused to prosecute the CIA operatives who illegally tortured people under the Bush-Cheney administration?[39] Or the fact that "Director of National Intelligence James Clapper perjured himself on camera with little or no fallout"?[40] Another example of lawlessness is clear in the case of "the CEO of JPMorgan who presided over various scams that resulted in $20 billion worth of fines and, for his trouble, he was awarded a 74 percent raise," rather than prosecuted and put in jail.[41] Then there is the egregious example of banking giant HSBC, "which admitted to laundering $850 million for a pair of Central and South American drug cartels," and, once again, nobody went to jail.[42]

Inundated by apocalyptic catastrophes and their spectacularization, we seem to shrug off the reign of corrupt financiers and politicians who operate outside the law. As Lifton and Mitchell have argued, we also fail to see the plight of those living in our midst as we "become increasingly insensitive to violence and suffering around us, to killing in general, but also to poverty and homelessness."[43] This echoes the sentiments of Zygmunt Bauman and Leonidas Donskis who insist that "violence shown every day ceases to provoke amazement, or disgust. It, as it were, grows on you. At the same time, it stays unreal—it still seems it cannot happen to us."[44] Furthermore, rather than being alarmed, for example, over the defense industry, which "embodies the primeval archetype of unencumbered raw violence,"[45] growing numbers of intellectuals mimic, through their silence, if not tacit support, an American public that seeks out more spectacular bloodshed as a way to ramp up the pleasure quotient and fulfill a collective desire for instant gratification and the need to feel something, anything. How else to explain the muteness of intellectuals regarding the legislation being passed in a number of states that will require teachers to carry weapons in their classrooms and allow people to take weapons into bars, thus clearly promoting a toxic gun culture that gives rise to, among other things, vigilante and militia groups patrolling the borders of the Southwest hunting for illegal immigrants?[46] How else to understand the silence in the face of an endless spate of violence against black urban youth in the past decade, which until recently has been barely reported in the media except in terms that describe it as routine policing rather than as acts of exceptional and unacceptable brutality?[47] As Antonio Thomas points out, according to the 2010 National Police Misconduct Statistics and Reporting Project, within a time frame of 16 months, there were

> 5,986 reports of police brutality that are reported resulting in 382 deaths, [of which] a great majority of these individuals have been black men and women. But due to the amount of fear that police use to terrorize the black community . . . most victims of police brutality do not report it to the proper authorities for fear of retali-

ation from a police force who has sworn to serve and protect them. What is wors[e] is that out of those 5,986 reports only 33% went through conviction, [of those convicted] only 64% has received a prison sentence and on an average the police only serve a maximum of 14 months.[48]

How is it that intellectuals have so little to say publicly about the overt racism in law enforcement, not to mention the way the media report on the shootings of poor minority youth in the nation's cities often as defensible homicides. This is especially disturbing at a time when those responsible for protecting the public indicate that they would rather inflict violence on young people and incarcerate them than provide them with decent education, training, health care, and employment? As intellectuals surrender their civic courage and intellectual capacities to the dictates of a neoliberal regime, it becomes all the more difficult to recognize that a pervasive inattentiveness to the lessons of history will inevitably breed these kinds of horrors.

As the spectacle of neoliberal terrorism, violence, and misery becomes one of the major organizing principles of daily life, it is all the more imperative for intellectuals, educators, artists, parents, students, and others to examine the myriad of cultural apparatuses that currently represent not only powerful political and pedagogical forces in shaping a culture of fear and violence—invoked by state and non-state groups to legitimize lawlessness—but also a new technology and pedagogical machinery for redefining the very nature of power itself. This is all the more crucial to recognize since the central elements of the spectacle of terrorism and the aesthetics of catastrophe are unlike anything many intellectuals have faced in the past—given their enshrinement of hyper-real violence, unadulterated appeal to fear, resistance to state authority and the rule of law, and elevation of the visual image to a place of social, cultural, and political dominance. Given how such cultural apparatuses have the power to work pedagogically and politically to wage a war on communal relations, the social state, and the radical imagination, it is crucial to remember, as Hannah Tennant-Moore reminds us, that "fear loves nothing so much as punishment."[49]

The spreading orgy of global violence that characterizes the twenty-first century can be traced from at least the birth of the atomic age extending to the 9/11 attacks on the Twin Towers. This historical trajectory links the power of violent images with the culture of fear, constituting a new space that has opened up for intellectuals to engage the political as a pedagogical force and the spectacle as the new language of politics.[50] C. Wright Mills raised this issue in his analysis of the importance of what he called the pedagogical role of the cultural apparatuses in capitalist societies, as did Raymond Williams in his astute definition of what he called "permanent education":

> What [permanent education] valuably stresses is the educational force of our whole social and cultural experience. It is therefore concerned not only with continuing education, of a formal or informal kind, but with what the whole environment, its institutions and relationships, actively and profoundly teaches.[51]

The tangible effects of extreme violence are now made visible through the theatrical staging efforts of both state and non-state terrorists. Shock videos such as the strangling by a New York police officer of Eric Garner and the shooting of Tamir Rice are aired repeatedly on the nightly news right alongside references to beheading videos (though the actual act is never shown on mainstream media outlets). In these circumstances, such horrific violence is removed from any historical context and aired within the registers of a smothering disimagination machine of shock, hyper-violence, and an aesthetics of destruction, rendering almost impossible any serious analysis of such events. Dwight Macdonald once argued after the firebombing of Tokyo that liberal intellectuals "have grown callous to massacre," dismissing them as "totalitarian liberals."[52]

One might argue that the tepidness of intellectuals has gotten worse in that they now find themselves living under a regime of neoliberalism in which virtually everyone is at risk of homelessness, facing a life of uncertainty and temporary jobs, and cut off from larger social issues. This is especially true for academics, given the current state of higher education in which the concept of the intellectual has been reduced to the status of a Walmart worker or technician. Professionalism has become corporatized, thus banishing the imperative for intellectuals to relate their academic interests and scholarship to larger social issues. Increasingly, broader political engagement is neglected in an attempt to survive in institutions that now resemble corporations governed by a business culture and that view students as customers whose education involves nothing more than job training.

Under the reign of the neoliberal dystopian dream machine, war, violence, and politics have taken on a new disturbing sense of urgency. As politics is constituted increasingly outside the law, one of its first victims is any viable sense of the relationship between private troubles and larger public considerations. The public sphere withers into privatized orbits of desire and understanding, and not surprisingly, the diverse realms of public life decay. American intellectuals now inhabit an amnesiac, if not psychopathic, society—one that under the reign of a depoliticizing neoliberalism appears to forget Hannah Arendt's warning that "humanity is never acquired in solitude."[53] For many intellectuals, the radical imagination has dissolved into a dystopian nightmare as marketplace values and the dictates of financialization define politics, the national zeitgeist, and the country's utopian possibilities. Charles Pierce is right in suggesting that intellectuals along with the American public have allowed themselves "to become mired in the habits of oligarchy, as though no other politics is possible."[54]

When the struggle to survive is removed from the much needed fight for justice, the results will be increasingly limited political horizons. In the United States, the specter of militarism, the ongoing pursuit of perpetual war, and commodification of just about everything have provided the conditions for the production of a new form of politics and a disimagination machine—which raises serious questions that intellectuals need to address. These include: how are fear and anxiety marketed; how is terrorism used to recruit people in support of authoritarian causes; how is the neoliberal theater of violence being produced in a vast array of pedagogical sites created by the old and new media; how does the state use mediated images of violence to justify its monopoly over the means of coercion; and how does the aesthetics of catastrophe manifest itself in an age of enormous injustices, deep insecurities, disembodied social relations, fragmented communities, and a growing militarization of everyday life? Totalitarian politics, militaristic violence, and a life-draining social atomization not only mutually inform one another, they have become the most important elements of power as mediating forces that shape identities, desires, and social relations. Given these circumstances, it is no wonder that the legacy of Hiroshima has dissolved into a neoliberal culture of violence, cruelty, and disposability.

The United States is in a new historical conjuncture defined largely by global neoliberal capitalism in which the relationships among cultural institutions, political power, and everyday life have become central to how we understand politics and the work it does.[55] At one level, the market has eroded the affective and symbolic relationships that create public trust, public life, and the bonds of social life. At the same time, politics has become intensely educative in terms of how it constructs the ways in which people understand themselves, their relations to others, and the wider society. Doreen Massey is right in arguing that "it is the internalization of the system that can potentially corrode our ability to imagine that things could be otherwise."[56] And that is precisely why, as the late Pierre Bourdieu argued, progressive intellectuals can no longer underestimate "the symbolic and pedagogical dimensions of struggle" if they are going to forge "appropriate weapons to fight on this front."[57]

If intellectuals are going to address the legacy of Hiroshima and the ongoing threat of nuclear annihilation, they will have to recognize that the struggle for a democratic formative culture will need to come from below; it will simply not take place at the behest of prevailing economic and political power. Moreover, they will have to acknowledge that matters of subjectivity, culture, and identity cannot be separated from material circumstances and commanding institutions, however complex that relationship often is. On the contrary, for such institutions and relations to be challenged collectively, they must be viewed as inextricably related, and they also have to be made visible—connected to the dynamics of everyday life—in order to become part of a transformative consciousness and struggle in which pedagogy becomes central to politics.

The need for a democratic formative culture in which critical intellectuals can thrive raises crucial questions about the educative nature of politics, and how the public pedagogy produced by the old and new media can be used to expand rather than close down democratic relations. Central to such a task is the attempt on the part of educators, intellectuals, artists, and other cultural workers to address what agents, conditions, contents, and structural transformations are necessary to rethink the importance of both the new media and a democratic formative culture in an advanced society so as to configure social practices within rather than outside of the realm of a substantive democracy.

If American intellectuals are to confront the horrors of Hiroshima, the long shadow of nuclear warfare that has developed since the rise of the atomic age, and the memory of the horrors visited upon thousands of civilians, must be revisited and made discernible. This is especially necessary if intellectuals are going to remember and condemn the bombing of Hiroshima and Nagasaki, call for the elimination of nuclear weapons and the oligarchic militarized governments that profit from them, and renounce the killing of civilians in the name of military necessity—a legacy that extends from Hiroshima to the slaughter of civilians in present-day Gaza.

But such struggles will only succeed if they are understood within a new political discourse and a new sense of crisis informed by an awareness of the world of images, digital technologies, the Internet, and alternative pedagogical spaces and cultural apparatuses so that they can be used in the struggle for a new type of agency, new modes of collective resistance, and an organized and long-term transformative struggle for a radical democracy. The struggles for justice and a radically new, democratically inspired society in which nuclear weapons and the dictates of perpetual war will no longer exist will only come when intellectuals and the wider public both understand and feel connected to the struggles of which they are asked to be a part. This is what Stuart Hall has called the "educative nature of politics." Hall spells this out in his claim that such a politics is sorely lacking on the left:

> The left has no sense of politics being educative, of politics changing the way people see things. . . . The left is in trouble. It's not got any ideas, it's not got any independent analysis of its own, and therefore it's got no vision. It just takes the temperature: "Whoa, that's no good, let's move to the right." It has no sense of politics being educative, of politics changing the way people see things.[58]

Hall is arguing, rightly in my view, that the left and its intellectuals need to take seriously what it means to change the subjectivities, desires, and consciousness of people so that they can act as critically informed and engaged agents, capable of learning how to lead and govern rather than simply be assailed, subjugated, and ruthlessly controlled.

Democracy is under assault and appears to have fallen over the edge into what Hannah Arendt once called "dark times." But, as Catherine Clément has noted, "every culture has an imaginary zone for what it excludes, and it is that zone that we must remember today."[59] Such memory work can start with the seventieth anniversary of Hiroshima so that its horrible legacy and effects are no longer part of a purposeful zone of forgetting. I believe that such zones of exclusion are crucial to remember because they make evident the long history of struggle by labor, unions, workers, young people, feminists, civil rights advocates, gay activists, progressive educators, and others who believe in the promise of a radical democracy along with the necessity to struggle with a renewed sense of urgency and collective strength. Such historical memories also make it easier for intellectuals and others to dispute the myth that governments should be trusted because they always act in the best interest of the people.

The time is ripe for the long historical struggle to ban nuclear weapons technology to come alive once more so as to shake off the authoritarian nightmare now engulfing the globe. It is time for intellectuals once again to question the deadly missions of the sixth and ninth of August. As Howard Zinn observed, if we "declare nuclear weapons an unacceptable means, even if it ends a war a month or two earlier," then it may lead to larger questions regarding what role intellectuals might play in creating the conditions for questioning political leaders and stopping monstrous acts before they happen.[60] The old familiar ways of defining and engaging politics no longer work. It is a time to reclaim the struggles and movements of resistance to nuclear weapons and once again take up the quest for global nuclear disarmament, on a different terrain, under new conditions, and with a renewed sense of urgency and hope.

I conclude by recalling Hannah Arendt's notion of "instants of truth" discussed in the epigraph of this chapter. Such instants often come in the form of images, narratives, and stories that shock. They don't accommodate reality as much as they turn it upside down, eviscerating common-sense assumptions a culture has about itself while revealing an intellectual and emotional chasm that runs through established modes of rationality and understanding. Such flashpoints not only rupture dominant modes of consciousness, they give rise to heated passions and debates, sometimes leading to massive displays of collective anguish and resistance, even revolutions. We have seen such "instants of truth" in Ferguson, Missouri, where images of Michael Brown's shooting and death helped to inspire huge waves of protests throughout the United States. These images of violence and human suffering inflamed a society to connect heated emotional investments to a politics in which unthinkable acts of violence are confronted as part of a larger "commitment to political accountability, community, and the importance of positive affect for both belonging and change."[61] Hiroshima provides another "instant of truth" through which intellectuals can confront the crimes of the past in order to develop a collective struggle and an energized politics for a democratically inspired present and future. There may be no greater challenge than this one facing intellectuals in the twenty-first century. As terrorism becomes normalized in the United States, it is imperative that the ethical, radical imagination once again makes visible the horrors of crimes against humanity not just as historical memories but as looming threats to the future of humankind.

12

Flipping the Script: Rethinking Working-Class Resistance in the Age of Terrorism

I HAVE OFTEN THOUGHT ABOUT the moment in which my working-class sensibility turned into a form of critical class consciousness. For most of my youth I was defined by ruling-class types and mainstream institutions through my deficits, which amounted to not having the skills and capacities to do anything but become either a cop or a firefighter. For many working-class youth, this is standard procedure. We are told that we are too angry when we display passion, and too dumb when we speak in the restricted code. Our bodies were the only cultural capital we had to define our sense of agency, either through an expression of solidarity, overdetermined masculinity, or through a commodified and sexualized notion of the body. The message was always the same. We were incomplete, unfinished, excess, and disposable. For many of us that meant a life governed by poverty, poor schools, and the ever expanding reach of the criminal justice system.[1]

I came alive and began to recognize my own agency when I realized that what the ruling-class types (in a variety of institutions, especially school) called my deficits were actually my strengths, that is, a sense of solidarity, compassion, a merging of the mind and the body, learning and willingness to take risks, embracing passion, connecting knowledge to

power, and being attentive to the injuries of others while embracing a
sense of social justice. I then realized that I had to flip the script to survive and became acutely aware that the alleged strengths of ruling-class
types, such as their cold, hyper-masculine modes of embodiment, along
with their ruthless sense of competitiveness, their suffocating narcissism,
their view of unbridled self-interest as the highest virtue, their ponderous
and empty elaborated code, and their often savage and insensitive modes
of interaction, were actually vicious deficits. That was a turning point in
my being able to narrate and free myself from one of the most sinister
forms of ideological domination, "those unexamined prejudices that keep
us from thinking."[2]

For me, this involved a slow process of unlearning the poisonous
sedimented histories working-class youth often have to internalize and
embody in order to survive. Unlearning meant becoming attentive to the
histories, traditions, daily rituals, and social relations that offered both a
sense of resistance and allowed people to think beyond the inflicted misery
and suffering that marked our neighborhoods and daily lives. It meant not
only learning about resistance in our lost histories but also how to narrate
oneselves from the perspective of understanding both the toxic cultural
capital that shored up ruling-class power and those modes of cultural capital, a kind of underground literacy, that allowed us to challenge it. It also
meant unlearning those modes of oppression that many working-class
youth had internalized, obvious examples being the rampant sexism, racism, and hyper-masculinity we had been taught were matters of common
sense and reputable badges of identity.

The struggle to redefine my sense of agency was about more than a
perpetual struggle between matters of intelligence, competency, and low
self-esteem, it was about reclaiming a sense of history, opening the door to
dangerous memories, and taking risks that enabled a new and more radical
sense of identity and what it meant to be in the world from a position of
strength. I found signposts of such resistance in my youth in black music,
stories about union struggles, the warm solidarity of my peers, and later
in the powerful displays of public intellectuals whose lectures I attended at

Brown University. The people who moved me at those lectures were not academics reading papers I barely understood, intellectuals who seemed frozen emotionally spewing out a kind of jargon reserved for the already initiated, smug in their insularity and remoteness.

They were public intellectuals such as William Kunstler, Stanley Aronowitz, Angela Davis, and Dick Gregory who provided me with an alternative understanding and representations of what a working-class public intellectual might be like. They were larger than life and passionate as they spoke about social injustices. They took over the stage in a display that was as smart as it was performative—their words matched by a stylized display of emotion, empathy, anger, and hope. They broke open and destabilized the stale language of the academy, "smuggling in sound, rhythm, and image."[3] Watching and listening to them, my political sensibility changed and I never looked back.

Once again we see working-class black, brown, and white youth reclaiming their histories in the face of massive state violence and terrorism, especially black youth in Black Lives Matter and other emerging movements. They are flipping the script in order to rewrite themselves into a massive movement not for reform but for economic and political change—real change in which a radical democracy comes alive with justice and hope for a better future. They are not concerned simply about naming and reforming injustices but about changing the economic, political, educational, and cultural structures that produce them. Such movements cannot emerge fast enough, given the relentless death machine that now dominates American society.

Everywhere we look today there is the looming threat of totalitarianism and the eradication of those public spheres that produce the critical and energizing formative culture necessary for a radical democracy. Schools have been militarized, providing a feeder to the incarceration state for poor minority youth. In addition, a range of social behaviors has been criminalized, especially in the public schools where young people are arrested for violating a dress code or doodling on their desks. As I have mentioned throughout this book, a war is being waged not on poverty but on the poor, as they are subject to laws that increasingly put them in jail for their debts or for simply being black and poor. The recent killings and then demonization of unarmed African American youths and adults in cities throughout the United States by white police officers have made visible how a kind of military metaphysics now dominates American life, which increasingly resembles a police state. Under such circumstances, it is not surprising that the police have been turned into soldiers who view the neighborhoods in which they operate as war zones. The earth is now viewed as a resource to be plundered, on par with the extraction of wealth, labor, hopes, and dreams taken from other spheres of social life. A mad violence now rules American life as the dark cloud of domestic terrorism operates through appeals to fear, uncertainty, a hollow notion of resilience, and national insecurity.

Outfitted with full riot gear, submachine guns, armored vehicles, and other lethal weapons imported from the battlefields of Iraq and Afghanistan, their mission is to assume battle-ready behavior. Is it any wonder that violence rather than painstaking, neighborhood police work and community dialogue and engagement becomes the norm for dealing with alleged "criminals," especially at a time when more and more behaviors are being criminalized? At the same time, violence becomes the electrical current running through a society that refuses to deal with larger structural issues such as massive inequality in wealth and power, a government that now unapologetically serves the rich and powerful corporate interests, and makes lawlessness and violence the organizing principles of governance.

Barbarism is not simply a political concept; it is a practice forged in war and violence. Incapable of self-reflection, it smothers ethical considerations in the language of tactics so that the killing of children at home and abroad through the mechanisms of state terrorism is justified under the pretext of a military necessity—a notion of fear forged in the bowels of the rising surveillance and punishing state. Turning poor neighborhoods into war zones is the metric of the financial elite and ethical zombies, who without any semblance of moral conscience merge power and violence, and wage war against those expanding populations now considered disposable. Under such circumstances, the distinction between civilians and combatants disappears. This is truly the logic of disposability central to state terrorism and the new totalitarianism.

It is hard to disagree with a growing consensus that what we are witnessing in the United States is the legacy of slavery and the criminalization of people of color reasserting itself in a society in which justice has been willingly and aggressively replaced by racial injustice. And it is precisely this militarization that should inform any analysis about the growing dangers of totalitarianism in America. Racist killings, the loss of privacy, the rise of the surveillance state, the growing poverty and inequality, and the increasing corporatization of commanding institutions point to something more than civil unrest, spying, police violence, and other specific antidemocratic issues. What is truly at work here and unites all of these disparate issues is a growing threat of authoritarianism—or what might be otherwise called totalitarianism with elections.

But there is more at work in the madness of neoliberal capitalism than the oppression caused by its economic structures and the iniquitous gap in wealth, power, and income that it produces. Americans also live in an age of death-dealing loneliness, isolation, and militarized atomization. If you believe the popular press, loneliness is reaching epidemic proportions in wired advanced industrial societies. The usual suspect is the Internet, which isolates people in the warm glow of the computer screen while reinforcing their own isolation and sense of loneliness. The Facebook notions of "Friends" and "Likes" become disembodied categories in which human beings disappear into the black hole of abstractions and empty signifiers. Yet blaming the Internet is too easy when one lives in a society in which any conception of dependence, compassion, mutuality, care for the Other, and sociality is undermined by a neoliberal ethic in which possessive individualism becomes the organizing principle of one's life and a survival-of-the-fittest ethic breeds a culture that at best promotes an indifference to the plight of others and at worst a disdain for the less fortunate while fuelling a widespread culture of cruelty. Isolated individuals do not make up a healthy democratic society.

A more theoretical language produced by Marx talked about alienation as a separation from the fruits of one's labor and later through the Frankfurt School's notion of the culture of instrumental rationality, which has made a comeback in the new data-driven culture that is sweeping American society. Yet traditional forms of alienation and the audit culture we now live in have evolved into something new and more poisonous. The culture of atomization and isolation under the current regime of neoliberalism is more extensive and governs the entirety of social life in a consumer-based society run by the demands of commerce and the financialization of everything. Isolation, privatization, and the cold logic of instrumental rationality have created a new kind of social formation and social order in which it becomes difficult to form communal bonds, deep connections, a sense of intimacy, and long-term commitments. Neoliberalism has created a ruling-class society of monsters for whom pain and suffering are now viewed as entertainment, warfare a permanent state of existence, and militarism as the most powerful force shaping masculinity. Politics has taken an exit from ethics and thus the issue of social costs is divorced from any form of intervention in the world. This is the ideological metrics of political zombies. The key word here is atomization, which is the curse of both neoliberal societies and democracy itself.

What must be remembered is that American politics is not simply representative of the death of reason and the emergence of a raw, unblemished, intense stupidity; it is also about the death of the formative cultures that make thinking possible. Manufactured thoughtlessness produces not only an inattentiveness to the never-ending task of critique, it is the failure of conscience and moral witnessing. Reminiscent of Goya's "sleep of reason," the scourge of stupidity sweeping American culture represents a war against thought and critical agency, and flirts with a kind of fascistic irrationality that lies at the heart of the spectacle of violence engulfing American society. The triumph of stupidity and manufactured ignorance is on full display in American political life and is matched by a savage militarization of the culture, an intensified level of daily violence and aggression, the withering of the social, and the withdrawal into private obsessions.

Citizens have now become consumers, smothered in a fog of exaggerated self-interests.

Manufactured ignorance becomes the assembly line for producing the moral coma and flight from responsibility that enables the American public to avoid such registers of American terrorism as a growing nuclear arsenal, the proliferating high-tech weapons of death, and the ongoing assault on the ecosystem by the burning of fossil fuels. In the first instance, the ongoing investment in nuclear weapons by the United States makes all the more inevitable nuclear annihilation; second, the marriage of new technologies and more sophisticated weapons of destruction and death such as drone warfare has done little to produce an effective anti-terrorism policy and done a great deal in killing innocent civilians and serving as a recruitment tool for terrorists mad with the lust for revenge. As Tom Engelhardt observes, "No one should then be surprised that the drone has produced not an effective war on terror, but a war that seems to promote terror."[4] Progress linked to unsustainable growth and the unchecked burning of fossil fuels is at the heart of America's neoliberal economic policy. Climate change threatens both humanity and the life of the planet only to be ignored by the insane drive for profits and the plundering of the earth. Given the aggressive complicity by the financial elite in the United States and other global powers such as Canada, India, and China promoting this "slow-motion version of nuclear Armageddon,"[5] it is difficult not to view this as a form of domestic terrorism.

Ignorance has become a form of weaponized refusal—a refusal to know and a type of armed knowledge denial parading as common sense. How else to explain the pure idiocy that now permeates the political sphere with the climate change deniers, advocates of creationism, those urging a war against women's reproductive rights, and the financial elite who are waging an assault on all forms of public and higher education? And so it goes. In a society in which social relations are reduced to a form of social combat and thinking collapses into a hyper-masculine adulation of self-interest, there is no room for thinking critically, engaging in thoughtful dialogue, or addressing important social issues. On the contrary, all that remains is the madness of violence, cruelty, and misery, dressed up in the commonsense assumption that the market should govern all social relations. But the posture of stupidity has another, darker side; it becomes a way to flee from all forms of social responsibility and to hide the totalitarian interests that it legitimates. Power now thrives on stupidity, not simply the ignorance that ties the public to dominant forms of oppression, but to a form of stupidity that colonizes power and thrives on a form of mental and ethical tranquillization. James Baldwin was so right when he said, "It is certain, in any case, that ignorance, allied with power, is the most ferocious enemy justice can have."[6]

Absorbed in privatized orbits of consumption, commodification, and display, Americans vicariously participate in the toxic pleasures of the authoritarian state. Violence has become the organizing force of a society, driven by a noxious notion of privatization in which it becomes difficult for ideas to be lifted into the public realm. Under such circumstances, politics is eviscerated because it now supports a market-driven view of society that has turned its back on any viable notion of citizenship. Andrew Bacevich is right in arguing that the United States clings to a minimalist notion of citizenship:

> That conception privileges individual choice above collective responsibility and immediate gratification over long-term well-being. For Americans today, duties and obligations are few. Although the United States is not without "good citizens"—they exist in every community—active participation in civic life is entirely a matter of personal preference. The prevailing definition of citizenship requires simply that you pay your taxes and avoid flagrant violations of the law.[7]

It gets worse. In the age of hyper-consumerism, paying taxes is viewed as an unnecessary burden and violations of the law no longer hold much credibility in a country where lawlessness has become institutionalized as a mode of governance. Police brutality is now matched by the brutality exhibited in policies that condone drone warfare, targeted assassinations, state torture, and a plethora of legislation that violates civil liberties. This violence against the social mimics not just the death of the radical imagination, but also a notion of banality made famous by Arendt, who argued that at the root of totalitarian violence was a kind of thoughtlessness, an inability to think, and a type of outrageous stupidity in which "there's simply the reluctance ever to imagine what the other person is experiencing."[8]

Many Americans are asking questions about why there are not more people in the streets, as if economic turmoil or even the most overt expressions of state violence offer us a politics with guarantees. One reason of course is that the war on the imagination has been matched by the war on solidarity, communal relations, and values that can't be commodified. We all live in war zones now, regimes marked by the most insidious violence and displays of greed, cruelty, and lies. Made all the worse by the economic crisis, the new totalitarianism has not been matched by a crisis of ideas. Subjectivity has been stripped of any meaning, reduced to the gaze of public relations industries that feed the dispossession through the workings of a neoliberal extraction machine that commodifies and privatizes everything it touches, including desires, values, and thinking itself. Capitalism has reached its endpoint, blind to its death march. Fortunately, more and more young people and others are refusing to stand by and let state terrorism and market fundamentalism define their everyday lives.

As John Dewey, Pierre Bourdieu, Noam Chomsky, Paulo Freire, Gayatri Spivak, Martha C. Nussbaum, and others have reminded us, there is no democracy without an informed public. This is a lesson the right wing took very seriously after the democratic uprisings of the sixties. This is not a matter of blaming the public but of trying to understand the role of culture and power as a vital force in politics and how it is linked to massive inequities in wealth and income. The financial state promotes a form of ideological terrorism and the key issue is how to expose it and dismantle its cultural apparatuses with the use of the social media, new political formations, and ongoing collective educational and political struggles.

A central question here is how can conditions be changed, such as the expanding forms of indebted citizenship and mass incarceration that make students, low-income, and poor minorities disposable and unable to offer any collective resistance given their struggle either just to survive or suffer under harsh conditions of state repression. As Noam Chomsky, Jeffrey St. Clair, Paul Buchheit, Chris Hedges, and others have pointed out, capitalism is spreading like a tumor in American society and the key is to cut out its ability to convince people that there are no other alternatives, that the market should govern all of social life, and that the government's only role is to protect the benefits of big business and the interests of the super-rich.

The argument that things will now get much worse and push people into action is politically naive because there are never any political guarantees of how people will act in the face of massive repression. They could for all intents and purposes go either left or right. And that is why such outcomes have to be struggled over both educationally and politically in the interests of creating a radical democratic society. James Baldwin, in a different historical moment, stated: "Not everything that is faced can be changed; but nothing can be changed until it is faced."[9] His words are more true and relevant today than when they were first published. Now is the time for working-class people to join with others to rethink the meaning of the political, to create new political formations, to rethink the possibilities of democracy without capitalism, and to organize for both short-term gains and long-term fundamental changes. America's addiction to the spectacle of violence and a culture of fear cannot be abstracted from its addiction to domestic and foreign terrorism, especially since it succumbs to the cruel irony of mimicking the very terrorism it claims to be fighting. It is time to flip the script.

Notes

INTRODUCTION: THE NEOLIBERAL REIGN OF TERROR

1. John Hinkson, "War Culture," *Arena Magazine* 135 (April–May 2015): 2.
2. See, for instance, Amy Goodman, "Michelle Alexander: Ferguson Shows Why Criminal Justice System of 'Racial Control' Should Be Undone," *Democracy Now!*, March 4, 2015, http://www.democracynow.org/2015/3/4/michelle_alexander_ferguson_shows_why_criminal. See also MattTaibbi, *The Divide: American Injustice in the Age of the Wealth Gap* (New York: Spiegel and Grau, 2014); Maya Schenwar, *Locked Down, Locked Out* (San Francisco: Berrett-Koehler Publishers, 2014).
3. See, for example, these important works: Pierre Bourdieu, *Acts of Resistance*, trans. L. Wacquant (New York: New Press, 1998); Randy Martin, *Financialization of Daily Life* (Philadelphia: Temple University Press, 2002); Alfredo Saad-Filho and Deborah Johnston, *Neoliberalism: A Critical Reader* (London: Pluto Press, 2005); David Harvey, *A Brief History of Neoliberalism* (New York: Oxford University Press, 2007); Henry A. Giroux, *Against the Terror of Neoliberalism* (Boulder, CO: Paradigm, 2008); Manfred B. Steger and Ravi K. Roy, *Neoliberalism: A Very Short Introduction* (New York: Oxford University Press, 2010); Gérard Duménil and Dominique Levy, *The Crisis of Neoliberalism* (Cambridge, MA: Harvard University Press, 2011); Stuart Hall, "The March of the Neoliberals," *The Guardian*, September 12, 2011, online: http://www.guardian.co.uk/politics/2011/sep/12/march-of-the-neoliberals; Colin Leys, *Market-Driven Politics* (London: Verso, 2001); Henry A. Giroux, *Twilight of the Social* (Boulder, CO: Paradigm, 2013); Philip Mirowski, "The Thirteen Commandments of Neoliberalism," *The Utopian*, June 13, 2013, online: http://www.the-utopian.org/post/53360513384/the-thirteen-commandments-of-neoliberalism; Wendy Brown, *Undoing the Demos: Neoliberalism's Stealth Revolution* (Cambridge, MA: Zone Books, 2015).
4. Friedrich Hayek, *The Road to Serfdom: Text and Documents—The Definitive Edition* (Chicago: University of Chicago Press, 2007); Milton Friedman, *Capitalism and Freedom: 40th Anniversary Edition* (Chicago: University of Chicago Press, 2002).
5. Robert W. McChesney, *Digital Democracy* (New York: New Press, 2014).
6. Charles Ferguson, *Predator Nation: Corporate Criminals, Political Corruption, and the Hijack-*

ing of America (New York: Crown Business, 2013); Elliott Currie, "Market, Crime and Community: Toward a Mid-Range Theory of Post-Industrial Violence," *Theoretical Criminology* 1/2 (1997): 147–72.

7.   Charles Derber, *Sociopathic Society* (Boulder, CO: Paradigm, 2013).

8.   See, for example, Zygmunt Bauman and Carlo Bordoni, *State of Crisis* (London: Polity, 2014).

9.   Charles H. Ferguson, *Predator Nation: Corporate Criminals, Political Corruption, and the Hijacking of America* (New York: Crown Business, 2012).

10.   Martin Gilens and Benjamin I. Page, *Testing Theories of American Politics: Elites, Interest Groups, and Average Citizens* (Princeton: Princeton University Press, 2014), online: https://www.princeton.edu/~mgilens/Gilens%20homepage%20materials/Gilens%20 and%20Page/Gilens%20and%20Page%202014-Testing%20Theories%203-7-14.pdf; Tom McKay, "Princeton Concludes What Kind of Government America Really Has, and It's Not a Democracy," *Popular Resistance,* April 16, 2014, http://www.policymic.com/ articles/87719/princeton-concludes-what-kind-of-government-america-really-has-and-it-s-not-a-democracy.

11.   Gilens and Page, *Testing Theories.*

12.   Chris Hedges, "Democracy in America Is a Useful Fiction," *Truthdig,* January 24, 2010, http://www.truthdig.com/report/item/democracy_in_america_is_a_useful_fiction_20100124#.

13.   Henry A. Giroux, *America's Educational Deficit and the War on Youth* (New York: Monthly Review Press, 2013).

14.   Michelle Alexander, *The New Jim Crow: Mass Incarceration in the Age of Colorblindness* (New York: New Press, 2012); Angela Y. Davis, *The Meaning of Freedom* (San Francisco: City Lights Books, 2012).

15.   I am taking the term "punishment creep" from Anne-Marie Cusac, *Cruel and Unusual: The Culture of Punishment in America* (New Haven: Yale University Press, 2009), 74. On the modeling of schools after prisons, see Annette Fuentes, *Lockdown High* (London: Verso, 2013); Henry A. Giroux, *Youth in a Suspect Society* (Boulder, CO: Paradigm, 2009).

16.   Barbara Gurr, *Reproductive Justice: The Politics of Health Care for Native American Women* (New Jersey: Rutgers University Press 2014); Dorothy Roberts, *Shattered Bonds: The Color of Child Welfare* (New York: Basic Books, 2003).

17.   Brondon T. Mathis, *Hands Up Don't Shoot: Why Are African-American Young Men Being Gunned Down in Our Streets* (New York: CreateSpace Independent Publishing, 2014); Alexander, *The New Jim Crow*; Victor M. Rios, *Punished: Policing the Lives of Black and Latino Boys* (New York: New York University Press, 2011).

18.   On the mass incarceration of blacks, see Michelle Alexander, *The New Jim Crow: Mass Incarceration in the Age of Colorblindness* (New York: The New Press, 2010); Anthony DiMaggio, *The Rise of the Tea Party* (New York: Monthly Review Press, 2011).

19.   Harriet Mcleod, Alana Wise, and Luciana Lopez, "Families of S.C. church massacre victims offer forgiveness," *Toronto Sun,* June 19, 2015, http://www.torontosun. com/2015/06/19/suspect-charged-with-murder-in-attack-on-black-us-church.

20.   Scott Shane, "Homegrown Radicals More Deadly than Jihadis in U.S.," *New York Times,* June 24, 2015, http://www.nytimes.com/2015/06/25/us/tally-of-attacks-in-us-challenges-perceptions-of-top-terror-threat.html?action=click&contentCollection=U.S.&regio

n=Footer&module=WhatsNext&version=WhatsNext&contentID=WhatsNext&conf igSection=article&isLoggedIn=false&moduleDetail=undefined&pgtype=Multimedia. See also Tom Engelhardt, "Our Jihadis and Theirs: The Real (Armed) Dangers of American Life," *TomDispatch.com*, June 21, 2015, http://www.tomdispatch.com/post/176013/ tomgram%3A_engelhardt,_armed_violence_in_the_homeland/.

21. *The Guardian* provides a website that now tracks police violence. http://www.theguardian.com/us-news/ng-interactive/2015/jun/01/the-counted-police-killings-us-database.

22. Report, "Black Americans killed by police twice as likely to be unarmed as white people," *The Guardian* (June 1, 2015). Online: http://www.theguardian.com/us-news/2015/ jun/01/black-americans-killed-by-police-analysis.

23. Gloria Feld, *The War on Choice: The Right-Wing Attack on Women's Rights and How to Fight Back* (New York: Bantam, 2007).

24. Chris Hedges, *Wages of Rebellion* (New York: Penguin, 2015), 144.

25. Henry A. Giroux, *Education and the Crisis of Public Values* (New York: Peter Lang, 2012).

26. Glenn Greenwald, *No Place to Hide: Edward Snowden, the NSA, and the U.S. Surveillance State* (New York: Metropolitan Books, 2014).

27. Ibid.

28. Jamelle Bouie, "Dick Cheney's America: Of Course Americans Are OK with Torture. Look at How We Treat Our Prisoners," *Slate*, December 14, 2014, http://www.slate. com/articles/news_and_politics/politics/2014/12/why_americans_support_torture_ we_accept_the_abuse_and_cruel_punishment_of.htm.

29. Joseph E. Stiglitz, "In No One We Trust," *New York Times*, December 21, 2013, http:// opinionator.blogs.nytimes.com/2013/12/21/in-no-one-we-trust/?_php=true&_ type=blogs&_r=0.

30. Henry A. Giroux, *Zombie Politics and Culture in the Age of Casino Capitalism*, 2nd ed. (New York: Peter Lang, 2014).

31. Henry A. Giroux, "Neoliberalism and the Machinery of Disposability," *Truthout*, April 8, 2014, http://www.truth-out.org/opinion/item/22958-neoliberalism-and-the-machinery-of-disposability.

32. Jennifer M. Silva, *Coming Up Short: Working-Class Adulthood in An Age of Uncertainty*, (New York: Oxford University Press, 2013).

33. See, for instance, Robert D. Putnam, *Our Kids: The American Dream in Crisis* (New York: Simon and Schuster, 2015), and Susan Searls Giroux, *Between Race and Reason: Violence, Intellectual Responsibility, and the University to Come* (Stanford: Stanford University Press, 2010).

34. Henry A. Giroux, *Neoliberalism's War against Higher Education* (Chicago: Haymarket Press, 2014).

35. William Boardman, "Does an Honorary Degree Relate to Free Speech? Not Much," *Reader Supported News*, May 20, 2014, http://readersupportednews.org/opinion2/277-75/23766-does-an-honorary-degree-relate-to-free-speech-not-much.

36. Hannah Arendt, *Eichmann in Jerusalem: A Report on the Banality of Evil* (New York: Penguin Classics, 2006; original work published 1963).

37. Even the *New York Times* has called for a number of officials under the Bush administration to be prosecuted for war crimes. See Editorial, "Prosecute Torturers and Their Bosses," *New York Times*, December 21, 2014, http://www.nytimes.com/2014/12/22/

opinion/prosecute-torturers-and-their-bosses.html. See also Marjorie Cohn, "Torture Report Confirms Team Bush War Crimes," *Global Research*, December 17, 2014, http://www.globalresearch.ca/torture-report-confirms-team-bush-war-crimes/5420286; Amy Goodman, "War Criminals Shouldn't Be Honored: Rutgers Students Nix Condoleezza Rice from Commencement Speech," *Truthout*, May 2014, http://truth-out.org/news/item/23504-war-criminals-shouldnt-be-honored-rutgers-students-nix-condoleezza-rice-from-commencement-speech.

38. Henry A. Giroux, *The University in Chains: Confronting the Military-Industrial-Academic Complex* (Boulder, CO: Paradigm, 2007).

39. Henry A. Giroux, *The Violence of Organized Forgetting: Thinking beyond America's Disimagination Machine* (San Francisco: City Lights Books, 2014).

40. Arendt, *Eichmann in Jerusalem*.

41. Michael Halberstam, *Totalitarianism and the Modern Conception of Politics* (New Haven: Yale University Press, 1999).

42. See, for instance, Zoë Carpenter, "The Racist Roots of the GOP's Favorite New Immigration Plan," *The Nation* (August 19, 2015). http://www.thenation.com/article/the-racist-roots-of-the-gops-favorite-new-immigration-plan/.

43. Chris Hedges, "America's 'Death Instinct' Spreads Misery across the World," *AlterNet*, September 30, 2014, http://www.alternet.org/world/americas-death-instinct-spreads-misery-across-world.

44. Tzvetan Todorov, *Torture and the War on Terror*, trans. Gila Walker with photographs by Ryan Lobo (Chicago: Seagull Books, 2009), 2–3.

45. See, for instance, Mark Danner, *Torture and Truth: America, Abu Ghraib, and the War on Terror* (New York: New York Review Books, 2004); Jane Mayer, *The Dark Side: The Inside Story of How the War on Terror Turned into a War on American Ideals* (New York: Doubleday, 2008); and Phillipe Sands, *Torture Team* (London: Penguin, 2009). On the torture of children, see Michael Haas, *George W. Bush, War Criminal? The Bush Administration's Liability for 269 War Crimes* (Westport, CT: Praeger, 2009). Also see Henry A. Giroux, *Hearts of Darkness: Torturing Children in the War on Terror* (Boulder, CO: Paradigm, 2010).

46. Ajamu Baraka, "Obama's Legacy: Permanent War and Liberal Accommodation," *Counterpunch*, February 18, 2015, http://www.counterpunch.org/2015/02/18/obamas-legacy-permanent-war-and-liberal-accommodation/.

47. Steven Rosenfeld, "8 Ways Obama Is as Bad–or worse–Than Bush on Civil Liberties," *Alternet* (March 18, 2013). http://www.alternet.org/civil-liberties/8-ways-obama-bad-or-worse-bush-civil-liberties.

48. James Risen, *Pay at Any Price* (New York: Houghton Mifflin Harcourt, 2014)

49. Agamben cited in Malcolm Bull, "States Don't Really Mind Their Citizens Dying: They Just Don't Like Anyone Else to Kill Them," *London Review of Books*, December 16, 2004, 3.

50. Spencer Ackerman, "The Disappeared: Chicago Police Detain Americans at Abuse-Laden 'Black Site'," *The Guardian*, February 24, 2015, http://www.theguardian.com/us-news/2015/feb/24/chicago-police-detain-americans-black-site.

51. See Brad Evans and Henry A. Giroux, *Disposable Futures* (San Francisco: City Lights, 2015); Henry A. Giroux, "State Terrorism and Racist Violence in the Age of Disposability: From Emmett Till to Eric Garner—Expanded Version," *Truthout*, December 2014.

online: http://truth-out.org/opinion/item/27832-state-terrorism-and-racist-violence-in-the-age-of-disposability-from-emmett-till-to-eric-garner. For a timeline of the recent killing of black men and youth by the police, see: http://www.abc.net.au/news/2015-04-09/timeline-us-police-shootings-unarmed-black-suspects/6379472.

52. Oliver Laughland, Jon Swaine, and Jamiles Lartey, "US police killings headed for 1,100 this year, with black Americans twice as likely to die," *The Guardian* (July 2015). http://www.theguardian.com/us-news/2015/jul/01/us-police-killings-this-year-black-americans.

53. Jeffrey St. Clair, "When Torturers Walk," *Counterpunch* (March 20–22, 2015), http://www.counterpunch.org/2015/03/20/when-torturers-walk/.

54. David A. Fahrenthold, "In the Hunt to Be the 2016 GOP Pick, Top Contenders Agree on One Thing: Guns," *Washington Post*, March 28, 2015, http://www.washingtonpost.com/politics/republican-presidential-hopefuls-sticking-to-their-guns/2015/03/28/b2ef4a1c-d3c4-11e4-8fce-3941fc548f1c_story.html.

55. Rustom Bharacuha, "Around Adohya: Aberrations, Enigmas, and Moments of Violence," *Third Text* (Autumn 1993): 45.

56. Sontag cited in in Carol Becker, "The Art of Testimony," *Sculpture* (March 1997): 28.

57. John R. Bolton, "To Stop Iran's Bomb, Bomb Iran," *New York Times*, March 26, 2015, http://www.nytimes.com/2015/03/26/opinion/to-stop-irans-bomb-bomb-iran.html.

58. Jamie Tarabay, "Obama and Leakers: Who Are the Eight Charged under the Espionage Act?" *Al Jazeera*, December 5, 3013. http://america.aljazeera.com/articles/2013/12/5/obama-and-leakerswhoaretheeightchargedunderespionageact.html.

59. Ariel Dorfman, "Repression by Any Other Name," *Guernica* 26 (February 3, 2014), online: https://www.guernicamag.com/features/repression-by-any-other-name/.

60. Eric Alterman, "Patriot Games," *The Nation*, October 29, 2001, 10.

61. Cited in the National Public Radio/Kaiser Family Foundation/Kennedy School of Government Civil Liberties Poll. Available at http://sandbox.npr.org/programs/specials/poll/civil_liberties/civil_liberties_static_results_3.html.

62. Tom Engelhardt, "Walking Back the American Twenty-First Century," *TomDispatch*, February 17, 2015, http://www.tomdispatch.com/dialogs/print/?id=175957.

63. See Henry A. Giroux, "Celluloid Heroism and Manufactured Stupidity in the Age of Empire," *Counterpunch*, February 12, 2015, http://www.counterpunch.org/2015/02/12/celluloid-heroism-and-manufactured-stupidity-in-the-age-of-empire/.

64. Robert Jay Lifton, "American Apocalypse," *The Nation*, December 22, 2003, 12, 14.

65. Mike Davis, "The Flames of New York," *New Left Review* 12 (November–December 2001): 44.

66. Ibid., 45.

67. Don Hazen, "Fear Dominates Politics, Media and Human Existence in America—And It Is Getting Worse," *Alternet*, March 1, 2015, http://www.alternet.org/fear-america/fear-dominates-politics-media-and-human-existence-america-and-its-getting-worse.

68. Ibid.

69. Franco Bifo Berardi, *Precarious Rhapsody* (New York: Autonomedia, 2009), 52

70. Many valuable sources document this history. Some exemplary texts include: A. J. Langguth, *Hidden Terrors: The Truth about U.S. Police Operations in Latin America* (New York: Pantheon Books, 1979); Gordon Thomas, *Journey into Madness: The True Story of Secret CIA Mind Control and Medical Abuse* (New York: Bantam, 1989); Danner, *Torture and Truth*;

Jennifer K. Harbury, *Truth, Torture, and the American Way: The History and Consequences of U.S. Involvement in Torture* (Boston: Beacon Press, 2005); and Alfred McCoy, *A Question of Torture: CIA Interrogation from the Cold War to the War on Terror* (New York: Metropolitan Books, 2006).

71.   Tom Engelhardt, "My War on Terror: Letter to an Unknown U.S. Patriot," *TomDispatch*, March 1, 2015, http://www.tomdispatch.com/post/175962/tomgram%3A_engelhardt,_the_ten_commandments_for_a_better_american_world/.

72.   See, for instance, Adolph Reed, Jr., "Nothing Left," *Harper's Magazine*, March 2014, 28–36; Stanley Aronowitz, "Democrats in Disarray: This Donkey Can't Save Our Asses," *The Indypendent* 202 (December 16, 2014), https://www.indypendent.org/2014/12/16/democrats-disarray-donkey-can%E2%80%99t-save-our-asses.

1. AMERICA'S ADDICTION TO TORTURE

1.   Adam Goldman and Peyton Craighill, "New Poll Finds Majority of Americans Believe Torture Justified after 9/11 Attacks," *Washington Post*, December 16, 2014, http://www.washingtonpost.com/world/national-security/new-poll-finds-majority-of-americans-believe-torture-justified-after-911-attacks/2014/12/16/f6ee1208-847c-11e4-9534-f79a23c40e6c_story.html.

2.   Lawrence Wittner, "The U.S. Is Number One—But in What?" *AlterNet*, October 13, 2014, http://www.alternet.org/us-number-one-what.

3.   The report can be found at http://www.intelligence.senate.gov/study2014/sscistudy1.pdf.

4.   Cited in Edward S. Herman, "Folks Out There Have a 'Distaste of Western Civilization and Cultural Values,'" Centre for Research on Globalization, September 15, 2001, http://www.globalresearch.ca/articles/HER109A.html.

5.   On the Phoenix Program, see Douglas Valentine, *The Phoenix Program* (Lincoln, NB: iUniverse, 2000).

6.   Carl Boggs supplies an excellent commentary on the historical amnesia in the U.S. media surrounding the legacy of torture promoted by the United States in "Torture: An American Legacy," *CounterPunch.org*, June 17, 2009, http://www.counterpunch.org/boggs06172009.html.

7.   Ibid.

8.   Many valuable sources document this history. Some exemplary texts include: A. J. Langguth, *Hidden Terrors: The Truth about U.S. Police Operations in Latin America* (New York: Pantheon Books, 1979); Gordon Thomas, *Journey into Madness: The True Story of Secret CIA Mind Control and Medical Abuse* (New York: Bantam, 1989); Mark Danner, *Torture and Truth* (New York: New York Review Books, 2004); Jennifer K. Harbury, *Truth, Torture, and the American Way: The History and Consequences of U.S. Involvement in Torture* (Boston: Beacon Press, 2005); Alfred McCoy, *A Question of Torture: CIA Interrogation, from the Cold War to the War on Terror* (New York: Metropolitan Books, 2006); and Darius Rejali, *Torture and Democracy* (Princeton: Princeton University Press, 2007). See also Jane Mayer, *The Dark Side: The Inside Story of How the War on Terror Turned into a War on American Ideals* (New York: Doubleday, 2008); and Phillipe Sands, *Torture Team* (London: Penguin, 2009). On the torture of children, see Michael Haas, *George W. Bush, War Criminal? The Bush Administration's Liability for 269 War Crimes* (Westport, CT: Praeger, 2009). Also, see

Henry A. Giroux, *Hearts of Darkness: Torturing Children in the War on Terror* (Boulder, CO: Paradigm, 2010).

9. Amy Goodman, "From COINTELPRO to Snowden, the FBI Burglars Speak Out after 43 Years of Silence,"Part 2, *Democracy Now!*, January 8, 2014, http://www.democracynow.org/blog/2014/1/8/from_cointelpro_to_snowden_the_fbi.

10. For an excellent source, see Ward Churchill and Jim Vander Wall, *The COINTELPRO Papers: Documents from the FBI's Secret Wars against Dissent in the United States* (Boston: South End Press, 2001). Also see *The People's History of the CIA* website: http://www.thepeopleshistory.net/2013/07/cointelpro-fbis-war-on-us-citizens.html.

11. Chomsky quoted in Goodman, "From COINTELPRO to Snowden."

12. See, for example, Edward E. Baptist, *The Half Has Never Been Told: Slavery and the Making of American Capitalism* (New York: Basic Books, 2014); Angela Y. Davis, *Abolition Democracy: Beyond Empire, Prisons, and Torture* (New York: Seven Stories Press, 2005); and Loic Wacquant, *Punishing the Poor* (Durham, NC: Duke University Press, 2009). This section draws on ideas from my *Hearts of Darkness: Torturing Children in the War on Terror* (Boulder: Paradigm, 2010).

13. Ishmael Reed, "How Henry Louis Gates Got Ordained as the Nation's 'Leading Black Intellectual,'" *Black Agenda Report*, July 27, 2009, http://www.blackagendareport.com/?q=content/how-henry-louis-gates-got-ordained-nations-leading-black-intellectual.

14. Pepe Lozano, "Chicago Torture Probe Draws Worldwide Attention," *Political Affairs Magazine*, July 6, 2006, online: http://www.politicalaffairs.net/article/view/3770/1/196/. See also Susan Saulny, "Ex-Officer Linked to Brutality Is Arrested," *New York Times*, October 22, 2008, http://www.nytimes.com/2008/10/22/us/22chicago.html.

15. Flint Taylor, "Jon Burge, Torturer of Over 100 Black Men, Is Out of Prison after Less than Four Years," *In These Times*, October 2, 2014, http://inthesetimes.com/article/17213/jon_burge_torture_chicago_has_not_paid_for_his_crimes.

16. Lozano, "Chicago Torture Probe."

17. Mayer, *The Dark Side*, 8.

18. Mark Danner, "U.S. Torture: Voices from the Black Sites," *New York Review of Books*, April 9, 2009, 77.

19. Michel Chossudovsky, "The Senate CIA Torture Report. Dick Cheney: 'The Report Is Full of Crap,'" *Global Research*, December 12, 2014, http://www.globalresearch.ca/the-senate-cia-torture-report-dick-cheney-the-report-is-full-of-crap-highlights-executive-summary/5419604.

20. Scott Shane, "Backing C.I.A. Tactics, Cheney Ramps Up Criticism of Senate Torture Report," *New York Times*, December 14, 2014, http://www.nytimes.com/2014/12/15/us/politics/cheney-senate-report-on-torture.html.

21. Some of the ideas in the following sections draw upon my book, *Hearts of Darkness: Torturing Children in the War on Terror.*

22. Frank Rich, "The Banality of Bush White House Evil," *New York Times*, April 26, 2009.

23. The torture memos can be found at the American Civil Liberties Union website: http://www.aclu.org/safefree/general/olc_memos.html.

24. Andrew Sullivan, "The Bigger Picture," *The Daily Dish*, April 17, 2009, http://andrewsullivan.theatlantic.com/the_daily_dish/2009/04/the-bigger-picture.html.

25. Ewen MacAskill, "Obama Releases Bush Torture Memos: Insects, Sleep Deprivation and Waterboarding among Approved Techniques by the Bush Administration," *The Guardian,* April 16, 2009, http://www.guardian.co.uk/world/2009/apr/16/torture-memos-bush-administration.

26. Ibid.

27. Andy Worthington, "Five Terrible Truths about the CIA Torture Memos," *Future of Freedom Foundation,* April 22, 2009, http://www.commondreams.org/view/2009/04/22-6.

28. Editorial, "The Torturers' Manifesto," *New York Times,* April 19, 2009.

29. Ibid.

30. Bybee cited in Neil A. Lewis, "Official Defends Signing Interrogation Memos," *New York Times,* April 29, 2009.

31. Thomas C. Hilde, "Introduction," in *On Torture,* ed. Thomas C. Hilde (Baltimore: Johns Hopkins University Press, 2008), 141.

32. Mark Mazzetti, "Panel Faults CIA over Brutality and Deceit in Terrorism Interrogations," *New York Times,* December 9, 2014, http://www.nytimes.com/2014/12/10/world/senate-intelligence-committee-cia-torture-report.html.

33. Elias Isquith, "'I don't care what we did': What Nicolle Wallace's Rant Reveals about America's Torture Problem," *Salon,* December 9, 2012, http://www.salon.com/2014/12/09/i_dont_care_what_we_did_what_nicolle_wallaces_rant_reveals_about_americas_torture_problem/.

34. See the repudiations of the right-wing arguments by Rebecca Gordon, "American Torture – Past, Present, and… Future? Beyond the Senate Torture Report," *TomDispatch.com,* December 14, 2014, http://www.tomdispatch.com/post/175934/tomgram%3A_rebecca_gordon%2C_the_torture_wars/#more.

35. Hilde, "Introduction," in *On Torture,* 1.

36. Glenn Greenwald, "U.S. TV Provides Ample Platform for American Torturers, but None to Their Victims," *The Intercept,* December 16, 2014, https://firstlook.org/theintercept/2014/12/16/u-s-tv-media-gives-ample-platform-american-torturers-victims/.

37. Henry A. Giroux, *The Violence of Organized Forgetting: Thinking beyond America's Disimagination Machine* (San Francisco: City Lights Books, 2015).

38. On the Phoenix Program, see Douglas Valentine, *The Phoenix Program,* and Carl Boggs, "Torture: An American Legacy."

39. See, for one example of this type of analysis, Chauncey DeVega, "The Culture of Cruelty Is International: From Lynchings to Eric Garner and the CIA Torture Report," *We Are Respectable Negroes,* December 10, 2014, http://www.chaunceydevega.com/2014/12/the-culture-of-cruelty-is-international.html.

40. Robert Jay Lifton, *Death in Life: Survivors of Hiroshima* (Chapel Hill: University of North Carolina Press, 1987), 479.

41. Cited in Spencer Ackerman, "West Point Professor Calls on US Military to Target Legal Critics of War on Terror," *The Guardian* (August 29, 2015). http://www.theguardian.com/us-news/2015/aug/29/west-point-professor-target-legal-critics-war-on-terror. The paper that published this vile piece of terrorism has since disavowed the publication.

2. TERRORIZING THE SELF

1. Immanuel Kant, Nicholas Walker (editor), James Creed Meredith (translator), *Critique of Judgement*, rev. ed. (New York: Oxford University Press, 2009), 123.

2. Ariel Dorfman, "Repression by Any Other Name," *Guernica*, February 3, 2014, http://www.guernicamag.com/features/repression-by-any-other-name/.

3. Zygmunt Bauman and David Lyon, *Liquid Surveillance: A Conversation* (Cambridge, UK: Polity Press, 2013), 28.

4. Personal correspondence with my colleague David L. Clark, February 10, 2015.

5. Jenna Wortham, "Self-Portraits and Social Media: The Rise of the 'Selfie'," *BBC News Magazine*, June 6, 2013, http://www.bbc.com/news/magazine-22511650.

6. Anita Biressi and Heather Nunn, "Selfishness in Austerity Times," *Soundings* 56 (Spring 2014): 54–66,http://muse.jhu.edu/journals/soundings_a_journal_of_politics_and_culture/v056/56.biressi.pdf.

7. Patricia Reaney, "Nip, Tuck, Click: Demand for U.S. Plastic Surgery Rises in Selfie Era," *Reuters*, November 29, 2014, http://www.reuters.com/article/2014/11/29/life-selfies-surgery-idUSL1N0SW1FI20141129/.

8. Ibid.

9. Peter Fonagy, Ethel Person, and Joseph Sandler, eds.. *Freud's "On Narcissism: An Introduction"* ((New Haven: Yale University Press, 1991); and Christopher Lasch, *The Culture of Narcissism: American Life in an Age of Diminishing Expectations* (New York: W. W. Norton, 1991).

10. Lynn Stuart Parramore, "Can We Escape Narcissism in America? 5 Possible Antidotes," *Alternet.org,* December 30, 2014, http://www.alternet.org/culture/can-we-escape-narcissism-america-5-possible-antidotes.

11. Reaney, "Nip, Tuck, Click."

12. Brad Evans and Henry A. Giroux, *Disposable Futures* (San Francisco: City Lights Books, 2015).

13. Jonathan Crary, *24/7: Late Capitalism and the Ends of Sleep* (Brooklyn, NY: Verso Press, 2013), 5.

14. Ibid., 17.

15. D.K.A., "A *Different* Selfie Article: Decolonizing Representations of Women of Color!," *Browntourage*, March 17, 2015, http://www.browntourage.com/magazine/look-at-me/.

16. The kind of babble defending selfies without any critical commentary can be found in Wortham, "Self-Portraits and Social Media."

17. Rachel Simmons, "Selfies Are Good for Girls," *Slate,* November 20, 2013, http://www.slate.com/articles/double_x/doublex/2013/11/selfies_on_instagram_and_facebook_are_tiny_bursts_of_girl_pride.html.

18. Erin Gloria Ryan, "Selfies Aren't Empowering, They're a Cry for Help," *Jezebel,* November 21, 2013, http://jezebel.com/selfies-arent-empowering-theyre-a-cry-for-help-1468965365.

19. Michelle K. Wolf, "Disability Selfies," *Jewish Journal*, August 4, 2014, http://www.jewishjournal.com/lifestyle/article/disability_selfies.

20. Ibid.

21. Kate Murphy, "We Want Privacy but Can't Stop Sharing," *New York Times*, October 4, 2014.

22. Ibid.

23. Eli Wolfe, "How Social Media Is Shaping the Israeli-Palestinian Conflict," *Kicker*, July 24, 2014, http://gokicker.com/2014/07/24/heres-social-media-israeli-palestinian-conflict/. See also https://www.facebook.com/selfiesforpalestine.

24. Mark Fisher, *Capitalist Realism: Is There No Alternative?* (Winchester, UK: Zero Books, 2009), 74.

25. Quentin Skinner and Richard Marshall "Liberty, Liberalism and Surveillance: A Historic Overview," *Open Democracy*, July 26, 2013, http://www.opendemocracy.net/ourkingdom/quentin-skinner-richard-marshall/liberty-liberalism-and-surveillance-historic-overview.

26. Henry A. Giroux, "Totalitarian Paranoia in the Post-Orwellian Surveillance State," *Truthout*, February 10, 2015, http://truth-out.org/opinion/item/21656-totalitarian-paranoia-in-the-post-orwellian-surveillance-state.

27. Michael Hardt and Antonio Negri, *Declaration* (New York: Argo Navis, 2012), 23.

28. Tom Engelhardt, "Tomgram: Engelhardt, A Surveillance State Scorecard," *Tom Dispatch. com*, November 12, 2013, http://www.tomdispatch.com/blog/175771/.

29. I take up many of these issues in Henry A. Giroux, *The Violence of Organized Forgetting* (San Francisco: City Lights Publishing, 2014); *The Twilight of the Social* (Boulder, CO: Paradigm Press, 2012), and *Zombie Politics and Culture in the Age of Casino Capitalism* (New York: Peter Lang, 2011).

30. See for instance the following sites: http://www.browntourage.com/magazine/look-at-me/; http://www.dailydot.com/lifestyle/transgender-community-needs-selfies/; http://fusion.net/story/4844/transgender-selfies-are-acts-of-revolutionary-self-love/ and http://www.vivalafeminista.com/2013/12/365feministselfie-are-you-in.html.

31. Alicia Eler, "The Feminist Politics of #Selfies," *Hyperallergic.com*, November 25, 2013, http://hyperallergic.com/95150/the-radical-politics-of-selfies/.

32. D.K.A, "A *Different* Selfie Article."

33. Hannah Arendt, "Ideology and Terror: A Novel Form of Government," in *The Origins of Totalitarianism* (New York: Houghton Mifflin Harcourt, 2001), 475.

34. Alex Honneth, *Pathologies of Reason* (New York: Columbia University Press, 2009), 188.

35. Skinner and Marshall, "Liberty, Liberalism and Surveillance."

3. DEATH-DEALING POLITICS IN THE AGE OF EXTREME VIOLENCE

1. *Research Bulletin: A New Majority Low Income Students Now a Majority in the Nation's Public Schools* (Washington, D.C.. Southern Education Foundation, January 2015, http://www.southerneducation.org/getattachment/4ac62e27-5260-47a5-9d02-14896ec3a531/A-New-Majority-2015-Update-Low-Income-Students-Now.aspx.

2. Andre Damon, "More than Half of U.S. Public School Students Living in Poverty," *Global Research*, January 19, 2015, http://www.globalresearch.ca/more-than-half-of-us-public-school-students-living-in-poverty/5425563.

3. Jana Kasperkevic, "More than Half of U.S. Public School Students Live in Poverty, Report Finds," *The Guardian*, January 17, 2015, http://www.theguardian.com/money/us-money-blog/2015/jan/17/public-school-students-poverty-report.

4. Peter Wagner and Leah Sakala, "Mass Incarceration: The Whole Pie," *Prison Policy Initiative*, March 12, 2014, http://www.prisonpolicy.org/reports/pie.html; Campaign for Youth Justice, "Key Facts: Youth in the Justice System," April 2012, http://www.campaignforyouthjustice.org/documents/KeyYouthCrimeFacts.pdf.

5. I take up a number of these issues in Henry A. Giroux, *The Violence of Organized Forgetting* (San Francisco: City Lights Books, 2015); Henry A. Giroux, *Dangerous Thinking in the Age of the New Authoritarianism* (Boulder, CO: Paradigm, 2015); Henry A. Giroux, *America's Education Deficit and the War on Youth* (New York: Monthly Review Press, 2013).

6. Paul Buchheit, "The Reality Tale of Two Education Systems," *AlterNet*, January 11, 2015, http://www.alternet.org/education/reality-tale-two-education-systems-one-poor-and-one-rest.

7. Cited in William Robinson, "In the Wake of Ayotzinapa, Adonde va Mexico?" *Truthout* (December 8, 2014, http://truth-out.org/opinion/item/27862-in-the-wake-of-ayotzinapa-adonde-va-mexico.

8. Amy Goodman, 'Noam Chomsky: Austerity Is Just Class War," *Alternet* (July 2, 2015). http://www.alternet.org/economy/noam-chomsky-austerity-just-class-war

9. Guy Standing, *The Precariat: The New Dangerous Class* (London: Bloomsbury Academic, 2011), 179.

10. Allan Pyke, "To Make Up for His Massive Tax Cuts, Kansas Governor Proposes Cutting Schools," *Think Progress*, January 22, 2015, http://thinkprogress.org/economy/2015/01/22/3614508/kansas-short-term-thinking-budget/.

11. Chris Hedges, "We Are All Greeks Now," *Truthdig* (July 12, 2015). http://www.truthdig.com/report/item/we_are_all_greeks_now_20150712

12. Paul Krugman, "Hating Good Government," *New York Times*, January 18, 2015, http://www.nytimes.com/2015/01/19/opinion/paul-krugman-hating-good-government.html.

13. Susan Buck-Morss, "Democracy: An Unfinished Project," *boundary 2* 41/2 (2014): 87.

14. David Theo Goldberg, *Are We All Postracial Yet?* (London: Polity, 2015).

15. Keith Ellison, "The Link Between Police Tactics and Economic Conditions Cannot Be Ignored," *The Guardian*, June 8, 2015, http://www.theguardian.com/commentisfree/2015/jun/08/police-tactics-economic-conditions-republican-policies.

16. Ibid.

17. David Graeber, "Ferguson and the Criminalization of American Life," *Gawker*, March 19, 2015, http://gawker.com/ferguson-and-the-criminalization-of-american-life-1692392051.

18. Michael Martinez, Alexandra Meeks, and Ed Lavandera, "Policing for Profit: How Ferguson's Fines Violated Rights of African-Americans," *CNN.com*, March 6, 2015, http://www.cnn.com/2015/03/06/us/ferguson-missouri-racism-tickets-fines/.

19. Ibid.

20. See Hannah Arendt, *Hannah Arendt: The Last Interview and Other Conversations* (Brooklyn, NY: Melville House Publishing, 2013), 33–34.

21. There are many books analyzing the hijacking of America by the financial elite; see, for example, Charles H. Ferguson, *Predator Nation: Corporate Criminals, Political Corruption, and the Hijacking of America* (New York: Crown-Business, 2013).

22. Ellison, "The Link Between Police Tactics."

23. Stephen Lendman, "Police State France, New Anti-Terrorism Legislation, Threat to Civil Liberties," *Global Research*, January 10, 2015, http://www.globalresearch.ca/police-state-france-new-anti-terrorism-legislation-threat-to-civil-liberties/5423798.

24. Ibid.

25. Ibid.

26. Ibid.

27. Editorial, "Bill C-24 Is Wrong: There Is Only One Kind of Canadian Citizen," *Globe and Mail*, June 30, 2014, http://www.theglobeandmail.com/globe-debate/editorials/bill-c-24-is-wrong-there-is-only-one-kind-of-canadian-citizen/article19400982/.

28. See Richard Sennett's lecture on "Disposable Life" in the Histories of Violence Project, available at http://historiesofviolence.com/specialseries/disposable-life/.

29. John W. Whitehead, "Zero Tolerance Schools Discipline Without Wiggle Room," *Huffington Post* (August 5, 2015). Online at: http://www.huffingtonpost.com/john-w-whitehead/zero-tolerance-policies-schools_b_819594.html. See also John Whitehead, *A Government of Wolves: The Emerging American Police State* (New York: Select Books, 2013); John W. Whitehead, "Arrested Development: The Criminalization of America's Schoolchildren." *NJToday.net*, May 7, 2012, http://njtoday.net/2012/05/07/arrested-development-the-criminalization-of-americas-schoolchildren/.

30. Alex Chastain, "More American Cities Are Punishing the Homeless for Being Homeless," *Ring of Fire*, November 18, 2014, http://www.ringoffireradio.com/2014/11/more-american-cities-are-punishing-the-homeless-for-being-homeless/.

31. Mark Fisher, *Capitalist Realism* (London: Zero Books, 2009), 74.

32. Terry Eagleton, "Reappraisals: What is the worth of social democracy?" *Harper's Magazine*, (October 2010), p. 78.

33. Pierre Bourdieu, *Acts of Resistance* (New York: Free Press, 1998), 11.

34. Arun Gupta, "How the Democrats Became the Party of Neoliberals," *CounterPunch*, November 3, 2014, http://www.counterpunch.org/2014/11/03/how-the-democrats-became-the-party-of-neoliberalism/.

35. Editors, "15 Ways Bill Clinton's White House Failed America and the World," *AlterNet*, June 22, 2015, http://www.alternet.org/election-2016/15-ways-bill-clintons-white-house-failed-america-and-world.

36. Joseph Kishore, "The Democratic Party Implosion," *World Socialist Web Site*, November 6, 2014, https://www.wsws.org/en/articles/2014/11/06/pers-n06.html. It is worth noting that what the WSWS thinks are class issues and what the electorate does might be two different things.

37. Paul Bucheit, "The Carnage of Capitalism" *CommonDreams.org*, August 18, 2014, http://www.commondreams.org/views/2014/08/18/carnage-capitalism.

38. Jacques Derrida, interview with Jean Birnbaum, in *Learning to Live Finally: The Last Interview* (Brooklyn, NY: Melville House Publishing, 2007), 12–13.

4. CLASS WARFARE AND THE ADVANCE OF AUSTERITY POLICIES UNDER THE NEW AUTHORITARIANISM

1. See, for instance, Alice Ollstein, "Scott Walker Wants to Run the Country: Here Is How He Ran Wisconsin," *Thinkprogress.org*, July 13, 2014, http://thinkprogress.org/election/2015/07/13/3614885/scott-walker-wants-run-country-ran-wisconsin/.

2. Elisabetta Povoledo and Doreen Carvajal, "Increasingly in Europe, Suicides 'by Economic Crisis,'" *New York Times*, April 14, 2012.

3. Ibid.

4. Nikolaos Antonakakis and Alan Collins, "The Impact of Fiscal Austerity on Suicide: On the Empirics of a Modern Greek Tragedy," *Social Science & Medicine* 112 (July 2014): 39–50.

5. Former finance minister Yannis Varoufakis said just this to the troika, and this was one of the things the troika found so unpalatable that they began to hint they could not deal with him.

6. Joerg Bibow, "Time to End Europe's Disgrace of Holding Greek People Hostage," *The Conversation*, June 10, 2015, http://theconversation.com/time-to-end-europes-disgrace-of-holding-greek-people-hostage-42939.

7. Zygmunt Bauman, "Capitalism Has Learned to Create Host Organisms," *The Guardian*, October 18, 2011, http://www.guardian.co.uk/commentisfree/2011/oct/18/capitalism-parasite-hosts. On matters of disposability, see Zygmunt Bauman, *Wasted Lives* (London: Polity Press, 2004).

8. One of the best commentaries on inequality in the midst of a slew of high-profile books on the subject can be found in Michael Yates, "The Great Inequality," *Monthly Review* 63/10 (March 2012), http://monthlyreview.org/2012/03/01/the-great-inequality.

9. Suzanne Mettler, *Degrees of Inequality: How the Politics of Higher Education Sabotaged the American Dream* (New York: Basic Books, 2014).

10. On the issue of inequality, see especially Yates, *The Great Inequality* (Boulder, CO: Paradigm Publishers, 2016).

11. See, for instance, Henry A. Giroux, *The Violence of Organized Forgetting* (San Francisco: City Lights Books, 2014).

12. Richard D. Wolff, "Austerity: Why and for Whom?," *In These Times*, July 15, 2010, http://www.inthesetimes.com/article/6232/austerity_why_and_for_whom/.

13. Bauman, "Capitalism Has Learned."

14. The most famous proponent of creative destruction is Joseph A. Schumpeter, *Capitalism, Socialism, and Democracy*, 3rd ed. (New York: Harper, 2008). See also Kenneth J. Saltman, *Capitalizing on Disaster: Taking and Breaking Public Schools* (Boulder, CO: Paradigm Publishers, 2007); and Naomi Klein, *The Shock Doctrine: The Rise of Disaster Capitalism* (New York: Picador, 2008).

15. See, for example, what is happening in Greece, the epicenter of austerity measures. C. J. Polychroniou, "The Greek 'Success Story' of a Crushing Economy and a Failed State," *Truthout*, January 9, 2014, http://truth-out.org/news/item/21265-the-greek-success-story-of-a-crushing-economy-and-a-failed-state.

16. Suzanne Daley, "Greek Patience with Austerity Nears Its Limit," *New York Times*, December 29, 2014, http://www.nytimes.com/2014/12/30/world/europe/greek-patience-with-austerity-nears-its-limit-.html.

17. Thomas Piketty, Jeffrey Sachs, Heiner Flassbeck, Dani Rodrik, and Simon Wren-Lewis "Austerity Has Failed: An Open Letter from Thomas Piketty to Angela Merkel," *The Nation* (July 7, 2015). http://www.thenation.com/article/austerity-has-failed-an-open-letter-from-thomas-piketty-to-angela-merkel/.

18. C. J. Polychroniou, "Greek Referendum Is a Machiavellian Plot," *Al Jazeera*, June 28, 2015,

http://www.aljazeera.com/indepth/opinion/2015/06/greek-referendum-machiavel-lian-plot-tsipras-150628060443154.html.

19. C. J. Polychroniou, "Greek Austerity Is Dead, Long Live Austerity," *Al Jazeera*, July 12, 2015, http://www.aljazeera.com/indepth/opinion/2015/07/greek-austerity-dead-long-live-austerity-150712083735451.html; Henning Meyer, "What Are the Consequences of the Greek Deal?," *Social Europe*, July 13, 2015, http://www.socialeurope.eu/2015/07/what-are-the-consequences-of-the-greek-deal/.

20. Jennifer M. Silva, *Coming Up Short: Working Class Adulthood in an Age of Uncertainty* (New York: Oxford University Press, 2013), 25.

21. C. J. Polychroniou, "The Resurgence of Authoritarianism in Economically Beleaguered Greece: The Shaping of a Proto-Fascist State," *Truthout*, November 26, 2013, http://truth-out.org/news/item/20167-the-resurgence-of-authoritarianism-in-economi-cally-beleaguered-greece-and-the-shaping-of-a-neoliberal-proto-fascist-state. See also Ellen Brown, "Greece Takes on the Vampire Squid," *CounterPunch* January 7, 2015, http://www.counterpunch.org/2015/01/07/greece-takes-on-the-vampire-squid/.

22. Daley, "Greek Patience with Austerity Nears Its Limit."

23. Anita Biressi and Heather Nunn, "Selfishness in Austerity Times," *Soundings* 56 (Spring 2014): 56.

24. Michelle Chen, "Jeb Bush Wants You to Work Longer Hours," *The Nation*, July 10, 2015, http://www.thenation.com/article/jeb-bush-wants-you-to-work-longer-hours/.

25. Ibid.

26. Paul Krugman, "Twin Peaks Planet," *New York Times*, January 1, 2015, http://www.nytimes.com/2015/01/02/opinion/paul-krugman-twin-peaks-planet.html.

27. John Stauber, "The Progressive Movement Is a PR Front for Rich Democracies," *CounterPunch*, March 15–17, 2013, http://www.counterpunch.org/2013/03/15/the-progressive-movement-is-a-pr-front-for-rich-democrats/.

28. Michael Hudson, "The Coming War on Pensions," *CounterPunch*, January 5, 2015, http://www.counterpunch.org/2015/01/05/the-coming-war-on-pensions/.

5. RACISM, VIOLENCE, AND MILITARIZED TERROR IN THE AGE OF DISPOSABILITY

1. Hannah Arendt, "Ideology and Terror: A Novel Form of Government," *The Origins of Totalitarianism* (New York: Houghton Mifflin Harcourt, 2001), 464.

2. I take up this issue in great detail in Henry A. Giroux, *Dangerous Thinking in the Age of the New Authoritarianism* (Boulder, CO: Paradigm, 2015).

3. Nicholas Kristof, "When Whites Just Don't Get It, Part 5," *New York Times*, November 29, 2014, http://www.nytimes.com/2014/11/30/opinion/sunday/nicholas-kristof-when-whites-just-dont-get-it-part-5.html. Two important books on racism and mass incarcera-tion: Michelle Alexander, *The New Jim Crow: Mass Incarceration in the Age of Colorblindness* (New York: New Press, 2012); and Maya Schenwar, *Locked Down, Locked Out: Why Prison Doesn't Work and How We Can Do Better* (Oakland, CA: Berrett-Koehler Publishers, 2014).

4. Jon Ronson, *The Psychopath Test: A Journey through the Madness Industry* (New York: Riv-erhead Books, 2012); Desh Kapoor, "Are CEOs and Entrepreneurs Psychopaths? Mul-tiple Studies Say 'Yes,'" *Drishtikone*, October 1, 2013, http://www.patheos.com/blogs/drishtikone/2013/10/are-ceos-and-entrepreneurs-psychopaths-multiple-studies-say-yes.

5.   Personal correspondence with David L. Clark on September 1, 2015.

6.   Arif Dirlik, personal correspondence, December 5, 2014.

7.   Margaret Talbot, "Why Cameras on Police Officers Won't Save Us," *The New Yorker,* December 4, 2014, http://www.newyorker.com/news/daily-comment/camera-police-officers-wont-save-us.

8.   Lauren C. Regan, "The Secret Darkness of Grand Juries," *CounterPunch,* November 28-30, 2014, http://www.counterpunch.org/2014/11/28/the-secret-darkness-of-grand-juries/print; Ginia Bellafante, "Police Violence Seems to Result in No Punishment," *New York Times,* December 4, 2014, http://www.nytimes.com/2014/12/07/nyregion/police-violence-seems-to-result-in-no-punishment.html.

9.   Mychal Denzel Smith, "The System That Failed Eric Garner and Michael Brown Cannot Be Reformed," *The Nation,* December 3, 2014,http://www.thenation.com/blog/191929/system-failed-eric-garner-and-michael-brown-cannot-be-reformed.

10. Jelani Cobb, "No Such Thing as Racial Profiling," *The New Yorker,* December 4, 2014, http://www.newyorker.com/news/news-desk/eric-garner-racial-profiling.

11. Chase Madar, "Why It's Impossible to Indict a Cop," *The Nation* (November 25, 2014). http://www.thenation.com/article/why-its-impossible-indict-cop/.

12. Elijah Anderson, "What Caused the Ferguson Riot Exists in So Many Other Cities Too," *Washington Post,* December 3, 2014, http://www.washingtonpost.com/posteverything/wp/2014/08/13/what-caused-the-ferguson-riot-exists-in-so-many-other-cities-too/.

13. Eba Hamid and Benjamin Mueller, "Fatal Police Encounters in New York City," *New York Times,* December 3, 2014, http://www.nytimes.com/interactive/2014/nyregion/fatal-police-encounters-in-new-york-city.html.

14. David Theo Goldberg, "Revelations of 'Postracial Ferguson,' " *Truthout,* December 3, 2014, http://www.truth-out.org/news/item/27773-revelations-of-postracial-ferguson.

15. Chase Madar, "Why It's Impossible to Indict a Cop," *The Nation,* December 4, 2014. https://www.thenation.com/article/190937/why-its-impossible-indict-cop.

16. Editors, "Donald Trump's Presidential Announcement Speech," *Time,* June 16, 2015, http://time.com/3923128/donald-trump-announcement-speech/.

17. John Feffer, "Racial Apartheid in America," *CounterPunch,* December 4, 2014, http://www.counterpunch.org/2014/12/04/racial-apartheid-in-america/.

18. Ta-Nehisi Coates, "Take Down the Confederate Flag—Now," *The Atlantic,* June 18, 2015, http://www.theatlantic.com/politics/archive/2015/06/take-down-the-confederate-flag-now/396290/.

19. Frank Rich, "The Confederate-Flag Debate Spotlights the GOP's Moral Cowardice," *New York Times,* June 24, 2015, http://nymag.com/daily/intelligencer/2015/06/confederate-flag-debate-shows-gops-cowardice.html.

20. Ibid.

21. On domestic terrorism, see the important work of Ruth Gilmore, *Golden Gulag: Prisons, Surplus, Crisis, and Opposition in Globalizing California* (Oakland: University of California Press, 2009).

22. Jason Stanley, "The War on Thugs," *Chronicle of Higher Education,* June 10, 2015, http://chronicle.com/article/The-War-on-Thugs/230787.

23. Jennifer Gonnerman, "Kalief Browder, 1993-2015," *The New Yorker,* June 7, 2015, http://www.newyorker.com/news/news-desk/kalief-browder-1993-2015.

24.   Robin D. G. Kelley, "Why We Won't Wait," *Counter Punch*, November 25, 2014, http://www.counterpunch.org/2014/11/25/75039/.

25.   Arianna Skibell, "'We are fighting for our lives': The Little-Known Youth Movement Rising Against Police Brutality," *Salon*, February 25, 2015, http://www.salon.com/2015/02/25/we_are_fighting_for_our_lives; Danielle Allen and Cathy Cohen, "The New Civil rights Movement Doesn't Need an MLK," *Washington Post*, April 10, 2015, http://www.washingtonpost.com/opinions/the-new-civil-rights-movement/2015/04/10/e43d2caa-d8bb-11e4-ba28-f2a685dc7f89_story.html.

26.   Amy Goodman, "Michelle Alexander: Ferguson Shows Why Criminal Justice System of 'Racial Control' Should be Undone," *Democracy Now!*, March 4, 2015, http://www.democracynow.org/2015/3/4/michelle_alexander_ferguson_shows_why_criminal.

27.   Jody Sokolower, "Schools and the New Jim Crow: An Interview with Michelle Alexander," *Truthout*, June 4, 2013,http://www.truth-out.org/news/item/16756-schools-and-the-new-jim-crow-an-interview-with-michelle-alexander.

28.   Robin D. G. Kelley, "Why We Won't Wait," *CounterPunch*, November 25, 2014, http://www.counterpunch.org/2014/11/25/75039/.

6. THE FIRE THIS TIME: BLACK YOUTH AND THE SPECTACLE OF POST-RACIAL VIOLENCE

1.   James Baldwin, talk delivered October 16, 1963, as "The Negro Child—His Self-Image" at Stanford University; originally published in *The Saturday Review* (December 21, 1963), and reprinted in *The Price of the Ticket, Collected Non-Fiction 1948-1985* (New York: St. Martin's Press, 1985), 325–32.

2.   For a recent list of such killings, see Jamal Simmons, "Why Hope Has Turned to Fury in America," *Telegraph*, May 4, 2015, http://www.telegraph.co.uk/news/worldnews/northamerica/11580619/Why-hope-has-turned-to-fury-in-America.html.

3.   Isabel Wilkerson, "Mike Brown's Shooting and Jim Crow Lynchings Have Too Much in Common: It's Time for America to Own Up," *The Guardian*, August 24, 2014, http://www.theguardian.com/commentisfree/2014/aug/25/mike-brown-shooting-jim-crow-lynchings-in-common.

4.   Frank Rich, "The Right Is Race-Baiting on Baltimore: Hillary Clinton Needs to Take a Stand," *New York*, April 29, 2015, http://nymag.com/daily/intelligencer/2015/04/why-the-right-is-race-baiting-on-baltimore.html.

5.   Craig Harrington, "The Worst Conservative Media Reactions to the Baltimore Riots," *Media Matters*, April 28, 2015, http://mediamatters.org/research/2015/04/28/the-worst-conservative-media-reactions-to-the-b/203446.

6.   Alex Kane, "Miss a Traffic Ticket, Go to Jail? The Return of Debtor Prison (Hard Times, USA)," *Alternet*, February 3, 2013, http://www.alternet.org/miss-traffic-ticket-go-jail-return-debtor-prison-hard-times-usa.

7.   For a recent commentary on the history, Nicholas Powers, "Killing the Future: The Theft of Black Life," *Truthout*, April 29, 2015, http://www.truth-out.org/news/item/30489-killing-the-future-the-theft-of-black-life.

8.   Lauren Gambino, "Family of Black Man Fatally Shot by Police in Ohio Walmart Files Lawsuit," *The Guardian*, December 16, 2014, http://www.theguardian.com/us-news/2014/dec/16/ohio-walmart-police-shooting-lawsuit-crawford.

9. Ibid.

10. Chase Madar, "Why It's Impossible to Indict a Cop," *The Nation*, December 4, 2014, https://www.thenation.com/article/190937/why-its-impossible-indict-cop.

11. Amy Goodman, "The American Dream: Living to 18," *Truthdig*, May 6, 2015, ttp://www.truthdig.com/report/print/the_american_dream_living_to_18_20150506.

12. Cited in Chris Hedges, "Tariq Ali: The Time Is Right for a Palace Revolution," *Truthdig*, March 1, 2015, http://www.truthdig.com/report/item/tariq_ali_the_time_is_right_for_a_palace_revolution_20150301.

13. Valerie Harper, "Challenging a 'Disposable Future,' Looking to a Politics of Possibility—Interview with Brad Evans and Henry A. Giroux," *Truthout*, May 10, 2015, http://www.truth-out.org/progressivepicks/item/30594-challenging-a-disposable-future-looking-to-a-politics-of-possibility.

14. See, for example, Maya Schenwar, *Locked Down, Locked Out* (Oakland: Berrett-Koehler, 2014); Michelle Alexander, *The New Jim Crow: Mass Incarceration in the Age of Colorblindness* (New York: New Press, 2012); and Heidi Boghosian, *Spying on Democracy: Government Surveillance, Corporate Power and Public Resistance* (San Francisco: City Lights, 2013).

15. Hanqing Chen, "The Best Reporting on Federal Push to Militarize Local Police," *Truth Dig*, August 20, 2014, http://www.truthdig.com/report/item/the_best_reporting_on_federal_push_to_militarize_local_police_20140820.

16. On the concept of the culture of war, see John Hinkson, "War Culture," *Arena Magazine* 135 (April–May 2015): 2–3.

17. Chen, "The Best Reporting."

18. Ibid.

19. Angela Y. Davis, *The Meaning of Freedom* (San Francisco: City Lights Books, 2012).

20. Chris Hedges, "Rise of the New Black Radicals," *Truthdig*, April 26, 2015, http://www.truthdig.com/report/item/rise_of_the_new_black_radicals_20150426.

21. On this issue, see, for instance, the always insightful Robin D. G. Kelley, "Why We Won't Wait," *Counterpunch*, November 25, 2014, http://www.counterpunch.org/2014/11/25/75039/.

22. Andrew Kolin, cited in Jason Leopold, "Occupy the Police State," *Truthout*, December 8, 2011, http://www.truth-out.org/occupy-police-state/1323354633. The theme of the growing police state is developed extensively in Andrew Kolin, *State Power and Democracy: Before and during the Presidency of George W. Bush* (New York: Palgrave Macmillan, 2012).

23. ACLU, *War Comes Home: The Excessive Militarization of American Policing* (New York: ACLU, 2014), https://www.aclu.org/sites/default/files/assets/jus14-warcomeshome-report-web-rel1.pdf.

24. Radley Balko, "New ACLU Report Takes a Snapshot of Police Militarization in the United States," *Washington Post*, June 24, 2014, http://www.washingtonpost.com/news/the-watch/wp/2014/06/24/new-aclu-report-takes-a-snapshot-of-police-militarization-in-the-united-states/.

25. Stephanie Burnett, "SWAT Teams Treat U.S. Neighborhoods 'Like a War Zone,'" *Time*, June 24, 2014, http://time.com/2916554/aclu-police-militarized-report-swat-war-comes-home/.

26. Radley Balko, "New ACLU Report Takes a Snapshot of Police Militarization in the United States," *Washington Post*, June 24, 2014, http://www.washingtonpost.com/news/

the-watch/wp/2014/06/24/new-aclu-report-takes-a-snapshot-of-police-militarization-in-the-united-states/.

27. John Whitehead, "Arrested Development: The Criminalization of America's Schoolchildren," *NJToday.net*, May 7, 2012, http://njtoday.net/2012/05/07/arrested-development-the-criminalization-of-americas-schoolchildren/. For an extended development of this argument, see the excellent John W. Whitehead, *A Government of Wolves: The Emerging American Police State* (New York: SelectBooks, 2013). Also see Kenneth J. Saltman and David A. Gabbard, *Education as Enforcement: The Militarization and Corporatization of Schools*, 2nd ed. (New York: Routledge, 2010).

28. See Henry A. Giroux, *University in Chains: Challenging the Military-Industrial-Academic Complex* (Boulder, CO: Paradigm Publishers, 2007).

29. See Paul Buchheit, "The Numbers Are Staggering: U.S. Is 'World Leader' in Child Poverty," *Alternet*, April 13, 2015, http://www.alternet.org/economy/numbers-are-staggering-us-world-leader-child-poverty.

30. Ibid.

31. Alex Honneth, *Pathologies of Reason* (New York: Columbia University Press, 2009), 188.

32. See, for instance, Jonathan Simon, *Governing through Crime: How the War on Crime Transformed American Democracy and Created a Culture of Fear* (New York: Oxford University Press, 2007). Also see Michelle Alexander, *The New Jim Crow: Mass Incarceration in the Age of Colorblindness* (New York: New Press, 2012), and Maya Schenwar, *Locked Down, Locked Out: Why Prison Doesn't Work and How We Can Do Better* (Oakland, CA: Berrett-Koehler Publishers, 2014).

33. Dave Manoucheri, "5-Year-Old Handcuffed, Charged with Battery on Officer," KCRA, November 23, 2011, http://www.kcra.com/news/29847063/detail.html.

34. Kay Steiger, "Teen Kept in Solitary Confinement for 143 Days before Even Facing Trial," *Think Progress*, March 28, 2015, http://thinkprogress.org/justice/2015/03/28/3640234/teen-kept-solitary-confinement-143-days-even-facing-trial/.

35. Ibid.

36. Erica Goode, "Many in U.S. Are Arrested by Age 23, Study Finds," *New York Times*, December 19, 2011.

37. Michelle Alexander, "Michelle Alexander, The Age of Obama as a Racial Nightmare," *TomDispatch*, March 25, 2012, http://www.tomdispatch.com/post/175520/best_of_tomdispatch%3A_michelle_alexander,_the_age_of_obama_as_a_racial_nightmare.

38. Sonali Kolhatkar, "A Reflection of Our Barbarity: Jailing Immigrant Mothers and Babies," *Truthdig*, April 23, 2015, http://www.truthdig.com/report/item/a_reflection_of_our_barbarity_20150423.

39. Karen Dolan with Jodi L. Carr, *The Poor Get Prison: The Alarming Spread of the Criminalization of Poverty* (New York: Institute for Policy Studies, 2015), http://www.ips-dc.org/wp-content/uploads/2015/03/IPS-The-Poor-Get-Prison-Final.pdf.

40. Maya Schenwar, "Too Many People in Jail? Abolish Bail," *New York Times*, May 18, 2015, http://www.nytimes.com/2015/05/09/opinion/too-many-people-in-jail-abolish-bail.html.

41. Dolan with Carr, *The Poor Get Prison*.

42. Allie Gross, "In Georgia, a Traffic Ticket Can Land You in the Slammer," *Mother Jones*,

February 26, 2015, http://www.motherjones.com/politics/2015/02/georgia-probation-misdemeanor-poor-jail.

43. Dolan with Carr, *The Poor Get Prison*.

44. David Graeber, "Ferguson and the Criminalization of American Life," *Gawker*, March 19, 2015, http://gawker.com/ferguson-and-the-criminalization-of-american-life-1692392051.

45. Barbara Ehrenreich, "Foreword," in Dolan with Carr, *The Poor Get Prison*.

46. Zoe Carpenter, "How Ferguson Uses Cops and the Courts to Prey on Its Residents," *The Nation*, March 5, 2015, http://www.thenation.com/blog/200185/how-ferguson-missouri-uses-cops-and-courts-prey-its-residents. On this issue, see also the prescient article by Radley Balko, "How Municipalities in St. Louis County, Mo., Profit from Poverty," *Washington Post*, September 3, 2014, http://www.washingtonpost.com/news/the-watch/wp/2014/09/03/how-st-louis-county-missouri-profits-from-poverty/.

47. On the iniquitous race- and class-based workings of the criminal justice system, see Matt Taibbi, *The Divide: American Injustice in the Age of the Wealth Gap* (New York: Spiegel & Grau, 2014).

48. Marian Wright Edelman, "Criminalizing Poverty," *Children's Defense Fund*, May 8, 2015, http://cdf.childrensdefense.org/site/MessageViewer?dlv_id=41044&em_id=42725.0.

49. See, for instance, Hannah Rappleye and Lisa Riordan Seville, "The Town that Turned Poverty into a Prison Sentence," *The Nation*, April 14, 2014, http://www.thenation.com/article/178845/town-turned-poverty-prison-sentence.

50. Dolan with Carr, *The Poor Get Prison*.

51. Josh Sager, "Profitized Policing: When Courts Become Shakedown Rackets," *The Progressive Cynic*, March 9, 2015, http://theprogressivecynic.com/2015/03/09/profitized-policing-when-courts-become-shakedown-rackets/.

52. Graeber, "Ferguson and the Criminalization of American Life."

53. Bethania Palma Markus, "Journalist Calls for Accountability in Police Killings," *Truthout*, March 18, 2014, http://www.truth-out.org/news/item/22538-journalist-calls-for-accountability-in-police-killings.

54. Ibid.

55. Tom McCarthy, "Police Officer Who Fatally Shot Tamir Rice Judged Unfit for Duty in 2012," *The Guardian*, December 4, 2014, http://www.theguardian.com/us-news/2014/dec/03/officer-who-fatally-shot-tamir-rice-had-been-judged-unfit.

56. Ta-Nehisi Coates, "The Myth of Police Reforms," *The Atlantic*, April 15, 2015, http://www.theatlantic.com/politics/archive/2015/04/the-myth-of-police-reform/390057/.

57. I am paraphrasing from Michael Hardt and Antonio Negri, *Multitude: War and Democracy in the Age of Empire* (New York: Penguin Press, 2004), 15.

58. Cited in Kathleen Copps, "Omar Khadr and the Charter of Rights," *Rabble.Ca* (April 28, 2014). http://rabble.ca/news/2014/04/omar-khadr-and-charter-rights.

59. Laura Flanders, "Building Movements without Shedding Differences: Alicia Garza of #BlackLivesMatter," *Truthout*, March 24, 2015, http://www.truth-out.org/news/item/29813-building-movements-without-shedding-differences-alicia-garza.

60. Coates, "The Myth of Police Reforms."

61. Annette Fuentes, *Lockdown High: When the Schoolhouse Becomes a Jailhouse* (New York: Verso, 2011); Henry A. Giroux, *Youth in a Suspect Society* (New York: Palgrave, 2010).

62. See, for example, Brad Evans and Henry A. Giroux, *Disposable Futures* (San Francisco: City Lights, 2015); and Saskia Sassen, *Expulsions: Brutality and Complexity in the Global Economy* (Cambridge: Belknap, 2014).

63. Rev. Martin Luther King, Jr., "Beyond Vietnam: A Time to Break Silence," *American Rhetoric*, n.d., available at: http://www.americanrhetoric.com/speeches/mlkatimetobreaksilence.htm.

64. One interesting list produced in response to the Baltimore uprising can be seen in James C. Perkins, "Baltimore Riots against Police Violence—*Tikkun* and the Baptist Response," *Tikkun*, April 30, 2015, http://www.tikkun.org/nextgen/baltimore-riots-against-police-violence-tikkun-and-the-baptist-response.

65. Peter Bloom, "Baltimore's Dangerous Politics of Containment," *Open Democracy*, April 29, 2015, https://www.opendemocracy.net/peter-bloom/baltimore%E2%80%99s-dangerous-politics-of-containment.

66. Ibid.

67. Elijah Anderson, "What Caused the Ferguson Riot Exists in So Many Other Cities Too," *Washington Post*, December 3, 2014, http://www.washingtonpost.com/posteverything/wp/2014/08/13/what-caused-the-ferguson-riot-exists-in-so-many-other-cities-too/.

68. Matt Taibbi, "The Police in America Are Becoming Illegitimate," *Rolling Stone*, December 5, 2015, http://www.rollingstone.com/politics/news/the-police-in-america-are-becoming-illegitimate-20141205.

69. Richard J. Bernstein, *The Abuse of Evil: The Corruption of Politics and Religion since 9/11*, (London: Polity Press, 2005), 75.

70. Amy Goodman, "Michelle Alexander: Ferguson Shows Why Criminal Justice System of 'Racial Control' Should Be Undone," *Democracy Now!*, March 4, 2015, http://www.democracynow.org/2015/3/4/michelle_alexander_ferguson_shows_why_criminal.

71. Kelly Hayes, "To Baltimore with Love: Chicago's Freedom Dreams," *Truthout*, April 30, 2015, http://www.truth-out.org/opinion/item/30531-to-baltimore-with-love-chicago-s-freedom-dreams.

72. Cited in ibid.

7. HIGHER EDUCATION UNDER SIEGE AND THE PROMISE OF INSURGENT PUBLIC MEMORY

1. Epigraph: James Young, "The Holocaust as Vicarious Past: Art Spiegelman's *Maus* and the Afterimages of History," *Critical Inquiry* 24 (Spring 1998): 667.

2. John Dewey, cited in E. L. Hollander, "The Engaged University," *Academe*, July–August 2000, http://www.aaup.org/publications/Academe/2000/00ja/JA00Holl.htm.

3. This position has been developed fully in the works of a number of educators. See especially Kenneth Saltman, *The Failure of Corporate School Reform* (Boulder,CO: Paradigm, 2012); Alexander J. Means, *Schooling in the Age of Austerity: Urban Education and the Struggle for Democratic Life* (New York: Palgrave, 2013); Diane Ravitch, *Reign of Error: The Hoax of the Privatization Movement and the Danger to America's Public Schools* (New York: Vintage, 2014). See also Henry A. Giroux, *Schooling and the Struggle for Public Life* (Boulder, CO: Paradigm, 2005).

4. See John Hinck, "A Half Century after Mario Savio's Berkeley Speech and Today's Warming Planet." *CommonDreams,* December 2, 2014, http://www.commondreams.org/views/2014/12/02/half-century-after-mario-savios-berkeley-speech-and-todays-warming-planet.

5. Lewis F. Powell, Jr., "The Powell Memo," *ReclaimDemocracy.org,* August 23, 1971, http://reclaimdemocracy.org/corporate_accountability/powell_memo_lewis.html.

6. Ibid. I am drawing here on a previous analysis of the memo: see Henry A. Giroux, "The Powell Memo and the Teaching Machines of Right-Wing Extremists," *Truthout,* October 2009, http://truth-out.org/archive/component/k2/item/86304:the-powell-memo-and-the-teaching-machines-of-rightwing-extremists. I have also taken up this issue in Henry A. Giroux, *The University in Chains: Challenging the Military-Industrial-Academic Complex* (Boulder: Paradigm, 2007).

7. Many of the ideas here and in the next chapter are drawn from Henry A. Giroux, *Youth in a Suspect Society: Democracy or Disposability* (New York: Palgrave, 2009).

8. Editorial, "Targeting the Academy," *Media Transparency,* March 2003, http://www.mediatransparency.org/conservativephilanthropy.php?conservativePhilanthropyPageID=11.

9. Editorial, "Targeting the Academy."

10. Max Blumenthal, "How My Dispute with Joe Scarborough Sheds Light on the Civil War within the GOP," *Alternet,* October 13, 2009, http://www.alternet.org/story/143262/how_my_dispute_with_joe_scarborough_sheds_light_on_the_civil_war_within_the_gop.

11. For a brilliant source on this issue, see Christopher Newfield, *Unmaking the Public University: The Forty-Year Assault on the Middle Class* (Cambridge, MA: Harvard University Press, 2011).

12. Even the popular press had to acknowledge left-wing criticism of Silber. See, for example, Gail Jennes, "Colossus or Megalomaniac, Boston University's John Silber Keeps His Campus in Turmoil," *People,* June 2, 1980, http://www.people.com/people/archive/article/0,,20076633,00.html. For a more serious treatment of Silber's tyranny, see Nicholas D. Kristof, "John R. Silber: War and Peace at Boston University," *Harvard Crimson,* November 28, 1979, http://www.thecrimson.com/article/1979/11/28/john-r-silber-war-and-peace/. For an analysis of the post-9/11 turn to the culture of fear and its repression of educators, see Susan Searls Giroux, *Between Race and Reason: Violence, Intellectual Responsibility, and the University to Come* (Stanford, CA: Stanford University Press, 2010).

13. See, for instance, Michael D. Yates, "Us Versus Them: Laboring in the Academic Factory," *Cheap Hotels and a Hotplate: An Economist's Travelogue,* October 2, 2012, http://cheapmotelsandahotplate.org/2012/10/02/us-versus-them-laboring-in-the-academic-factory/.

14. Jerry L. Martin and Anne D. Neal, *Defending Civilization: How Our Universities Are Failing America and What Can Be Done about It,* ACTA Report, November 2001, http://www.la.utexas.edu/~chenry/2001LynnCheneyjsg01ax1.pdf. This statement was deleted from the revised February 2002 version of the report available on the ACTA website: http://www.goacta.org/publications/Reports/defciv.pdf.

15. Colman McCarthy, "Adjunct Professors Fight for Crumbs on Campus," *Washington Post,* August 22, 2014, http://www.washingtonpost.com/opinions/adjunct-professors-fight-for-crumbs-on-campus/2014/08/22/ca92eb38-28b1-11e4-8593-da634b334390_story.html.

16. Ibid.

17. Stacey Patton, "The Ph.D. Now Comes with Food Stamps," *Chronicle of Higher Education*, May 6, 2012, http://chronicle.com/article/From-Graduate-School-to/131795/.

18. On this issue, see the important collection: Carlo Fanelli and Bryan Evans, eds. *Neoliberalism and the Degradation of Education* (Toronto: Alternate Routes, 2015); also see, Henry A. Giroux, *Neoliberalism's War on Higher Education* (Chicago: Haymarket, 2014).

19. One good example of a group taking up this struggle can be found at http://www.cocal-international.org/.

20. Kate Jenkins, "The Tall Task of Unifying Part-Time Professors," *The Atlantic*, February 15, 2015, http://www.theatlantic.com/business/archive/2015/02/the-tall-task-of-unifying-part-time-professors/385507/.

21. William B. Stanley, *Curriculum for Utopia: Social Reconstructionism and Critical Pedagogy in the Postmodern Era* (New York: SUNY Series, 1992). See also Henry A. Giroux, *Schooling and the Struggle for Public Life*.

22. I take this issue up in great detail in Henry A. Giroux and Susan Searls Giroux, *Take Back Higher Education* (New York: Palgrave Macmillan, 2004); and Henry A. Giroux, *Against the Terror of Neoliberalism* (Boulder, CO: Paradigm, 2008). Also, see Henry A. Giroux, *The University in Chains: Challenging the Military-Industrial-Academic Complex* (Boulder, CO: Paradigm, 2011).

23. See Henry A. Giroux, *Neoliberalism's War on Higher Education*; Henry A. Giroux, *America's Educational Deficit and the War on Youth* (New York: Monthly Review Press, 2013); and Stanley Aronowitz, *Against Schooling: For an Education that Matters* (Boulder, CO: Paradigm Publishers, 2008).

24. Wendy Brown, *Regulating Aversion* (Princeton: Princeton University Press, 2006), 88.

25. John Dewey, *Individualism: Old and New* (New York: Minton, Balch, 1930), 41.

26. Richard J. Bernstein, *The Abuse of Evil: The Corruption of Politics and Religion since 9/11* (London: Polity, 2005), 45.

27. James B. Conant, "Wanted: American Radicals," *The Atlantic*, May 1943, http://www.theatlantic.com/issues/95sep/ets/radical.htm.

28. Doug Lederman, "Rethinking Student Aid, Radically," *Inside Higher Education*, September 19, 2008, http://www.insidehighered.com/news/2008/09/19/rethink.

29. For an excellent analysis of this attack, see Beshara Doumani, "Between Coercion and Privatization: Academic Freedom in the Twenty-First Century," in *Academic Freedom after September 11*, ed. Doumani (Cambridge, MA: Zone Books, 2006), 11–57; and Evan Gerstmann and Matthew J. Streb, *Academic Freedom at the Dawn of a New Century: How Terrorism, Governments, and Culture Wars Impact Free Speech* (Stanford, CA: Stanford University Press, 2006). A sustained and informative discussion of academic freedom after 9/11 can be found in Tom Abowd, Fida Adely, Lori Allen, Laura Bier, Amahl Bishara et al., *Academic Freedom and Professional Responsibility after 9/11: A Handbook for Scholars and Teachers* (New York: Task Force on Middle East Anthropology, 2006); Anthony J. Nocella II, Steven Best, and Peter McLaren, eds., *Academic Repression: Reflections from the Academic Industrial Complex* (Baltimore: AK Press, 2010); Edward J. Carvalho and David Downing, eds., *Academic Freedom in the Post 9/11 Era* (New York: Palgrave, 2011); Piya Chatterjee and Sunaina Maira, eds., *The Imperial University: Academic Repression and Scholarly Dissent* (Minneapolis: University of Minnesota Press, 2014).

30. *Daily Kos* Staff, "Gov. Scott Walker seeks $300 million in university cuts, but $220 million to build Bucks a new arena," *Daily Kos* (January 28, 2015) http://www.dailykos.com/story/2015/01/28/1360765/-Gov-Scott-Walker-seeks-300-million-in-university-cuts-but-220-million-to-build-Bucks-a-new-arena.

31. Mary Bottari and Jonas Persson, "Wisconsin Gov. Scott Walker Tripped Up by Truth," *CommonDreams,* February 6, 2015, http://www.commondreams.org/views/2015/02/06/wisconsin-gov-scott-walker-tripped-truth.

32. Colleen Flaherty, "Whose History?" *Inside Higher Education,* February 15, 2015, https://www.insidehighered.com/news/2015/02/23/oklahoma-legislature-targets-ap-us-history-framework-being-negative.

33. Judd Legum, "Oklahoma Lawmakers Vote Overwhelmingly to Ban Advanced Placement U.S. History," *Think Progress,* February 17, 2015, http://thinkprogress.org/education/2015/02/17/3623683/oklahoma-lawmakers-vote-overwhleming-ban-advanced-placement-history-class/.

34. Valerie Strauss, "Ben Carson: New AP U.S. History Course Will Make Kids Want to Sign Up for ISIS," *Washington Post,* September 29, 2015, http://www.washingtonpost.com/blogs/answer-sheet/wp/2014/09/29/ben-carson-new-ap-u-s-history-course-will-make-kids-want-to-sign-up-for-isis/.

35. Ibid.

36. Thom Hartmann and the Daily Take Team, "The Conservative Attempt to Rewrite the United States' Progressive History," *Truthout,* February 23, 2015, http://www.truth-out.org/opinion/item/29270-the-conservative-attempt-to-re-write-our-progressive-history.

37. For an insightful critique of Giuliani's hypocritical appeal to love, see Wayne Barrett, "What Rudy Giuliani Knows about Love—A Response to His 'Doesn't Love America' Critique of Obama," *New York Daily News,* February 20, 2015, http://www.newyorker.com/news/amy-davidson/rudy-giuliani-obama-meaning-love.

38. Giuliani's criticisms are almost always tinged with racism; see Janet Allon, "5 Absurd, Deeply Racist Things Rudy Giuliani Said This Week," *AlterNet,* November 27, 2014, http://www.alternet.org/news-amp-politics/5-absurd-deeply-racist-things-rudy-giuliani-said-week.

39. Pierre Bourdieu, *Acts of Resistance* (New York: Free Press, 1998).

40. Paulo Freire, *Pedagogy of Freedom* (Boulder, CO: Paradigm, 1998).

41. Mark Karlin, "Robert McChesney: We Need to Advocate Radical Solutions to Systemic Problems," *Truthout,* January 2015, http://www.truth-out.org/progressivepicks/item/28294-robert-mcchesney-we-need-to-advocate-radical-solutions-to-systemic-problems.

42. Pierre Bourdieu and Gunther Grass, "The 'Progressive' Restoration: A Franco-German Dialogue," *New Left Review* 14 (March–April, 2002): 2.

43. Chris Hedges, "Tariq Ali: The Time Is Right for a Palace Revolution," *Truthdig,* March 1, 2015, http://www.truthdig.com/report/print/tariq_ali_the_time_is_right_for_a_palace_revolution_20150301.

44. Bourdieu, *Acts of Resistance*, 11.

45. Sarah Stein Lubrano and Johannes Lenhard, "Crises and Experimental Capitalism: An Interview with Nancy Fraser," *King's Review Magazine,* April 11, 2014, http://kingsreview.co.uk/magazine/blog/2014/04/11/crises-and-experimental-capitalism-an-interview-with-nancy-fraser/.

46. Ibid.
47. Hedges, "Tariq Ali." For a somewhat different take, see Michael D. Yates, "Occupy Wall Street and the Significance of Political Slogans," *Counterpunch,* February 27, 2013, http://www.counterpunch.org/2013/02/27/occupy-wall-street-and-the-significance-of-political-slogans/.
48. Salvatore Babones, *Sixteen for '16: A Progressive Agenda for a Better America* (Chicago: Policy Press, 2015).
49. Bernie Sanders, "An Economic Agenda for America: 12 Steps Forward," *Huffington Post* (August 23, 2015), http://www.huffingtonpost.com/rep-bernie-sanders/an-economic-agenda-for-am_b_6249022.html.
50. Stanley Aronowitz, "Democrats in Disarray: This Donkey Can't Save Our Asses," *The Indypendent,* December 16, 2014), 13 https://indypendent.org/2014/12/16/democrats-disarray-donkey-can%E2%80%99t-save-our-asses.
51. Michael D. Yates, "The Growing Degradation of Work and Life and What We Might Do to End It," *Truthout,* March 21, 2015, http://www.truth-out.org/news/item/29643-the-growing-degradation-of-work-and-life-and-what-we-might-do-to-end-it.
52. Ibid.
53. See, for instance, Carlos Declós, "Radical Democracy: Reclaiming The Commons," *Countercurrents,* February 22, 2015, http://www.countercurrents.org/declos220215.htm.
54. David Price, "Memory's Half-Life: A Social History of Wiretaps," *Counterpunch* 20/6 (June 2013); 14.
55. See, Alicia Garza, "A Herstory of the #BlackLivesMatter Movement," *The FeministWire* (November 2014), http://www.thefeministwire.com/2014/10/blacklivesmatter-2/.

8. ACADEMIC TERRORISM, EXILE, AND POSSIBILITY OF CLASSROOM GRACE

1. In the title I borrowed the term "classroom grace" from Kristen Case, "The Other Public Humanities," *Chronicle of Higher Education,* January 13, 2014, http://m.chronicle.com/article/Ahas-Ahead/143867/.
2. I also reference this in Chapter 1. Cited in Spencer Ackerman, "West Point Professor Calls on US Military to Target Legal Critics of War on Terror," *The Guardian* (August 29, 2015). http://www.theguardian.com/us-news/2015/aug/29/west-point-professor-target-legal-critics-war-on-terror.
3. Murtaza Hussain, "Wesley Clark Calls for Internment Camps for 'Radicalized' Americans," *The Intercept* (July 20, 2015). https://theintercept.com/2015/07/20/chattanooga-wesley-clark-calls-internment-camps-disloyal-americans/
4. Rebecca Leber, "Canada's Government Won't Let Its Own Climate Scientists Speak to the Press: Our Northern Neighbors Are Taking a Page from George W. Bush's Playbook," *The New Republic,* August 20, 2014, http://www.newrepublic.com/article/119153/canadas-stephen-harper-government-muzzles-climate-scientists.
5. Carol Linnitt, "Harper's Attack on Science: No Science, No Evidence, No Truth, No Democracy," *Academic Matters,* May 2013, http://www.academicmatters.ca/2013/05/harpers-attack-on-science-no-science-no-evidence-no-truth-no-democracy/. See more at: http://www.timescolonist.com/news/local/harper-controlled-dfo-is-censoring-federal-scientists-with-research-rules-critics-say-1.75280#sthash.42UhaZul.dpuf.

6.   Tom Dart, "Bobby Jindal: Republican who brought creationism into schools to join election," *The Guardian* (June 24, 2015). http://www.theguardian.com/us-news/2015/jun/24/bobby-jindal-republican-creationism-2016-election.

7.   Many of these issues are discussed in Emily J. M. Knox, "Book Banning in 21st-Century America" (Boulder, CO: Rowman and Littlefield, 2015); Robert McChesney, *Rich Media, Poor Democracy: Communication Politics in Dubious Times* (New York: New Press, 2015); Henry A. Giroux, *Education and the Crisis of Public Values,* 2nd ed. (New York: Peter Lang, 2015).

8.   Much of this has been documented over the years by Noam Chomsky, Ed Herman, and Robert McChesney. See, for example, Edward S. Herman and Noam Chomsky, *Manufacturing Consent: The Political Economy of the Mass Media* (New York: Pantheon, 2002).Robert McChesney, *Rich Media, Poor Democracy: Communication Politics in Dubious Times*, new edition (New York: The New Press, 2015).

9.   Richard Rodriguez, "Sign of the Times," *New York Times Style Magazine,* October 19, 2014.

10.   Author's personal correspondence with Victoria Harper, November 17, 2014.

11.   Efrain Kristal and Arne De Boever, "Disconnecting Acts: An Interview with Zygmunt Bauman Part II," *Los Angeles Review of Books,* November 12, 2014, http://lareviewofbooks.org/essay/disconnecting-acts-interview-zygmunt-bauman-part-ii.

12.   Meara Sharma interviews Claudia Rankine, "Blackness as the Second Person," *Guernica,* November 17, 2014, https://www.guernicamag.com/interviews/blackness-as-the-second-person/.

13.   Case, "The Other Public Humanities."

14.   Cited in Maria Popova, AJames Baldwin on the Creative Process and the Artist's Responsibility to Society, *BrainPickings,* August 20, 2014, http://www.brainpickings.org/2014/08/20/james-baldwin-the-creative-process/.

15.   A useful book for this type of criticism is David Graeber, *The Utopia of Rules: On Technology, Stupidity, and the Secret Joys of Bureaucracy* (Brooklyn, N.Y.: Melville House, 2015).

16.   Leon Wieseltier, "Among the Disrupted," *International New York Times,* January 7, 2015, http://www.nytimes.com/2015/01/18/books/review/among-the-disrupted.html.

17.   Michael Yates, "Honor the Vietnamese, Not the Men Who Killed Them," *Monthly Review* 67/1 (2015), http://monthlyreview.org/2015/05/01/honor-the-vietnamese-not-those-who-killed-them/.

18.   See, for instance, Sheldon S. Wolin, *Democracy Incorporated: Managed Democracy and the Specter of Inverted Totalitarianism* (Princeton: Princeton University Press, 2008); and Henry A. Giroux, *The Violence of Organized Forgetting: Thinking beyond America's Disimagination Machine* (San Francisco: City Lights, 2014).

19.   Case, "The Other Public Humanities."

20.   See, for instance, "How America's Colleges Could Be Tuition Free," at http://www.collegerank.net/tuition-free-college/

21.   Blog of Junct Rebellion, "How The American University Was Killed, in Five Easy Steps," *The Homeless Adjunct,* August 12, 2012, http://junctrebellion.wordpress.com/2012/08/12/how-the-american-university-was-killed-in-five-easy-steps/.

22.   Scott Jaschik, "Making Adjuncts Temps—Literally," *Inside Higher Ed,* August 9, 2010, http://www.insidehighered.com/news/2010/08/09/adjuncts.

23.   Stacey Patton, "The Ph.D. Now Comes with Food Stamps," *Chronicle of Higher Education,* May 6, 2012, http://chronicle.com/article/From-Graduate-School-to/131795/.

24. Noam Chomsky, "How America's Great University System Is Being Destroyed," *Alternet,* February 28, 2015, http://www.alternet.org/corporate-accountability-and-workplace/ chomsky-how-americas-great-university-system-getting.

9. BARBARIANS AT THE GATES: AUTHORITARIANISM AND THE ASSAULT ON PUBLIC EDUCATION

1.   Thomas E. Mann and Norman J. Ornstein, *It's Even Worse than It Looks: How the American Constitutional System Collided With the New Politics of Extremism* (New York: Basic Books, 2013).
2.   Cited in Marie Luise Knott, *Unlearning with Hannah Arendt,* trans. David Dollenmayer (New York: Other Press, 2013), 10.
3.   Henry A. Giroux, *Education and the Crisis of Public Values,* 2nd ed. (NewYork: Peter Lang, 2015); Doug Martin, *Hoosier School Heist* (Indianapolis: Brooks Publishing, 2014); Diane Ravitch, *Reign of Error: The Hoax of the Privatization Movement and the Danger to America's Public Schools* (New York: Vintage, 2014); Kenneth J. Saltman, *The Failure of Corporate School Reform* (Boulder, CO: Paradigm Publishers, 2012).
4.   For an excellent critique of this position, see Kenneth J. Saltman, *The Failure of Corporate School Reform* (Boulder: Paradigm, 2012). See also, Henry A. Giroux, *Education and the Crisis of Public Values,* 2nd edition (New York: Peter Lang, 2015).
5.   David Sirota, "New Data Shows School 'Reformers' Are Full of It," *Salon,* June 3, 2013, http://www.salon.com/2013/06/03/instead_of_a_war_on_teachers_how_about_ one_on_poverty/.
6.   Henry A. Giroux, *America's Education Deficit and the War on Youth* (New York: Monthly Review Press, 2013).
7.   Mark Naison, "'The War on Teachers: Why Is the Public Watching It Happen?" *Common Dreams,* March 13, 2012. https://www.commondreams.org/view/2012/03/13-10.
8.   Hannah Arendt, "Ideology and Terror: A Novel Form of Government," in *The Origins of Totalitarianism* (New York: Houghton Mifflin Harcourt, 2001), 468.
9.   Diane Ravitch, "The People behind the Lawmakers Out to Destroy Public Education: A Primer," *Common Dreams,* May 2, 2012, http://www.commondreams.org/ views/2012/05/02/people-behind-lawmakers-out-destroy-public-education-primer.
10. Paul Buchheit, "How Our Public Schools Became a 'Communist Threat,'" *Common Dreams,* November 18, 2013, http://www.commondreams.org/views/2013/11/18/ how-our-public-schools-became-communist-threat.
11. Robert Hunziker, "A Neoliberal Spring?" *CounterPunch,* December 18, 2014, http://www. counterpunch.org/2014/12/18/a-neoliberal-spring/.
12. See, for instance, Roger Cohen, "Capitalism Eating Its Children," *New York Times,* May 29, 2014, http://www.nytimes.com/2014/05/30/opinion/cohen-capitalism-eating-its-children.html.
13. Aaron Kase, "Public School Asks Parents to Pay $613 per Student as Right-Wing Governor Destroys Public Education with Insane Defunding," *AlterNet,* August 22, 2013, http:// www.alternet.org/education/public-school-asks-parents-pay-613-student-right-wing-governor-destroys-public-education.
14. Ibid.
15. See, for example, Catherine Y. Kim, Daniel J. Losen, and Damon T. Hewitt, *The School-to-Prison Pipeline: Structuring Legal Reform* (New York: New York University Press, 2010).

16. Henry A. Giroux, *America's Education Deficit and the War on Youth* (New York: Monthly Review Press, 2013).

17. The growing resistance to these mind-numbing modes of teaching can be found in Jesse Hagopian, *More than a Score: The New Uprising against High-Stakes Testing* (Chicago: Haymarket Books, 2014).

18. See, for instance, the classic work on zero tolerance: William Ayers, Bernardine Dohrn, and Rick Ayers, eds., *Zero Tolerance: Resisting the Drive for Punishment in Our Schools* (New York: New Press, 2001). See also Annette Fuentes, *Lockdown High: When the Schoolhouse Becomes a Jailhouse* (New York: Verso, 2013).

19. Henry A. Giroux, *Dangerous Thinking in the Age of the New Authoritarianism* (Boulder: Paradigm, 2015).

20. Hannah Arendt, *Hannah Arendt: The Last Interview and Other Conversations* (Brooklyn, NY: Melville House, 2013), 123.

21. Michael D. Yates, "Public School Teachers: New Unions, New Alliances, New Politics," *Truthout*, July 24, 2013, http://truth-out.org/opinion/item/17756-public-school-teachers-new-unions-new-alliances-new-politics.

22. Anita Biressi and Heather Nunn, "Selfishness in Austerity Times," *Soundings* 56 (Spring 2014): 55.

23. Lorenzo Del Savio and Matteo Mameli, "Anti-Representative Democracy and Oligarchic Capture," *Open Democracy*, August 16, 2014, https://www.opendemocracy.net/lorenzo-del-savio-matteo-mameli/antirepresentative-democracy-and-oligarchic-capture.

24. Robin D. G. Kelley, "Why We Won't Wait: Resisting the War against the Black and Brown Underclass," *Counterpunch*, November 25, 2014, http://www.counterpunch.org/2014/11/25/75039/.

25. Stanley Aronowitz, "Democrats in Disarray," *The Indypendent*, December 16, 2014, 12.

26. Ibid.

27. Ibid.

28. Ibid.

29. See Michael Yates, *The Great Inequality* (Boulder, CO: Paradigm Publishers, 2016).

30. Rabbi Michael Lerner, "The Environmental and Social Responsibility Amendment to the U.S. Constitution," *Huffington Post* (June 22, 2015). http://www.huffingtonpost.com/rabbi-michael-lerner/the-environmental-and-soc_b_7115984.html.

31. One recent example of this kind of pie-in-the-sky politics can be found in Scott Galindez, "2014: The Beginning of the End for the GOP?" *Reader Supported News*, December 26, 2014, http://readersupportednews.org/opinion2/277-75/27704-focus-2014-the-beginning-of-the-end-for-the-gop.

32. Ursula K. Le Guin, "We Will Need Writers Who Can Remember Freedom," speech delivered at the National Book Awards, November 19, 2014, http://parkerhiggins.net/2014/11/will-need-writers-can-remember-freedom-ursula-k-le-guin-national-book-awards/.

10. HOLLYWOOD HEROISM IN THE AGE OF EMPIRE: FROM *CITIZENFOUR* AND *SELMA* AND *AMERICAN SNIPER*

1. Nick Turse, *The Complex: How the Military Invades Our Everyday Lives* (New York: Metropolitan Books, 2009); Andrew J. Bacevich, *Washington Rules: America's Path to Perma-*

nent War (New York: Metropolitan Books, 2010); Melvin Goodman, "American Militarism: Costs and Consequences," *Truthout*, March 5, 2013, http://truth-out.org/news/item/14926.

2. Glenn Greenwald, *No Place to Hide: Edward Snowden, the NSA, and the U.S. Surveillance State* (New York: Metropolitan Books, 2014).

3. Peter Bradshaw, "*Citizenfour* Review: Gripping Snowden Documentary Offers Portrait of Power, Paranoia and One Remarkable Man," *The Guardian*, October 16, 2014, http://www.theguardian.com/film/2014/oct/16/citizen-four-review-edward-snowden-documentary.

4. I want to thank John Pilger for reminding me of the need to bring the depoliticization issue to the forefront when interpreting this film. Personal correspondence, February 12, 2015.

5. Douglas Valentine, "*CitizenFour*: The Making of an American Myth," *CounterPunch*, March 2, 2015, http://www.counterpunch.org/2015/03/02/citizen-four-the-making-of-an-american-myth/.

6. Howard Zinn, *SNCC: The New Abolitionists*, 2nd ed. (Chicago: Haymarket, 2013).

7. Richard Cohen, "How 'Selma' Insults LBJ, and Our History," New York *Daily News*, January 5, 2015, http://www.nydailynews.com/opinion/richard-cohen-selma-insults-lbj-history-article-1.2066666.

8. Glen Ford, "Selma: Black History According to Oprah," *Black Agenda Report*, January 21, 2015, http://blackagendareport.com/node/14624.

9. See, for instance, Cornel West, ed., *Martin Luther King, Jr.: The Radical King* (Boston: Beacon Press, 2015).

10. Steven Rea, "*Selma*: A Clear Sense of the Mission and the Man," *Philly.com*, January 9, 2015, http://www.philly.com/philly/entertainment/20150109__Selma___A_clear_sense_of_the_mission_and_the_man.html#zBzQP2YFJr5ZkPyY.99.

11. Dennis Trainor, Jr., "'The Truth Is Unspeakable': A Real American Sniper Unloads on *American Sniper*," *Salon*, February 4, 2015, http://www.salon.com/2015/02/04/this_american_sniper_didnt_keep_track_of_his_kills_and_hates_that_i_ask_him/.

12. Joseph E. Lowndes, "'American Sniper,' Clint Eastwood and White Fear," *CounterPunch*, February 3, 2015, http://www.counterpunch.org/2015/02/03/american-sniper-clint-eastwood-and-white-fear/.

13. Jeremy Scahill, quoted in Michael B. Kelley, "US Special Ops Have Become Much, Much Scarier Since 9/11," *Business Insider*, May 10, 2013, http://www.businessinsider.com/the-rise-of-jsoc-in-dirty-wars-2013-4.

14. Jeremy Scahill, *Dirty Wars: The World Is a Battlefield* (New York: Nation Books, 2014).

15. See T. P. Wilkinson, "Harry's Gone a Huntin," *Dissident Voice*, January 29, 2015, http://dissidentvoice.org/2015/01/harrys-gone-a-huntin/.

16. Amanda Terkel, "Rudy Giuliani Says White Cops Are Needed to Stop Black People from Shooting Each Other," *Huffington Post*, November 24, 2014, http://www.huffingtonpost.com/2014/11/23/rudy-giuliani-ferguson_n_6207608.html.

17. *ProPublica*, cited in ibid.

18. Amy Nelson, "Clint Eastwood's *American Sniper* Is One of the Most Mendacious Movies of 2014," *Slate*, January 9, 2015, http://www.slate.com/articles/arts/the_movie_club/features/2014/the_movie_club_2014/worst_movies_of_2014_american_sniper_glosses_over_chris_kyle_s_lies.html.

19. Trainor, "'The Truth Is Unspeakable.'"
20. Olivia Ward, "Why Hollywood Won't Win an Oscar for History," *Toronto Star,* February 21, 2015, http://www.thestar.com/news/world/2015/02/21/why-hollywood-wont-win-an-oscar-for-history.html.
21. Michael Lerner, "Henry Giroux on Hysterical Authoritarianism: Terrorism, Violence and the Culture of Madness," *Tikkun,* March 30, 2015, http://www.tikkun.org/nextgen/henry-girous-on-hysterical-authoritarianism-terrorism-violence-and-the-culture-of-madness.
22. Stuart Hall, "The March of the Neoliberals," *The Guardian,* September 12, 2011, http://www.guardian.co.uk/politics/2011/sep/12/march-of-the-neoliberals.
23. Naomi Klein, "Greed Is Good, for Some," *New York Times Book Review,* March 22, 2015.
24. Ibid.

11. HIROSHIMA, INTELLECTUALS, AND THE CRISIS OF TERRORISM

1. Epigraph: Hannah Arendt, cited in Georges Didi-Huberman, *Images in Spite of All: Four Photographs from Auschwitz* (Chicago: University of Chicago Press, 2008), 31. Jennifer Rosenberg, "Hiroshima and Nagasaki (Part 2)," 20th Century History, *About.com,* March 28, 201, http://history1900s.about.com/od/worldwarii/a/hiroshima_2.htm. A more powerful atom bomb was dropped on Nagasaki on August 9, 1945, and by the end of the year an estimated 70,000 had been killed. For the history of the making of the bomb, see Richard Rhodes's monumental *The Making of the Atomic Bomb* (New York: Simon & Schuster, 2012).
2. The term "technological fanaticism" comes from Michael Sherry who suggested that it produced an increased form of brutality. Quoted in Howard Zinn, *The Bomb* (San Francisco: City Lights, 2010), 54–55.
3. Oh Jung, "Hiroshima and Nagasaki: The Decision to Drop the Bomb," *Michigan Journal of History* 1/2 (Winter 2002), http://michiganjournalhistory.files.wordpress.com/2014/02/oh_jung.pdf.
4. See, in particular, Ronald Takaki, *Hiroshima: Why America Dropped the Atomic Bomb* (Boston: Back Bay Books, 1996).
5. Kensaburo Oe, *Hiroshima Notes* (New York: Grove Press, 1965), 114.
6. Ibid., 117.
7. Robert Jay Lifton and Greg Mitchell, *Hiroshima in America* (New York: Avon Books, 1995), 314–15, 328.
8. Jung, "Hiroshima and Nagasaki."
9. Robert Jay Lifton, "American Apocalypse," *The Nation,* December 22, 2003, 12.
10. This reference refers to a collection of interviews with Michel Foucault. See "What our present is," in *Foucault Live: Collected Interviews, 1961–1984,* ed. Sylvere Lotringer, trans. Lysa Hochroth and John Johnston (New York: Semiotext(e), 1989 and 1996), 407–15.
11. Zygmunt Bauman and Leonidas Donskis, *Moral Blindness: The Loss of Sensitivity in Liquid Modernity* (Cambridge, UK: Polity Press, 2013), 33.
12. Daniel Sandstrom, interview with Philip Roth, "My Life as a Writer," *New York Times,* March 2, 2014, http://www.nytimes.com/2014/03/16/books/review/my-life-as-a-writer.html.
13. Of course, the Occupy movement in the United States and the Quebec student movement are exceptions to this trend. See, for instance, David Graeber, *The Democracy Project:*

A History, A Crisis, A Movement (New York, NY: The Random House Publishing Group, 2013); and Henry A. Giroux, *Neoliberalism's War against Higher Education* (Chicago: Haymarket, 2014).

14.   Quoted in Lifton and Mitchell, *Hiroshima In America,* 351.

15.   Ibid., 345.

16.   Peter Bacon Hales, *Outside the Gates of Eden: The Dream of America from Hiroshima to Now* (Chicago: University of Chicago Press, 2014), 17.

17.   Jacques Derrida, "No Apocalypse, Not Now (Full Speed Ahead, Seven Missiles, Seven Missives)," *Diacritics* 14/ 2 (Summer 1984): 22, 29.

18.   Arendt quoted in Georges Didi-Huberman, *Images in Spite of All* (Chicago: University of Chicago Press, 2012), 31.

19.   I have taken this term from Sandstrom, "My Life as a Writer."

20.   Susan Sontag famously pursued this theme in "The Imagination of Disaster," *October* (1965), 42–48.Available at: http://americanfuturesiup.files.wordpress.com/2013/01/sontag-the-imagination-of-disaster.pdf.

21.   Michael Levine and William Taylor, "The Upside of Down: Disaster and the Imagination 50 Years On," *M/C Journal* 16/ 1 (2013), http://journal.media-culture.org.au/index.php/mcjournal/article/viewArticle/586.

22.   Sontag, "The Imagination," 42.

23.   Ibid.

24.   Brad Evans, "The Promise of Violence in the Age of Catastrophe," *Truthout,* January 5, 2014, http://www.truth-out.org/opinion/item/20977-the-promise-of-violence-in-the-age-of-catastrophe.

25.   Zygmunt Bauman and Leonidas Donskis, *Moral Blindness: The Loss of Sensitivity in Liquid Modernity* (Cambridge, UK: Polity Press, 2013), 33.

26.   Zinn, *The Bomb,* 23–24.

27.   I have taken up this issue in detail in Henry A. Giroux, *Neoliberalism's War on Higher Education* (Chicago: Haymarket Books, 2014).

28.   João Biehl, *Vita: Life in a Zone of Social Abandonment* (Los Angeles: University of California Press, 2005), 2.

29.   This theme is taken up extensively in Brad Evans and Henry A. Giroux, *Disposable Futures: Violence in the Age of the Spectacle* (San Francisco: City Lights, 2015).

30.   Glenn Greenwald, *No Place to Hide* (New York: Macmillan, 2014); Henry A. Giroux, *Zombie Politics in the Age of Casino Capitalism,* 2nd ed. (New York: Peter Lang, 2014).

31.   Peter Bacon Hales, *Outside the Gates of Eden: The Dream of America from Hiroshima to Now* (Chicago: University of Chicago Press, 2014), 17.

32.   David Graeber, *The Democracy Project: A History, a Crisis, a Movement* (New York: Random House, 2013), 281.

33.   Tom Englehardt, "Noam Chomsky, Why National Security Has Nothing to Do with Security," *TomDispatch.com,*August 5, 2014, http://www.tomdispatch.com/post/175877/tomgram%3A_noam_chomsky%2C_why_national_security_has_nothing_to_do_with_security/.

34.   Susan Sontag, *Regarding the Pain of Others* (New York: Farrar, Straus and Giroux, 2003), 81.

35.   Paul Virilio, *Art and Fear* (New York: Continuum, 2004), 28.

36. Lifton and Mitchell, *Hiroshima in America,* 338.

37. Evans and Giroux, *Disposable Futures.*

38. Étienne Balibar, "Outline of a Topography of Cruelty: Citizenship and Civility in the Era of Global Violence," in *We, The People of Europe: Reflections on Transnational Citizenship* (Princeton: Princeton University Press, 2004), 115–32.

39. Jeremy Scahill, "It's Official: Obama Will Not Prosecute CIA Torturers," *Common Dreams,* April 16, 2009, http://www.commondreams.org/news/2009/04/16/its-official-obama-will-not-prosecute-cia-torturers. On the state of exception, see Giorgio Agamben, *State of Exception,* trans. Kevin Attell (Chicago: University of Chicago Press, 2005).

40. Bill Blunden, "The Zero-Sum Game of Perpetual War," *CounterPunch,* September 2, 2014, http://www.counterpunch.org/2014/09/02/the-zero-sum-game-of-perpetual-war/.

41. Ibid.

42. Ibid.

43. See Lifton and Mitchell, *Hiroshima in America.*

44. Bauman and Donskis, *Moral Blindness,* 39.

45. Blunden, "The Zero-Sum Game of Perpetual War."

46. Mark Memmott, "Let Teachers Carry Guns? Some State Lawmakers Say Yes," *National Public Radio.org,* December 19, 2012, http://www.npr.org/blogs/thetwo-way/2012/12/19/167622812/let-teachers-carry-guns-some-state-lawmakers-say-yes.

47. German Lopez, "The Shooting of Michael Brown Was the Final Straw for People in Ferguson," *Vox,* August 14, 2014, http://www.vox.com/2014/8/14/5999929/shooting-mike-brown-final-straw-ferguson-st-louis-missouri. See also Bryan Winston, "Ferguson in Context," *CounterPunch,* August 22, 2014, http://www.counterpunch.org/2014/08/22/ferguson-in-context/.

48. Antonio Thomas, "Petition—Stop Police Brutality against Black People," *Change.Org,* petition started in June 2010, http://www.change.org/p/stop-police-brutality-against-black-people.

49. Hannah Tennant-Moore, "The Awakening," *New York Times Book Review,* June 19, 2014.

50. This theme is brilliantly explored in Hales, *Outside the Gates of Eden.*

51. Raymond Williams, "Preface to Second Edition," *Communications* (New York: Barnes and Noble, 1967), 15.

52. Quoted in Zinn, *The Bomb,* 58.

53. Hannah Arendt, *Hannah Arendt: The Last Interview and Other Conversations* (Brooklyn, NY: Melville House, 2013), 37.

54. Charles P. Pierce, "Why Bosses Always Win If the Game Is Always Rigged," *Esquire,* October 18, 2012, http://www.esquire.com/blogs/politics/mitt-romney-boss-13852713.

55. Stanley Aronowitz has taken this theme up in a number of articles. See, for instance, Stanley Aronowitz, "What Kind of Left Does America Need?," *Tikkun,* April 14, 2014, http://www.tikkun.org/nextgen/what-kind-of-left-does-america-need.

56. Doreen Massey, "Vocabularies of the Economy," *Soundings,* 2013, http://lwbooks.co.uk/journals/soundings/pdfs/Vocabularies%20of%20the%20economy.pdf.

57. Pierre Bourdieu, *Acts of Resistance* (New York: Free Press, 1998), 11.

58. Zoe Williams, "The Saturday Interview: Stuart Hall," *The Guardian,* February 11, 2012, http://www.guardian.co.uk/theguardian/2012/feb/11/saturday-interview-stuart-hall.

59. Hélène Cixous and Catherine Clément, *The Newly Born Woman,* trans. Betsy Wing, Theo-

ry and History of Literature Series, vol. 24 (Minneapolis: University of Minnesota Press, 1986), ix.

60.   Howard Zinn, "The Bombs of August," *The Progressive,* August 2000, http://www.com-mondreams.org/views/073000-108.htm.

61.   Clare Hemmings, "Invoking Affect: Cultural Theory and the Ontological Turn," *Cultural Studies* 19/ 5 (September 2005): 557–58.

12. FLIPPING THE SCRIPT

1.   For an excellent source on what it means to come of age in the working class, see Michael D. Yates, *In and Out of the Working Class* (Winnipeg, MB: Arbeiter Ring Publishing, 2009).

2.   Marie Luise Knott, *Unlearning with Hannah Arendt,* trans. David Dollenmayer (New York: Other Press, 2011), 87.

3.   Ibid., 73.

4.   Tom Engelhardt, "The Superpower Conundrum: The Rise and Fall of Just About Everything," *TomDispatch,* July 2, 2015, http://www.tomdispatch.com/post/176018/tomgram%3A_engelhardt%2C_what_happened_to_war/#more.

5.   Ibid.

6.   James Baldwin, *No Name in the Street* (New York; Dial Press, 1972), 149.

7.   Andrew J. Bacevich, *Washington Rules: America's Path to Permanent War* (New York: Metropolitan Books, 2010), 242.

8.   The quote by Karl Jaspers is from Hannah Arendt, *The Last Interview and Other Conversations* (Brooklyn, NY: Melville House, 2013), 37.

9.   James Baldwin, "As Much Truth as One Can Bear," *New York Times Book Review,* January 14, 1962.

Index

CPSIA information can be obtained at www.ICGtesting.com
Printed in the USA
BVOW08*0902160416

444403BV00001B/1/P